Transit Street
Design Guide

ABOUT ISLAND PRESS

Since 1984, the nonprofit Island Press has been stimulating, shaping, and communicating the ideas that are essential for solving environmental problems worldwide. With more than 800 titles in print and some 40 new releases each year, we are the nation's leading publisher on environmental issues. We identify innovative thinkers and emerging trends in the environmental field. We work with world-renowned experts and authors to develop cross-disciplinary solutions to environmental challenges. Island Press designs and implements coordinated book publication campaigns in order to communicate our critical messages in print, in person, and online using the latest technologies, programs, and the media. Our goal: to reach targeted audiences—scientists, policymakers, environmental advocates, the media, and concerned citizens—that can and will take action to protect the plants and animals that enrich our world, the ecosystems we need to survive, the water we drink, and the air we breathe. Island Press gratefully acknowledges the support of its work by the Agua Fund, Inc., The Margaret A. Cargill Foundation, Betsy and Jesse Fink Foundation, The William and Flora Hewlett Foundation, The Kresge Foundation, The Forrest and Frances Lattner Foundation, The Andrew W. Mellon Foundation, The Curtis and Edith Munson Foundation, The Overbrook Foundation, The David and Lucile Packard Foundation, The Summit Foundation, Trust for Architectural Easements, The Winslow Foundation, and other generous donors. The opinions expressed in this book are those of the authors and do not necessarily reflect the views of our donors.

Transit Street
Design Guide

NACTO

National Association of
City Transportation Officials

ISLANDPRESS

WASHINGTON | COVELO | LONDON

NACTO
National Association of
City Transportation Officials

ABOUT NACTO

The National Association of City Transportation Officials is a 501(c)(3) nonprofit association that represents large cities on transportation issues of local, regional, and national significance. NACTO views the transportation departments of major cities as effective and necessary partners in regional and national transportation efforts and promotes their interests in federal decision making. The organization facilitates the exchange of transportation ideas, insights, and best practices among large cities, while fostering a cooperative approach to key issues facing cities and metropolitan areas. As a coalition of city transportation departments, NACTO is committed to raising the state of practice for street design and transportation by building a common vision, sharing data, peer-to-peer exchange in workshops and conferences, and regular communication among member cities.

**National Association of
City Transportation Officials**
120 Park Avenue, 23rd Floor
New York, NY 10017
www.nacto.org

© Copyright 2016 National Association of City Transportation Officials

ISBN: 978-1-61091-747-6

Library of Congress Catalog Control Number: 2016933373

NACTO EXECUTIVE BOARD

Seleta Reynolds, President
General Manager, Los Angeles
Department of Transportation

Scott Kubly, Vice President
Director, Seattle Department
of Transportation

Crissy Fanganello, Secretary
Director of Transportation for Public Works,
City and County of Denver

Danny Pleasant, Treasurer
Director of Transportation, City of Charlotte

Robin Hutcheson,
Affiliate Member Representative
Director of Transportation, Salt Lake City

Janette Sadik-Khan, Chair

NACTO MEMBER CITIES

Atlanta
Austin
Baltimore
Boston
Charlotte
Chicago
Denver
Detroit
Houston
Los Angeles
Minneapolis
New York
Philadelphia
Phoenix
Pittsburgh
Portland
San Diego
San Francisco
San José
Seattle
Washington, DC

**AFFILIATE
MEMBERS**
Arlington, VA
Boulder, CO
Burlington, CT
Cambridge, MA
Chattanooga, TN
El Paso, TX
Fort Lauderdale, FL
Hoboken, NJ
Indianapolis, IN
Louisville, KY
Madison, WI
Memphis, TN
Miami Beach, FL
Oakland, CA
Palo Alto, CA
Salt Lake City, UT
Santa Monica, CA
Somerville, MA
Vancouver, WA
Ventura, CA

**INTERNATIONAL
MEMBERS**
Montréal, QC
Puebla, Mexico
Toronto, ON
Vancouver, BC

NACTO PROJECT TEAM

Linda Bailey
Executive Director

Matthew Roe
Director, Designing Cities Initiative

Corinne Kisner
Director of Policy and Special Projects

Craig Toocheck
Program Analyst/Designer,
Designing Cities Initiative

Aaron Villere
Designing Cities Fellow

ACKNOWLEDGMENTS

The *Transit Street Design Guide* would not have been possible without the support and guidance of TransitCenter and the Summit Foundation. Many thanks to Darryl Young of the Summit Foundation and David Bragdon, Shin-pei Tsay and Stephanie Lotshaw of TransitCenter. The project team would like to thank all of the members of the steering committee, as well as contributors and representatives of partner organizations, who contributed their expertise to the development of this guide, including the Institute of Transportation Engineers and the American Public Transportation Association.

Special thanks to Heather Boyer, Rachel Miller, Sharis Simonian, and all the staff at Island Press for bringing this publication into print. Finally, thanks to Laurie Alemian-Derian, Kate Fillin-Yeh, and Ted Graves of NACTO, for their tireless support and contributions to the project.

THE SUMMIT
FOUNDATION

Contents

Foreword

Transit and cities grow together. As cities strive to become more compact, sustainable, and healthy, their work is paying dividends: in 2014, Americans took 10.8 billion trips on public transit, a stunning reversal of 20th century trends and the highest ridership since the dawn of the freeway era. The growing vitality of cities is bringing more and more people to our bus and rail networks, at the same time that the explosive growth of bicycling and walking has demonstrated the urgent priority of designing streets as public spaces.

This is a thrilling opportunity and a big challenge. Simply put, our critical transit lines and streets need to move more people without more space, and technology alone isn't going to balance that equation. Neither will highways that treat transit and its riders as an afterthought at best. We have to change the purpose of the street—from traffic alone to active modes, from moving machines to moving people. The NACTO *Transit Street Design Guide* is part of this movement of cities to put people and transit right where they belong, at the heart of city street design. It's about a shift in mindset and recognizing priorities.

Cities are rising to the challenge. From Seattle's RapidRide to Houston's New Bus Network, from the Los Angeles Metro Rapid to Toronto's Queen's Quay, we're seeing renewed attention and investment in transit and streets together. City leaders are pushing forward because they want to create the kinds of healthy, active neighborhoods and downtowns that residents increasingly demand, and that wouldn't be possible without excellent transit systems that take people where they need to, when they need to.

Some of this is simple math: allocating scarce space to transit instead of private automobiles greatly expands the number of people a street can move. But bringing these changes to complex city streets takes a lot more than good intentions. Cities need to know how to manage streets to keep transit moving. Street design and everyday engineering and design decisions made by cities, from how signals are timed to how long a bus stop will be, can dramatically change how transit works and how people use it. Transit service can be smarter, too: fewer stops means faster trips, and a chance to upgrade stops into comfortable, sustainable places to do more than just wait. Some of the finest public spaces in the world are transit streets, because transit does so much more with so much less space than any other mode. So it's not just about making city streets into convenient places to ride, but also great places to arrive. Paying attention to the public realm and pedestrian space is what distinguishes good transit streets from great ones.

The *Transit Street Design Guide* arrives at a critical moment. Since the NACTO *Urban Street Design Guide* and *Urban Bikeway Design Guide* were first published a few short years ago, a design revolution has taken hold in cities around the world. More and more cities are reimagining their streets, replacing outdated highway-based practices with fresh ideas that prioritize people and the quality of their lives. The immense popularity of walkable urban places, built in part on transit investments over decades, has helped lay the groundwork for a new paradigm in how we think about streets.

Now the cities at the forefront of this movement are bringing their attention to transit as a core function of the street. The *Transit Street Design Guide* forges a much-needed link between transit service providers and city transportation departments. Through the National Association of City Transportation Officials, leaders from around the country have brought together innovative ideas in street design with the best service practices in transit, to create a new blueprint for transit streets in cities. This guide is the result of a professional collaboration between transit planners and street designers, city traffic engineers and project managers—people who understand and care how public transportation works in and for a city.

I know firsthand how important it is to bring together the professionals and policies that affect transit. We're fortunate that the SFMTA is responsible for both transit and streets. We know that the day-to-day operational decisions about streets can keep transit rolling—or grind it to a halt. So our transit service planners sit right next to the engineers and designers responsible for our key transit streets. That's made it possible to do great things at the fast pace of a busy city, even when the design solutions take real work.

Here in San Francisco, our Muni Forward program has brought together smarter operations and on-street priority to make the whole transit system work better. That means rolling out the red carpet of dedicated transit lanes, for buses and light rail alike. It means investing in stops to create boarding islands and bulbs that give space to transit vehicles, passengers, and people on bikes all at the same time. Ultimately, it means saving time, and that means more transit service on the street.

We're creating a Rapid Network of both bus and rail lines with frequent service spanning the entire city, and upgrading the country's premier transit street in the Better Market Street project. Muni also has the distinction of being the first big transit system in the country with universal all-door boarding on both buses and rail, reducing the amount of time spent boarding by 38%. There's less waiting, less fare evasion, less crowding at the front, and faster trips for everyone. San Francisco is a transit-first city, but these are techniques that every city can use to make their streets and transit work better together.

We have a lot riding on this: every day, the streets of San Francisco move hundreds of thousands of people in buses, light rail vehicles, historic streetcars, and, of course, cable cars, in one of the biggest municipally-operated transit systems in the world. So we have to manage our streets in a way that supports transit, regardless of the type of transit vehicle or mode that serves it.

With this guide, cities around the country and around the world have a new resource illustrating how streets of every size can be shaped to create great transit streets. Transit streets are an indispensable part of the movement among cities to make their streets into places, and the *Transit Street Design Guide* gives us the tools we need to design for any mode of transit on streets in cities.

Ed Reiskin
NACTO President Emeritus (2014–2015)
Director, San Francisco Municipal Transportation Agency

South Jackson Street, **SEATTLE, WA**

About the Guide

The *Transit Street Design Guide* sets a new vision for how cities can harness the immense potential of transit to create active and efficient streets in neighborhoods and downtowns alike. Building on the *Urban Street Design Guide* and *Urban Bikeway Design Guide*, the *Transit Street Design Guide* details how reliable public transportation depends on a commitment to transit at every level of design. Developed through a new peer network of NACTO members and transit agency partners, the Guide provides street transportation departments, transit operating agencies, leaders, and practitioners with the tools to actively prioritize transit on the street.

Using the Guide

PURPOSE AND ORIGIN

The *Transit Street Design Guide* provides design guidance for the development of transit facilities on city streets, and for the design and engineering of city streets to prioritize transit, improve transit service quality, and support other goals related to transit. The guide has been developed on the basis of other design guidance, as well as city case studies, best practices in urban environments, research and evaluation of existing designs, and professional consensus. These sources, as well as the specific designs and elements included in the guide, are based on North American street design practice.

STRUCTURE & GUIDANCE TYPES

The contents of the *Transit Street Design Guide* are presented in a non-linear fashion, suitable for reference during the design process. Internal cross-references, a list of further resources by topic, and endnotes are provided to assist the reader in developing a deep understanding of the subject. The *Transit Streets* chapter incorporates elements presented in greater depth throughout the guide, with *Elements* sections providing the greatest level of detail.

Some sections of the guide include a **CONTEXT** or **APPLICATION** discussion. The specific applications are provided for reference, and include common existing uses, rather than an exhaustive or exclusive list of all potential uses.

For most topics and treatments in this guide, the reader will find three levels of guidance:

» **CRITICAL** features are elements for which there is a strong consensus of absolute necessity.

» **RECOMMENDED** features are elements for which there is a strong consensus of added value. Most dimensions and other parameters that may vary, as well as accommodations that are desirable but not universally feasible, are included in this section to provide some degree of flexibility.

» **OPTIONAL** features are elements that may vary across cities and may add value, depending on the situation.

Note: Certain sections contain a only general **DISCUSSION** section and have no **CRITICAL**, **RECOMMENDED**, or **OPTIONAL** points.

Key points on renderings are highlighted in yellow. Highlights refer to either the treatment or topic being discussed or the main idea of the image shown.

Dimension guidance is sometimes presented in multiple levels within the guide, to be applied based on the specific needs and constraints of real streets on a case-by-case basis.

» **MINIMUM DIMENSIONS** are presented for use in geometrically constrained conditions. Lanes or other elements that use minimum dimensions will typically not provide a comfortable operating space for relevant users over long distances. Nonetheless, minimum dimensions often allow dedicated transit and other facilities to be constructed where space constraints and competing uses are present, especially when seeking to provide a balanced cross-section in a retrofit of existing streets.

» **DESIRED MINIMUM DIMENSIONS** provide basic operating spaces in normal operational conditions. Larger dimensions are generally encouraged and can have comfort, operational, or other performance benefits. In other respects, desired minimum dimensions are similar to the lower end of recommended dimensions.

» **RECOMMENDED DIMENSIONS** provide for comfortable operations in many common conditions. Where a range of dimensions is provided, choose a dimension based on location, context, local experience. In some cases, such as turn radii and mixed-traffic lane widths, larger than recommended dimensions are less safe. However, if presented with factors not considered in the guidance, smaller or larger dimensions may perform better than recommended dimensions.

» **MAXIMUM DIMENSIONS**, if exceeded, may result in undesirable uses, such as overly high speeds or disallowed passing maneuvers.

GUIDE CONTEXT

Underlying assumptions are discussed here and in specific sections of the guide.

Transit service operates across the full spectrum of built environments and rights-of-way, with bus and rail vehicles of a variety of sizes and configurations. "Transit" and "public transportation" refer to transportation services on fixed routes intended to move many people at once, with multiple origins and destinations, and open to any paying passenger. Both publicly and privately owned operators exist for these services.

The guide assumes a variety of conditions for transit. Importantly, pre-existing streets are assumed to accommodate but not always prioritize the presence of transit vehicles, their passengers, and people walking. These modes, as well as bicycles, taxis, private motor vehicles, trucks, and emergency vehicles are assumed to exist in varying numbers by context. Design typologies and elements included in the guide assume the presence of these modes, as well as specific conditions such as on-street parking or loading, some driveways, and a moderate to high volume of movement on foot or on bicycle. Sidewalks and pedestrian crossings are assumed to exist in some form in all cases.

This guide is aimed at filling the gap that exists in transit street design guidance for city street conditions. However, most of the elements and concepts covered in the guide are applicable to streets typically found in lower-density urbanized areas, including streets with frequent or large driveways, no on-street parking, and higher traffic speeds. Many urban areas with primarily non-urban existing street design can be addressed through the application of this guide, in combination with the NACTO *Urban Street Design Guide* and other guidance.

Nearly all transit vehicles can be deployed on each of the transit street types presented, in a wide variety of service patterns. With a few exceptions, vehicle type and size as well as service frequency or demand are treated as inputs in street design, and street configurations are not intended here to prescribe vehicle types. Transit street types, facility types, and service types are not inherently linked to specific vehicles. Several designs in the guide are based on existing conditions whose best North American examples are associated with a specific vehicle type, but even these examples are not meant to prescribe the use of specific vehicles for specific designs.

This guide does not address transit design on controlled-access freeway facilities or grade-separated rights-of-way, or stations on off-street lots. Readers are referred to the TCQSM and the AASHTO **Guide for Geometric Design of Transit Facilities on Highways and Streets** for transitway design in controlled-access conditions.

For complementary information on safely designing streets for walking and bicycling, readers are referred to the NACTO **Urban Street Design Guide**, NACTO **Urban Bikeway Design Guide**, and other guidance. NACTO design guides may be accessed online at http://nacto.org.

The treatments and topics discussed in this guide must be tailored to individual situations and contexts. NACTO encourages good engineering judgment in all cases. Decisions should be thoroughly documented. To assist with this, this guide links to references and cites relevant materials and studies.

RELATION TO OTHER GUIDANCE

Several major national guidance documents exist that are relevant to transit and street design in ways that overlap with the NACTO *Transit Street Design Guide*.

As a national document in the United States adopted and modified by individual states, the **Manual for Uniform Traffic Control Devices** (MUTCD) has a special significance in street engineering and design guidance. In instances where a particular sign, signal, or marking should be used, the guide highlights its specific reference in the MUTCD. Geometric design features, such as vertical and horizontal elements that create exclusive transit, bike, or pedestrian facilities, are not traffic control devices.

The vast majority of design elements included in the guide are consistent with MUTCD standards. Some specific signal, markings, and signage elements described in the guide have been developed or adopted in the years since the last major revision of the MUTCD. Since the status of these treatments may change in pending revisions to the MUTCD, this guide does not specify the status of each item in each place where it is used. Several included signage, markings, and signal elements have received interim approval for inclusion in the next edition of the MUTCD and do not involve experimentation. Several other important design elements in widespread use in the United States are available through experimentation as of the publication of this guide. These include red/terra cotta colored transit lanes, bus-only transit signals and displays, bike boxes and two-stage turn queue boxes. NACTO strongly encourages the use of the Federal Highway Administration's (FHWA) MUTCD experimentation process for new or innovative traffic control devices, an important method of expanding the options available to designers and engineers.

The **Transit Capacity and Quality of Service Manual**, *3rd Edition* (TCQSM) is assumed to be the basis of most service decisions, and is a foundational tool for understanding transit passenger service needs and outcomes.

Specific standards in the **Americans with Disabilities Act Accessibility Guidelines** (ADAAG)—developed by the US Access Board, adopted by the US Department of Justice and Department of Transportation—are cited where applicable to transit facilities.

The U.S. Access Board's **Public Rights-Of-Way Accessibility Guidelines** (PROWAG)—proposed in 2011 and under consideration for adoption as US Federal standard as of publication — includes detailed accessibility guidance developed specifically for streets. These proposed rules differ from the ADAAG, and are cited where applicable.

Many transit operators have developed transit stop criteria and station siting or equipment criteria, often connected with a transit service manual. Many cities have developed local street design guidance that discusses transit stop design in the context of street design, including bikeway design. NACTO references materials from a selection of these guides and urges municipalities to use the *Transit Street Design Guide* as a basis for creating or updating local standards.

1. Introduction

Transit is returning to its central place in the life of cities. With more people using buses, streetcars, and light rail than ever before, our street design paradigm is shifting to give transit the space it deserves. People are choosing to live, work, and play in walkable neighborhoods, and cities are prioritizing highly productive modes like transit as the key to efficient, sustainable mobility for growing urban populations. Transit agencies and street departments are working together to create streets that not only keep buses and streetcars moving, but are great places to be. Cities are extending light rail systems, investing in streetcar lines, and creating new rapid bus lines at a stunning pace, with ridership growing even faster in city centers. Transit agencies are rethinking their networks to serve neighborhoods at a high level all day, not just at commute times, while bike share and active transportation networks make it even easier to not only reduce driving, but to avoid the expense of owning a car.

At the heart of these changes is the need for cities to grow without slowing down. Transit is a key that unlocks street space, bringing new opportunities to create streets that can move tremendous numbers of people and be enjoyed as public spaces at the same time.

Cities around the country and around the world are finding new ways to create these places. To codify and advance best practices in transit design, the National Association of City Transportation Officials has brought together practitioners and leaders from the transit and street sectors to develop the *Transit Street Design Guide*. This new framework for designing transit corridors as public spaces will help cities and their residents work together to create the streets that are the foundation of a vibrant urban future.

Key Principles

BETTER STREETS, BETTER SERVICE

Making transit work in cities means raising the level of design across the entire street network. Cities can take the lead on transit, creating dedicated lanes and transitways, designing comfortable stops and stations, and coordinating action with transit agencies on intersections and signals.

Transit-first street design also means treating walking as the foundation of the transportation system. Ultimately, the efficiency of transit creates room for public space, biking and walking networks, and green infrastructure—allowing cities to remake their streets as safer, more sustainable public spaces.

TRANSIT CREATES URBAN PLACES

Cities and transit are deeply linked. In vibrant, bustling cities, people are on the move, and transit plays an indispensable role in keeping them moving. Walkable urban places have a critical mass of people and activities that support and rely on transit to connect them to other places. Cities can strengthen this synergy by creating transit streets: places that move people.

With the majority of US residents preferring walkable, bikeable urban environments,[1] the value of better transit accrues not only to existing transit passengers and newly attracted ones, but to people who will decide where to live and start businesses—in which neighborhood, city, or region—based on the availability of transit-served walkable neighborhoods. These location decisions affect the competitiveness of the entire metropolitan area and justify transit-first policies in street design and investment.

A MOBILITY SERVICE FOR THE WHOLE CITY

Making it possible to quickly and reliably go anywhere by transit is a way for cities to significantly improve quality of life. A transit system designed as a mobility service focuses on its value to the rider, providing prompt, seamless, and safe connections to where people want and need to go. A public transit-based mobility system, open to people of all ages and abilities, is fundamentally more equitable than one based primarily on private vehicles.

A crucial complement to the transit network is a suite of flexible, convenient, and affordable mobility choices—walking, bicycling, shared mobility, and on-demand rides—that, together with fixed-route transit, allow residents to avoid the costs of car ownership and make proactive decisions about each trip they take.

GROWTH WITHOUT CONGESTION

Transit streets allow growth in economic activity and developmental density without growth in traffic congestion by serving more people in less space. Transit is most productive for a city and most effective for riders when a large number of people want to travel along one street, but these types of streets are inherently prone to automobile congestion, with unreliable travel times when the most people need to travel.

Streets designed for rapid transit reverse this equation, making transit trips fastest on streets with high travel demand, where frequency is greatest. A public transit-based mobility system benefits everyone in a city, whether or not they choose to ride transit, as people using transit and private vehicles alike can access more destinations in the same amount of time after transit has been improved and density increased.

SAFE MOVEMENT AT A LARGE SCALE

With transit's order-of-magnitude safety advantage over private automobiles, promoting transit is integral to policies that seek sustained improvements in pedestrian, bicyclist, and vehicle occupant safety. Transit mode share and transit-supportive infrastructure are directly correlated to lower traffic fatality rates.[2]

Improving transit does not mean creating speedways, since higher top speeds have little benefit for transit on city streets. Transit streets designed with people in mind are safe places to walk and bike, and transit improvements go hand in hand with better pedestrian access, safer crossings, and more enjoyable public space.

PERMANENT ECONOMIC BENEFITS

Transit streets save both time and money, making frequent service into a financially sustainable proposition and setting off a virtuous cycle of more riders, more service, and more street space for people. Beyond the well-documented local economic benefits of transit-friendly street design, savings are accrued by transit agencies, which can provide mobility to more people at a lower cost, as well as to passengers who can access more destinations faster. And since transit supports higher-value, more compact development, it is a more fiscally sustainable investment than highway infrastructure. These savings are good for businesses and residents along a transit corridor and far beyond.

Powell Street, **SAN FRANCISCO, CA**

Why Transit Streets Matter

High-quality transit allows a city to grow without slowing down. When prioritized, transit has the potential to stem the growth of vehicle congestion, provide environmentally efficient and responsible transportation, and reduce both personal mobility expenses and overall public infrastructure expenses. And transit that can be relied on makes it possible to build walkable urban places—the kinds of places that city residents increasingly demand.

Accomplishing all of this requires that cities set priorities and make investments, both in transit service itself and in the streets on which transit operates. Much of the transit street design challenge lies in aligning the priorities and demands of city departments with those of transit operators, and in demonstrating the value of investments and dedicated street space to city residents and leaders. Balancing multiple modes in a limited right-of-way calls for a considered approach, with short-term successes building to long-term gains.

Designing to Move People

Transit streets are designed to move people, and should be evaluated in part by their ability to do so. Whether in dense urban cores, on conventional arterials, or along neighborhood spines, transit is the most spatially efficient mode.

Traditional volume measures fail to account for the entirety of functions taking place on urban streets, as well as the social, cultural, and economic activities served by transit, walking, and bicycling. Shifting trips to more efficient travel modes is essential to upgrading the performance of limited street space.

Using person throughput as a primary measure relates the design of a transit street to broader mode shift goals.

While street performance is conventionally measured based on vehicle traffic throughput and speed, measuring the number of people moved on a street—its person throughput and capacity—presents a more complete picture of how a city's residents and visitors get around. Whether making daily commutes or discretionary trips, city residents will choose the mode that is reliable, convenient, and comfortable.

Transit has the highest capacity for moving people in a constrained space. Where a single travel lane of private vehicle traffic on an urban street might move 600 to 1,600 people per hour (assuming one to two passengers per vehicle and 600 to 800 vehicles per hour),[3] a dedicated bus lane can carry up to 8,000 passengers per hour. A transitway lane can serve up to 25,000 people per hour per travel direction.[4]

PRIVATE MOTOR VEHICLES
600–1,600/HR

MIXED TRAFFIC WITH FREQUENT BUSES
1,000–2,800/HR

TWO-WAY PROTECTED BIKEWAY
7,500/HR

DEDICATED TRANSIT LANES
4,000–8,000/HR

SIDEWALK
9,000/HR

ON-STREET TRANSITWAY, BUS OR RAIL
10,000–25,000/HR

The capacity of a single 10-foot lane (or equivalent width) by mode at peak conditions with normal operations.[5]

Reliability Matters

Unlocking the enormous potential of transit requires active measures to make trips take less time. To achieve this, the *Transit Street Design Guide* details street design strategies to improve transit reliability and reduce overall travel times.

Transit service that is reliable and efficient brings value to people and cities, but slow and inconsistent service will discourage passengers and jeopardize local benefits. If a trip takes significantly longer by transit than by other modes, or if actual trip time ranges so widely as to be unpredictable, people may choose not to take transit and cities will miss out on opportunities to reduce congestion and spur development.

For urban transit, getting to a destination faster means removing sources of delay rather than raising top travel speeds. The most significant sources of transit delay are related to both street design and transit operations, calling for coordinated action by transit and street authorities.

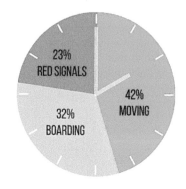

MINNEAPOLIS, MN: In the Twin Cities, the transit agency estimates that the majority of transit runtimes on a major corridor are when transit vehicles are not moving. (Source: Metro Transit).

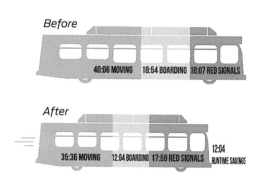

NEW YORK, NY: After implementing a series of street and service improvements including all-door boarding and dedicated lanes on First and Second Avenues, New York's Metropolitan Transportation Authority and Department of Transportation observed substantial travel time improvements on the M15 Select Bus Service compared with the previous M15 Limited service. (Source: NYC DOT).

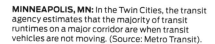

TRAFFIC & INTERSECTION DELAY

In mixed traffic, transit is limited by prevailing traffic conditions, and will be delayed by all the factors that delay the cars it shares space with. Time spent waiting for signals or slowing for stop signs, known as intersection delay or traffic control delay, increases as traffic volume nears the capacity of the street, and as cross streets are more frequent or reach their own capacity. Providing transit lanes (see page 110) and using signal strategies (see page 149) can help cut travel times by half, with the greatest benefits made available by using transitways (see page 126). While these levels of priority stop short of grade-separated facilities, they can be the foundation of every city's transit design toolbox, and are inherently adaptable to a variety of street conditions.

While signal delay is relatively easy to address through active TSP if traffic queues are short, signals with long or variable queues can add up to very long delays for buses and streetcars in mixed-traffic conditions. Time spent slowly approaching red signals or stop signs in heavy traffic can also contribute to overall delay.

Unreliable travel times are a major issue for transit operations because short delays can quickly snowball as more passengers try to board a late-arriving vehicle. Missing one green signal can cause a bus or streetcar to fall behind enough to delay the transit vehicle behind it.[6]

DWELL TIME

Dwell time related to passenger boarding and payment is a large component of total travel time on productive routes, especially in downtowns and destination areas. Level or near-level boarding (see page 64), multi-door boarding and advanced payment options (see page 182), and better passenger information can cut dwell time in half or more. Stop consolidation also reduces the amount of time spent dwelling at stops.[7]

Savings from Transit Improvements

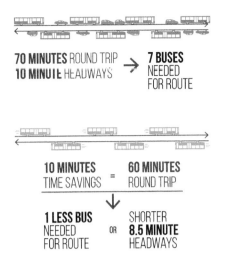

Example of operational savings from transit improvements.

Responding to development

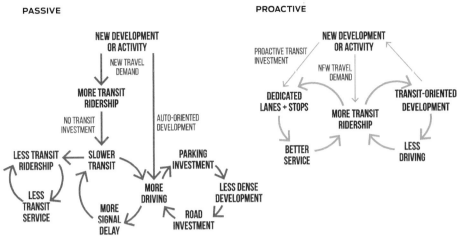

Examples of the compounding benefits from responding proactively to development through transit investment (right), and the compounding issues from auto-oriented development without transit investment (left).[8]

TIME IN MOTION: ACCELERATION, MERGING, AND ROUTE DIVERGENCE

Acceleration, deceleration, and door operation time approaching or leaving a stop can add 15–30 or more seconds per stop. Consolidating from stops to stations (see page 181) and introducing rapid services (see page 10) can dramatically reduce this time expenditure.

For buses in particular, merging into or re-entering the flow of general traffic after a conventional curbside pull-out stop is a perennial source of delay. Reduce this delay by providing in-lane stops and stop-related signal treatments (see *Signals & Operations* on page 149, and *Stop Placement & Intersection Configuration* on page 60), or by enforcing a yield-to-bus law.

Circuitous routes and turns can be time consuming for transit operators and confusing for passengers, often adding significantly to travel time. Keeping transit lines simple and direct serves to minimize this delay, improving transit travel times. While this may increase the time spent walking to a stop, it can benefit overall trip times. Evaluate any changes based on a walking network model and transit travel times.

PASSENGER ACCESS AND WAIT TIME

In addition to on-board transit time, a passenger's trip time also includes time spent walking to a stop, waiting for transit to arrive, making any transfers, and accessing a destination. Since passengers place 2.5 times more value on a shorter wait than on a shorter amount of time spent in motion or a shorter walk to transit, a small improvement in wait time can provide a larger benefit to passengers and a greater boost to ridership than a similar improvement in speed.[9]

Reliability affects how passengers perceive wait times. If wait time and travel time vary significantly, or are routinely much longer than the scheduled time, passengers build this time into their trips, and transit becomes less useful for them.

Transit and street design can make wait time valuable to passengers by providing comfortable waiting areas at stops (see *Stations & Stops*, page 57), by providing real-time information to reduce start-of-trip wait times, and by reducing the time needed for transfers through network design (see *Transit System Strategies*, page 175). Quality urban street design can make walking to a transit stop a positive feature of transit trips.

UNLOCKING OPERATIONAL EFFICIENCIES

Addressing the main sources of transit delay has two related benefits. It shortens door-to-door time for a passenger trip, improving the competitiveness of transit. It also reduces the time and cost of each transit vehicle's run, enabling a transit agency to provide more frequent service to each stop with the same number of vehicles and drivers. In this context a small travel time savings is a large cost savings.

Buses in mixed traffic are susceptible to a downward service spiral, in which increased congestion—exacerbated over the long term by designing streets primarily to accommodate private motor vehicles—results in lower ridership and revenue, resulting in service cuts and lower ridership and revenue.

This cycle can be reversed by improving on-street transit travel times. Shorter travel time allows transit operators to run more frequent service, with more runs per hour using the same number of vehicles and drivers. Greater frequency and shorter trip time yields higher ridership, raising revenue and permitting still greater service frequency.

For detailed information and analysis of transit delay, see the Transit Capacity and Quality of Service Manual, 3rd Edition.

16th Street, **DENVER, CO**

Service Context

Different transit services call for different facilities. While street design practice has historically focused on motor vehicle movement and has treated transit capacity as primarily influenced by stop design, street design processes are increasingly recognizing that key transit lines—those with higher ridership, higher frequency, and more potential for growth—both need and justify greater accommodation than lower-ridership routes.

Designing for the type and frequency of transit service on a street means providing transit with priority treatments and the space necessary to perform at a high level. Whether a route uses bus, light rail, or streetcar, service decisions in an urban transit network are made based on a complex combination of capacity, reliability, comfort, and the need to accommodate passengers in a network. Some projects involve a simultaneous change in transit service on a street along with transit prioritization or streetscape investments, but all street design projects have a service context.

This section provides designers and planners with a basis of discussion of the needs of transit, by linking specific design elements and comprehensive street designs, found later in the *Guide*, with concepts of transit service frequency and the type of transit route supported by a street.

Transit Route Types

Different streets, neighborhoods, and cities have different transportation needs, and a wide range of service types are available to meet them. Likewise, service can be complemented by a range of design elements depending on service needs and street context.

When prioritizing street investments, differentiate between "structural" and "non-structural" transit routes. Structural routes form the bones of the transit network, and yield the greatest results from upgrades. Non-structural routes serve to fill gaps in the transit network.

Robust evidence-based service planning using realistic data can identify new service and growth opportunities, especially opportunities to add rapid routes. These can be supported by street design to create broader transit benefits.

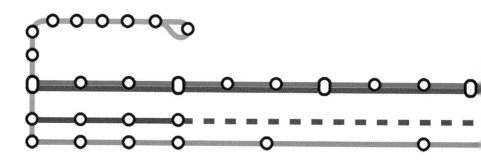

DOWNTOWN LOCAL

Downtown local routes, often frequent, serve an area with a very high demand for short trips and are sometimes operated by a city transportation department or civic group. Unlike conventional loop circulators, downtown locals provide a core transit function for short distances, sometimes parallel to longer local or rapid routes. If planned to complement rather than compete with other structural routes, they can become a permanent feature of the city.

APPLICATION

Downtown locals can be used to connect a high-capacity node (such as a commuter rail terminal) with a broader destination area.

Downtown locals provide extra capacity where dense residential areas are close to major employment or education centers.

Complementary designs:*

- » In-lane stops
- » Transit lanes

*Complementary Designs are detailed in Chapters 4 (*Lane Elements*), 5 (*Stop Typologies*), 6 (*Stop Elements*), and 7 (*Intersection Strategies*).

SERVICE DETAILS

- » Stop Frequency: 4 or more per mile.
- » Service Area: Compact, dense.

LOCAL

Local routes, whether served by bus or rail, are the basic building blocks of urban transit. Local service must balance access—usually considered in terms of stop frequency—with speed. For passengers and operators alike, reliability is often more important than running time. To be effective, local service must be as direct as possible. Deviating from a direct route to serve areas of relatively low ridership will degrade the quality of service.

APPLICATION

Appropriate for all urban contexts, local service serves trips within and between neighborhoods, downtowns, and other hubs.

Provide stop and intersection investments, potentially tied to modest increases in stop distance, to reduce delay on local routes.

Complementary designs:

- » Enhanced shared lanes
- » Dedicated transit lanes
- » Conversion from stops to stations
- » Multi-door boarding
- » Transit signal progressions and short cycle lengths

SERVICE DETAILS

- » Stop Frequency: 3–5 per mile.
- » Service Frequency: Moderate to high, depending on context.
- » Service Area: While route length is variable, riders typically use for short- to medium-length trips (less than 3 miles).

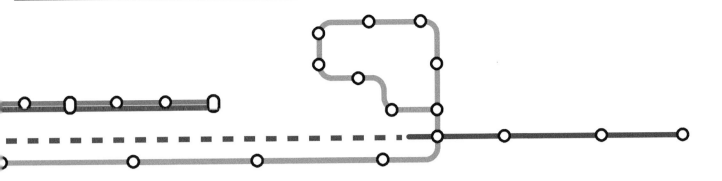

RAPID

With less frequent stops and higher capacity vehicles, rapid (or "limited") service can provide a trunkline transit service for longer trips and busy lines, or can run along the same route as a local service. Most bus rapid transit, light rail transit, rapid streetcars, and limited-stop bus lines run on this service pattern.

COVERAGE

In low-density areas, or where street networks are poorly connected, basic transit accommodation often results in indirect or infrequent service. In these areas, routes have to be circuitous to serve small pockets of ridership. This is best done by using a coverage route rather that adding a deviation to a local route. Keeping coverage routes as direct as is reasonable can be a prelude to a more productive service as density and demand increases.

EXPRESS

Provide direct point-to-point service with few stops using limited-access highways, sometimes in dedicated or HOV lanes, to reach destinations quickly. Express bus operation is usually more expensive per passenger than limited service, since it often uses one central boarding/alighting point. Many express services run coach buses.

APPLICATION

On long, direct, or high-demand transit routes, especially on priority corridors such as those connecting downtowns to dense neighborhoods.

Rapid service can make transfers worthwhile to more passengers on routes that intersect many other transit routes.

Complementary designs:
- » Separated transitways
- » Dedicated transit lanes
- » Stations or high-amenity stops
- » Transit signal priority
- » All-door boarding

APPLICATION

In less densely populated urban edges, coverage service provides a functional connector to regional hubs and destinations, and to the full transit network.

If coverage service is provided to a planned development corridor, include transit-supportive design in initial capital projects.

Complementary designs:
- » Enhanced stops
- » Complementary mobility services, such as taxi, for-hire vehicles, and car sharing can reduce the need for coverage service in some areas.

APPLICATION

Connecting neighborhoods with peak-period ridership directly to downtown or other destinations such as airports.

Where freeways or other limited access routes are available.

Primarily serving long-distance commuter routes.

Complementary designs:
- » Access to on-street terminals and other high-capacity stops
- » Passenger queue management
- » Dedicated transit lanes, especially in access routes to freeways or in downtowns

SERVICE DETAILS

- » Stop Frequency: 1 to 3 per mile.
- » Service Frequency: Moderate to high.

SERVICE DETAILS

- » Stop Frequency: 2 to 8 per mile.
- » Service Frequency: Low.
- » Service Area: Low density, feeder to intermodal hubs.

SERVICE DETAILS

- » Stop Frequency: Non-stop "express segments" between service areas that have more frequent stops.
- » Service Frequency: Scheduled, often infrequent and concentrated at peak periods. Schedule adherence is critical.

Transit Frequency & Volume

The volume of transit vehicles and passengers moving through and stopping on a street are key factors in both the selection of street elements and their detailed design. Street design has an interactive effect on transit frequency, both supporting transit at different volumes, and attracting passengers to different degrees. For decisions about street space and time allocation, the combined frequency of all routes is more significant than the frequency of any given route.

Frequency is discussed here in the context of standard buses during peak periods. For larger vehicles, consider both ridership and vehicle frequency in determining spatial needs.

Santa Fe Depot, **SAN DIEGO, CA**

LOW VOLUME

- » Over 15 minute headways
- » 4 or fewer buses per hour
- » Typically fewer than 100 passengers per hour

Street design must accommodate transit vehicle geometry, but passenger and pedestrian safety and access are often larger issues on lower-use routes. Many express and coverage routes have low frequencies, with schedule adherence and general reliability the primary concern for passengers and operators alike.

Active transit signal priority (TSP) has relatively strong benefits for transit and minimal impacts on other modes.

Enhancing stops improves comfort and customer confidence.

Passenger information both at stops and online is critical to basic usability of the service.

Elements & Strategies:
- » Enhanced stops
- » Intermodal stations
- » Active transit signal priority
- » Passenger information
- » Access to dedicated lanes
- » Combined queue jump/turn lanes

MODERATE VOLUME

- » 10–15 minute or shorter headways, generally 5–10 at peak
- » 4–10 buses per hour
- » 100–750 passengers per hour

Providing a qualitatively different service than low frequency routes, transit lines that are part of a frequent network should be kept prompt and reliable for easy transfers, overall usability, and a good passenger experience. These transit streets have room for growth, and services must be as competitive as possible.

Traffic delay, rather than dwell time, is usually the main source of delay. Intersection priority focused on reliability, and dedicated lanes at slow points, can put these services on the path to growing ridership.

Street design should prioritize transit stop convenience and provide transit vehicles with a preferred position in traffic, including in-lane stops and other priority treatments.

Moderately frequent service can be integrated into spaces shared with active modes, including shared streets.

Elements & Strategies:
- » Active transit signal priority (all service)
- » Transit approach lanes and queue jumps
- » In-lane stops
- » Boarding islands/bulbs; near-level boarding
- » Multi-door boarding
- » Dedicated transit lanes
- » Dedicated peak-only lanes
- » Shared bus-bike lanes

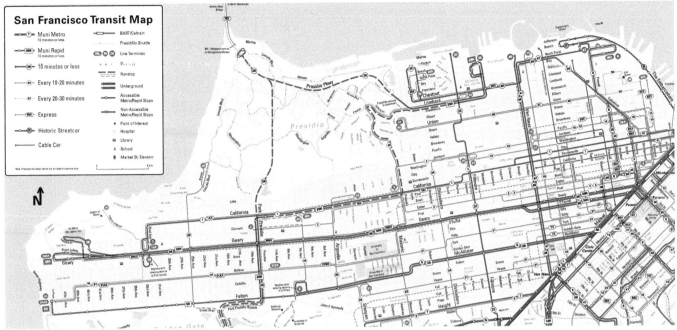

San Francisco's transit map clearly distinguishes route headways, helping riders consider wait times when making trips (MUNI map by David Wiggins & Jay Primus).

HIGH VOLUME

- » 2–6 minute combined headways
- » 10–30 buses per hour
- » 500–2,000 passengers per hour

With transit arriving every few minutes, schedule adherence is less important to passengers than wait time, and maintaining headways matters for reliability as well as speed.

At these high service frequencies, buses and rail vehicles have a major influence on general traffic operations, and might account for a majority of travel on the street. Providing dedicated lanes or improving existing dedicated lanes can expand total street capacity, attracting more passengers. Transit can easily become the fastest mode on a street if given space.

If multiple routes operate or long dwell times occur, refer to very high volume guidance.

Elements & Strategies:

- » Dedicated transit lanes or peak transit lanes
- » In-lane stops
- » Boarding islands/bulbs
- » Low-speed signal progression
- » Active transit signal priority (late vehicles only)
- » Robust stops or stations
- » All-door boarding

VERY HIGH VOLUME

- » Combined headways under 2–3 minutes
- » More than 20–30 buses per hour
- » Over 1,000 passengers per hour on multiple routes, or over 2,500 per hour on one route with multi-unit vehicles

The performance of transit on streets where multiple routes converge at key points in the network often determines the fate of the entire transit network. On these highly productive transit streets, transit will dominate the streetscape whether or not the design prioritizes it effectively. Exclusive transit lanes are crucial for maintaining speed and reliability.

At headways of 3 minutes and shorter, buses and rail vehicles carry thousands of passengers per hour, and must be insulated from general traffic delay. Dedicated lanes or transitways are indispensable for the efficient movement of people. Stop capacity is a critical operational factor.

Signal and intersection operations should favor transit, with transit-friendly signal progressions or dedicated transit phases providing stronger benefits than active transit signal priority.

Elements & Strategies:

- » Transitways or dedicated transit lanes with turn management
- » Dual transit lanes or dedicated lanes with pull-out stops
- » On-street terminals
- » Boarding islands/bulbs
- » Transit signal progression

Case Study: Houston Metro System Reconfiguration

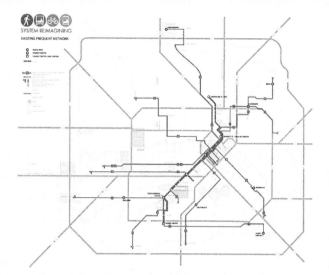

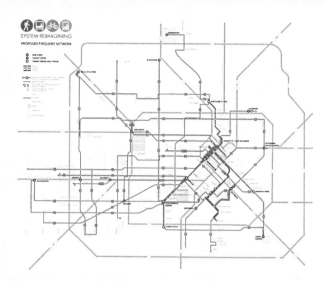

On August 16, 2015, Houston's Metro transit system implemented one of the largest bus network changes in US history. All local routes, including routes that had not been rethought since the 1920s, were redesigned and integrated with recently opened light rail lines.

Just a few months after implementation of the New Bus Network, local bus ridership had increased 4.3%, and total local network ridership increased 11% from November 2014 to November 2015. Weekends in particular received much more frequent service, resulting in a Sunday ridership jump of 30%. The fast success of this effort demonstrates the value that cities can generate by matching the transit network to the street network.

The New Bus Network replaced a mostly peak-oriented low-frequency radial network with a high-frequency all-times grid. The first major aspect of this change is turning a radial system focused on Downtown Houston into a grid that reaches Houston's polycentric employment clusters. The second aspect is a focus on frequency, doubling the number of routes that have service every 15 minutes or better. This change provides dramatic improvements in midday, evening, and weekend service, transforming the network into a full-time system. Routes now operate as frequently on a Sunday morning as they do at midday on a Monday.

The grid network allows simpler, more direct, and faster routes by creating logical transfer locations. Riders are no longer forced to go through Downtown, and routes are both easier to use and more efficient. About 95% of the city's population now lives within one quarter of a mile of a frequent service, and less than half a percent of existing riders moved beyond a quarter mile of service.

The network was created through a planning process that took a "blank sheet" look at the network, convened a policy discussion on whether to focus resources on ridership or coverage goals, and involved extensive public discussion and consultation. The result was a decision to intentionally shift service hours towards ridership goals, and to rethink all routes—even successful ones. Rail and bus are complementary rather than competitive in the new network; the new light rail lines are used as high-capacity network spines for access to Downtown, carrying riders who previously used buses. By making each route more productive, the network change was implemented with almost no increase in bus operating costs. Ridership growth building on these service changes is expected to continue, as people make decisions on where to live and work based on it and as the system becomes easier to use through better passenger information, real-time arrival information by text messaging, three-hour tickets, and longer-term investments in stops and pedestrian improvements.

2. Transit Streets

Realizing the full potential of transit calls for the transformation of transit's operating environment: the street. As the most spatially efficient mode for moving people, transit is the foundation for high-demand city streets.

Designing streets for transit involves making every passenger's trip work as well or better using transit as with other modes. When streets prioritize transit service and active modes, transit can be prompt and effective, and accessing and using it can be easy and comfortable. This strategy may be called development-oriented transit: enhancing and supporting the community, business, and civic value of a street by removing barriers to efficient movement in the most sustainable motorized mode.

By attracting new riders and activity, the design and operational concepts shown in this section help make the entire street work better for everyone.

Washington/LaSalle LoopLink Station, **CHICAGO, IL**

Transit Streets

Transit can be integrated into a full variety of urban streetscapes, from one-lane shared streets to multi-lane boulevards. The street compositions in this section reflect a series of design packages that combine complementary treatments and service types in relevant urban contexts. They demonstrate ways to efficiently integrate on-street transit vehicle facilities, service-enhancing stops and stations, pedestrian and bicycle infrastructure, and general traffic lanes in a variety of street sizes and types. They also illustrate how street design elements work together to form a vibrant streetscape with transit as its spine.

Transit Street Principles

TRANSIT STREETS ARE LIVING STREETS

Great transit brings more people to a street in less space than other modes, creating nodes of activity around stations and along routes. Designing transit streets as linear public spaces enhances both the attractiveness of transit and its ability to support healthy urbanism.[1] Shift vehicular priority from cars to transit to unlock space for parklets, plazas, bike lanes, and sidewalk cafes.

PRIORITIZE TRANSIT AT EVERY SCALE

On streets of every size and context, design can directly improve transit travel time, reliability, and capacity. Major projects like dedicated transitways can substantially increase transit speeds and the total person capacity of a street.[2] On smaller streets, fine-grained improvements like bus bulbs and signal timing combine to transform the way the street works.

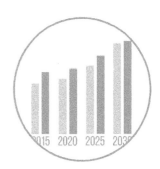

DESIGN FOR GROWTH

Streets that comprehensively prioritize transit create an upward spiral of higher ridership, better service, local economic growth, and more compact, sustainable development. Basic transit accommodations are not enough to support future growth; high-quality transit calls for efficient and comfortable stops, coordinated signals, and dedicated space. Combine these with mixed-use zoning and expanded city services to fundamentally remake a transit corridor.

TRANSIT STREETS ARE ACTIVE STREETS

Transit streets are built around safe, low-stress, and complete pedestrian and bicycling infrastructure. Transit riders are active users of the street, relying on comfortable sidewalks and bikeways—and orderly motor vehicle traffic moving at safe speeds. Intuitive travel paths and frequent opportunities to cross the street make it easy and safe for people to get to transit stops, and are essential to building ridership.[3]

DESIGN CHANGES DEMAND

As streets become more heavily traveled, repurposing space for transit can dramatically increase ridership, bringing more activity to the street. Investments in transit-supportive infrastructure attract new riders and reveal latent demand for better transit service. Street design powers a shift to transit, walking, and bicycling by making them the most attractive travel modes—safe, convenient, efficient, and enjoyable.

NEAR-TERM PROJECTS, LONG-TERM PLANS

Implementing transit improvements quickly with interim materials can demonstrate the value of dedicating space to transit and can build support for broader change, while informing public discussions around street design. Use low-cost materials to change street geometry, unlocking opportunities for new types of transit service, improving walking conditions, and testing new ideas while preparing for longer-lasting capital construction.

Street Environments

Three basic street environments are discussed in this guide: Neighborhood, Corridor, and Downtown transit streets. Just as each of these contexts has distinct design needs related to its role in the transportation network, each context presents unique challenges to designing for transit.

Infrastructure options for transit stops, lanes, and intersections are affected by the existing design of a street and the types of transit vehicles in use, but priorities in the allocation of space are often defined by factors beyond the transit service or vehicle itself—from the nature of local businesses to the length of blocks.

NEIGHBORHOOD STREETS

Neighborhood streets, including both mixed-use main streets and residential streets, are both important multi-modal routes as well as urban living spaces. Typically no wider than a lane in each direction, neighborhood streets have moderate pedestrian and bicycle traffic, with low-speed vehicular traffic.[4] Local transit has an important relationship with neighborhood streets, which provide all-week demand and ridership. Limited street capacity presents challenges for transit reliability.

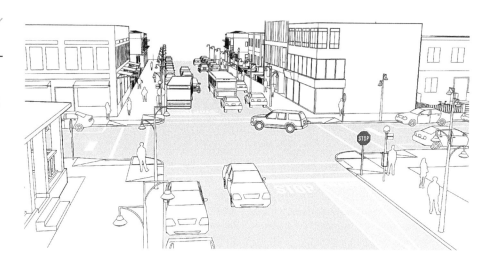

CORRIDOR STREETS

Long and direct, transit corridor streets are critical venues for high-frequency transit service at the center of regional mobility. But these streets have often been designed as highway-like arterials, with minimal or substandard pedestrian and bicycle facilities and high motor vehicle speeds—a high-risk combination. Prioritizing transit throughput and pedestrian safety on these corridors can support higher transit capacity at a citywide level, while attracting local investment.

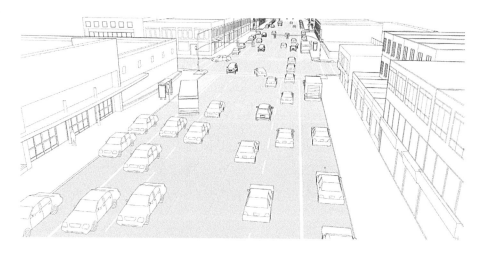

DOWNTOWN STREETS

Located in major urban activity centers, downtown streets have high pedestrian and transit volumes due to a high density of nearby destinations like shops, restaurants, offices, and cultural attractions—a concentration of activity only made possible by transit. Separation of transit from general traffic is often necessary to achieve safe and efficient transit performance while supporting pedestrian activity on such vibrant streets.

Techniques that keep local buses prompt on small neighborhood streets are insufficient for downtown streets with multiple types of service, heavy boardings and unpredictable traffic speeds. The mix of walking, bicycling, driving, parking, and staying activities inform design goals, as do the buildings, institutions, and businesses that form the urban character.

This approach to transit design emphasizes the experience of people using and accessing transit and public space, along with the value of time. It treats streets as linear public spaces that support transit by making it both reliable and attractive as a means of urban travel.

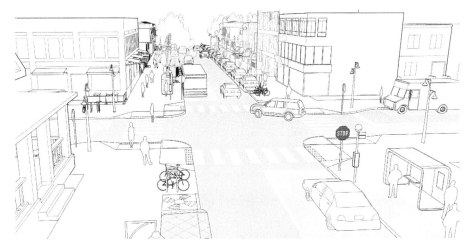

Boarding bulbs and careful curbside management make transit service more reliable without dramatic changes to the street section. On a neighborhood-scale street, improved transit stops provide a significantly better pedestrian realm, and are a focal point for other neighborhood improvements and mobility hubs. Designating space for deliveries and drop-offs, and setting a fair price for curbside parking, relieve common sources of delay for transit and private vehicles alike, and create a safer place to bike as well.

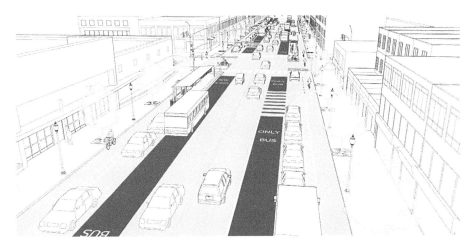

Wide corridor streets are sometimes-overlooked candidates for the assignment of general-traffic lanes to transit, making the street more organized, easier to use, and more predictable, while reducing aggressive driving.[5] Providing exclusive spaces for walking, biking, transit, and driving accommodates the different speeds and distinct operational needs of each mode.

Downtown transit streets can be premier public spaces, and transit reliability is key in an intensively used downtown. Exclusive transit space or space shared with other active modes can create large time savings and radical improvements to the social and economic life of the street.[6] Creative use of one-way streets can support a productive transit grid. Transit signal progressions, stations with near-level platforms, longer spacing of stops, and all-door boarding can all speed up the boarding process, benefiting both transit operations and the experience of the street.

Roncesvalles Avenue, **TORONTO, ON**

Two-Way Streets

Two-way streets are one of the basic building blocks of modern cities. They can provide all levels of transit service depending on their size, and, compared to one-way streets, they can make transit routes visible and easier to understand, with service running in both directions on the same street.

In all contexts, improving the transit function of congested two-way streets remains a challenge of balancing dynamic traffic movements, local access, and an inviting public realm. Multiple modes may be competing for scarce street space, and often require management to keep them moving efficiently. Street design tools can improve transit function at all scales and reduce the need for ongoing enforcement.

Enhanced Neighborhood Transit Street

Neighborhood main streets and residential streets alike can be enhanced with simple measures, making the most of available transit improvements in often narrow rights-of-way. Boarding bulbs and other streetscape measures improve transit reliability, provide upgrades to the pedestrian realm, support the street as a living space, and improve safety for all users by moderating traffic speeds.

RECOMMENDATIONS

1 A combination of street design and operation measures, especially Transit Signal Priority (TSP) and boarding bulbs or islands, can provide benefits where transit is a moderate priority, or where more robust measures like dedicated transit lanes cannot fit. Facilitating in-lane stops with boarding bulbs or islands allows buses to remain in a priority position in the street while at stops (see page 72).

Design stops and stations for the expected peak boarding volumes, when passenger impacts on sidewalk conditions are highest.

Near-level boarding platforms, complementary with all-door boarding, reduce dwell time and improve operational efficiency (see page 64).

2 Boarding bulbs create space for transit shelters even where sidewalk space is limited, contributing to higher-visibility service. Bulbs have safety benefits, including improved sightlines that allow bus drivers to see waiting passengers more easily, prevention of high-speed turns, and shorter pedestrian crossing distances. These facilitate shorter signal cycles, bringing general traffic progression in line with bus speeds and potentially improving travel time for several modes.

3 Along signal controlled corridors, alternating between near-side and far-side stop placement may help balance the signal progression around planned stops; the bus can arrive at a far-side stop near the end of green phases, and arrive at the subsequent near-side stop during a red phase. Site stops for easy transfer at transit route intersections. Stops should be near-side at stop-controlled intersections (see *Stop Placement & Intersection Configuration* on page 60).

Speed cushions can calm vehicle traffic without adversely affecting transit vehicles. As buses' wheels are spaced more widely than those on cars, these elements should be built to a width that allows bus tires to straddle and pass over the cushion.[1]

Turn bays or restrictions may be applied at intersections of larger streets where delay is common.

Manage curbside activities. Consider implementing or modifying meter pricing as a method to better allocate scarce space. Dynamic (or "smart") parking systems have been shown to provide a small but steady supply of available parking near businesses, reducing the need for vehicles to circle in search of parking.[2]

4 Designated freight loading zones relieve the loading and double-parking conflicts that frequently inhibit transit service, while providing essential business access. Freight deliveries may also be limited to off-peak periods.

Integrate stormwater management and other green infrastructure on neighborhood streets.

Electric or hybrid buses and streetcars have smoother and quieter acceleration, making them friendlier in smaller-scaled or residential streetscapes.

Use transit stops as mobility hubs, placing bike share or car share stations within the sightlines of alighting passengers.

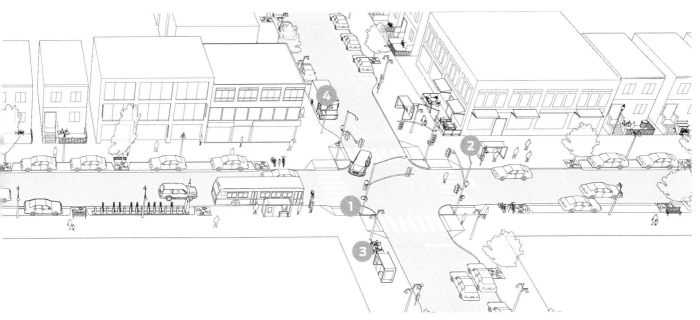

Neighborhood main street (38 feet curb-to-curb, 62-foot ROW)

Case Study: NW 23rd Avenue, Portland

Portland's boarding bulb program, originally developed to improve pedestrian and bicycling operation, has also yielded benefits to transit operations. The installation of enhanced boarding space on NW 23rd Avenue by the City of Portland and TriMet, the region's transit agency, shows how this treatment confers benefits across modes and activates on neighborhood main streets.

NW 23rd Avenue, the first street in Portland where boarding bulbs were implemented, is a main street in the Nob Hill neighborhood. The mile-long corridor has a strong mix of residential, retail, and recreational destinations, in an actively used 60-foot right-of-way. This neighborhood main street serves a frequent bus line with roughly 10-minute headways, and draws substantial bicycling, walking, and driving volumes, with one lane in each direction, parallel parking on both sides, and tree-lined 12-foot sidewalks. The Portland streetcar serves the northern portion of the corridor.

Providing both multi-modal capacity and safe, transit-friendly traffic speeds were key project goals. The city installed bus bulbs at each of the transit stops along NW 23rd Avenue, expanding the pedestrian space and

allowing transit vehicles to make in-lane stops. The shared bus-streetcar stops also feature a dual-height curb profile, with a rear streetcar-level section (14 inches high) and a front bus section (6 inches high), allowing both vehicles to offer accessible boardings from the same platform. Additionally, stops were consolidated to a 750-foot (three-block) spacing, allowing higher boarding volumes at fewer stops, along with the addition of shelters and green infrastructure.

In-lane stops have had a variety of benefits. Prior to the project, transit operators noted that buses rarely

pulled out of traffic to reach the existing sidewalk stops, either due to difficult turning maneuvers or vehicles blocking the bus zone. Since implementation, motor vehicle travel times and traffic speeds have remained unchanged, while the percentage of cars speeding has declined.

Satisfaction with the stop enhancements is high; transit operators report easier loading, especially for riders using wheelchairs, and pedestrians have improved perceptions of traffic stress and walking comfort.

Dual-height curb profile at a boarding bulb stop on NW 23rd Ave., **PORTLAND, OR**

Neighborhood Transit Street with Bike Lane

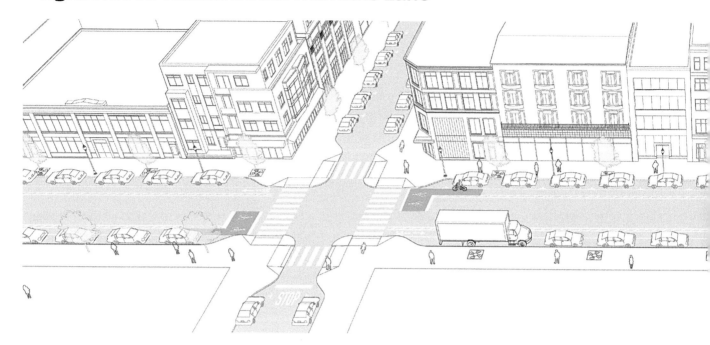

Many neighborhood transit streets and small transit corridors also serve as important bicycle routes. Whether bike lanes are conventional, buffered, or protected, converting to in-lane stops with boarding islands can improve transit speeds and bicycle comfort and safety at the same time, while also making it easier to access transit by bicycle. These robust stop designs also raise the profile of transit on the street, consistent with a high-quality service.

RECOMMENDATIONS

1 On streets with buffered bike lanes, most stops can be converted to in-lane stops. Buses are no longer required to pull to the curb and re-enter traffic, a major advantage on a street with one lane per direction.

Boarding islands direct bicyclists behind transit stops, reducing or eliminating most conflicts between transit vehicles and bicyclists, and expanding available sidewalk space. Eliminating the interaction between buses and bicycles at the curb has potentially large safety benefits for bicyclists, while refuge areas on boarding islands improve pedestrian safety and access by reducing exposure and crossing time.

Boarding islands ensure that all-door boarding will be available by keeping other vehicles from blocking the bus stop. With investments in level or near-level stops that permit all-door boarding, increasing the distance between stops (primarily by consolidating stops) can have even stronger travel time benefits. Provide shelters, seating, and off-board fare collection to improve the passenger experience and reduce common sources of delay.

High turn volumes are a potential source of delay for through-moving transit. Provide left turn bays for high-volume movements, and place bus stops far-side or at intersections with lower turn volumes where feasible.

For streets with tiered local-rapid service, provide occasional pull-out stops, giving rapid and express services and other motor vehicle traffic opportunities to pass the local service.

2 Design boarding islands with pedestrian refuges, shortening crossing distances and enabling shorter signal cycles. Small deflector islands protect pedestrians and tighten turn radii (for additional guidance, see *Side-Boarding Islands*, page 73).

3 Transit and bicycle signal delay can both be reduced with low-speed signal progressions, short cycles, and/or active signal priority to improve transit speeds and reduce corridor-wide travel times (see page 149).

4 Position bicyclists using intersection crossing markings, and apply green color as the bike lane passes the boarding island. Bicyclists can be positioned in front of motor vehicles at intersections using bike boxes, or left turns can be made using two-stage turn queue boxes. On streetcar routes, use two-stage turn queue boxes to encourage bicyclists to cross tracks at a safe angle. Refer to *Bicycle Rail Crossings* (page 166) and the *Urban Bikeway Design Guide* for additional guidance.

Manage parking demand, freight deliveries, and curbside access with dedicated curb space or time-of-day restrictions in retail areas, to reduce blockages of the bike lane or motor vehicle lane. On-street parking can activate underutilized corridor streets and provide a buffer to biking or the pedestrian realm.[3] On-board camera enforcement can be used to deter double-parking, a significant contributor to transit delay on small streets.[4]

Robust stop designs draw attention to high-quality transit service.

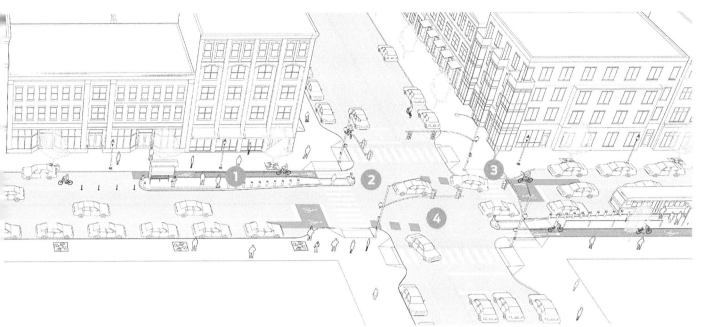

Neighborhood transit street or small transit corridor, with buffered bike lanes (50 feet)

Case Study: Dexter Avenue, Seattle

The Seattle Department of Transportation (SDOT) uses in-lane stops to improve transit and bike safety and operations. During a scheduled resurfacing project of 1.5 miles of Dexter Avenue between Westlake Avenue North and Mercer Street—a segment with frequent bus service—SDOT seized an opportunity to reallocate space to transit by removing an existing center two-way left turn lane. The new configuration features one travel lane, a buffered bike lane, and a curbside parking lane in each direction, with left-turn pockets only where needed. To improve transit travel time and efficiency, bus stops were consolidated to an approximately quarter-mile spacing, allowing SDOT to build more robust and comfortable stops. At 10 of the 12 bus stops on the corridor, SDOT constructed dedicated transit islands, allowing buses to make in-lane stops for boarding passengers. The boarding islands are 10 feet wide and 80 feet long, and constructed using standard concrete. The islands are typically located at far-side stops at intersections with existing curb ramps at the sidewalk, simplifying the provision of accessible paths. Detectable warning strips were used to mark the edge of curb ramps, and all boarding islands are fully accessible.

At boarding islands, the buffered bike lane transitions to the right and is routed behind the bus stop, preventing conflicts between cyclists and stopped buses. The boarding island and bike channel is situated in the shadow of the parking lane, which resumes downstream of the island after the bike lane transitions back to the left. The corridor includes a pull-out stop approximately once per mile to allow vehicles queued behind the bus to pass, maintaining a balanced traffic flow.

Since implementation, bus boardings have increased by 23% along the corridor, and a motor vehicle traffic volume increase of 13% was accommodated, while vehicle travel time has been unchanged. The safety of the corridor has been measurably improved, with a 19% drop in the collision rate. Despite increased boardings at island locations, no conflicts have been reported between bicyclists and passengers. The enhanced stop design has successfully met the need for expanded transit capacity and overall street efficiency, while proving an attractive stop design for transit riders.

Dexter Ave., **SEATTLE, WA**

Downtown Shared Transitway

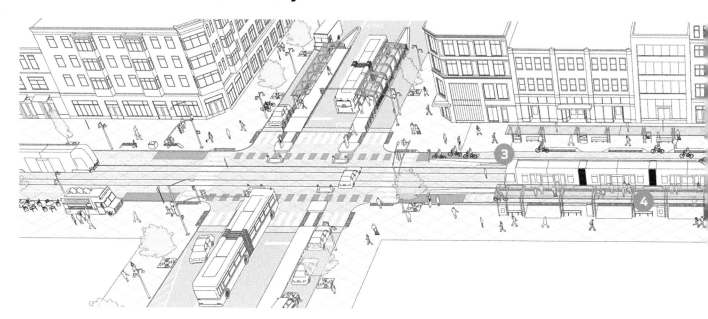

Transit malls with large sidewalks and a central transitway, once a mainstay of North American downtown planning, have sometimes struggled with inadequate local activity levels. By creating a single surface, these malls can be retrofitted to emphasize active use by people on foot across the transitway, and provide for limited access by other street users. Designing the entire right-of-way as a public space provides a sense of place, making an underused mall into a vibrant destination, with high pedestrian volumes, frequent transit, and low-speed bicycle access.

The shared transit street provides both the clear transit space and level of destination access needed on a key downtown route, integrated into a marquee public space that acts as a destination in its own right.

RECOMMENDATIONS

This street has been reconstructed from a conventional curbed transit mall to provide a nearly flush surface with low, mountable curbs defining the right-of-way. A center-running transit street, with a similar right-of-way but narrower existing sidewalks, can also be converted into a shared transit street by reconstructing with widened sidewalks.

Transit capacity is extremely high, supporting bus or rail transit with tens of thousands of passengers per hour. Capacity depends on platform height, signal priority and other conditions. Transit and other speeds are low, prioritizing safe pedestrian movement.

1 A low-curb or, optionally, curbless surface increases pedestrian permeability across the entire street, maximizing available public space and emphasizing the shared condition of the street. Pedestrians can cross a shared transit street at any point, but are discouraged from walking along the central transitway by the high volume of transit vehicles.[5]

Street furniture—including bollards, benches, planters, street lights, and bicycle parking—is sited to provide definition for a shared space and integrated into the cohesive street design. Design elements provide guidance for the visually impaired and subtly delineate the traveled way from the pedestrian-exclusive area. Where less permeability is desired, including just ahead of stations, use plantings and furniture to concentrate activity in desired areas and channelize pedestrian travel paths.

2 The addition of bikeways between the transitway and the exclusive pedestrian space adds further person-capacity to the street. Especially at peak times, the bikeway insulates the shared transitway from the exclusive pedestrian space.

3 At station locations, the bikeway and a portion of the side pedestrian space rise to create a level boarding platform. Where transit shelters are provided, they must be placed on the raised portion of the exclusive pedestrian space. If they are not provided, a lean bar or other furnishings should be used to prevent tripping on the back of the platform (see *Shared Cycle Track Stop*, page 76).

4 Detectable warning strips should be used along the platform edge and at the ends of the platform where the bikeway slope begins. An accessible path must be provided on both sides of the street. At intersections, mark crosswalks and provide detectable warning strips at the end of the exclusive pedestrian area.

Low-emissions and quiet-running transit vehicles, such as battery-electric or hybrid-electric vehicles, are more compatible with the pedestrian environment than an internal-combustion bus fleet, but any transit vehicle can be used.

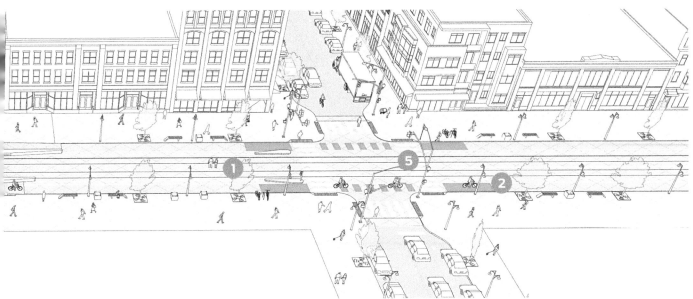

Shared two-way light rail street (40 feet)

5 Auto traffic is either prohibited or limited using volume management techniques that filter out through-traffic and permit local vehicle access, especially for deliveries. These strategies include forced turns, single-block prohibitions, and time-of-day restrictions. Bicycle traffic may also be restricted if a safe alternate route is provided without significant detour requirement.

Limited delivery and private vehicle traffic can be permitted at off-peak transit hours, and delivery vehicles can be permitted to use the street in early morning hours. Fully prohibiting auto traffic on blocks with transit stops prevents lane blockages and cross-street delay. Provide dedicated parking space for loading and delivery vehicles at locations where these vehicles will use the street during daytime hours.

Programming is essential to activating the shared street, and can be coordinated with a local maintenance partner. Shared transit streets are well configured for special events. If nearby parallel streets can accommodate transit service, temporary street closures can be used at off-peak times. Transit detours require robust passenger communications in advance of special events and on site.

Trench drains can be useful for providing both drainage along the street without sewer relocation, and a detectable edge to the transitway.

For additional guidance on Shared Streets, refer to the *Urban Street Design Guide.*

Case Study: Granville Street, Vancouver

In 2010, the City of Vancouver, BC, reconstructed a segment of Granville Street, a primary transit spine and downtown destination. This reconstruction provided the opportunity to improve upon the existing transitway and shared street, by providing wide sidewalks, high-quality custom street furniture, and a better balance of local access and transit movement.

Bus and trolleybus service operates at very high frequency on Granville Street, with headways averaging 80 seconds at peak periods. Deliveries are accommodated through design and regulation; commercial vehicles are allowed to enter the street at off-peak times and to park for short periods on the sidewalk, maintaining a clear transitway but enabling freight deliveries. Bicycling is permitted, as on other bus lanes in Vancouver, and the route is popular among people using bikes for downtown access. Taxis are also permitted to drop off or pick up passengers, but other private motor vehicles are not permitted on the transitway.

Given Granville Street's importance as a destination and nightlife magnet, a primary goal of the project was to create a street that pedestrians would find safe and comfortable to cross throughout each block, not just at intersections. The concrete transitway transitions gently over a mountable curb up to an aggregate sidewalk; pedestrians are alerted by the curb when crossing into the transitway, but are not discouraged from doing so. This design was enabled by an ordinance modifying pedestrian regulations that allows people to cross the street at any point. The result is a linear public space that provides full access, supporting entertainment businesses and activity along the street, while moving transit passengers and vehicles at a large scale.

Granville Street, VANCOUVER, BC

Center-Running Transit Street

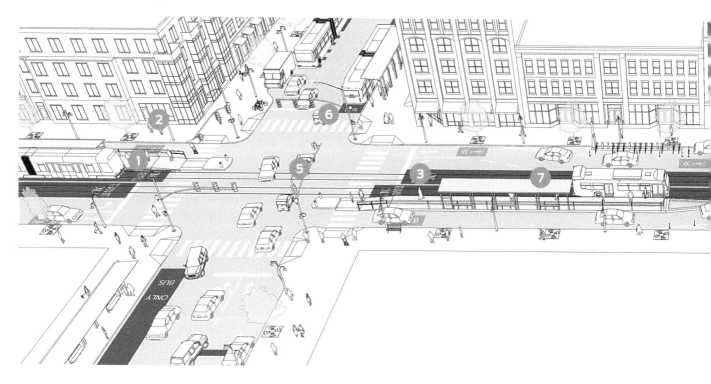

Center-running transit lanes are particularly suited to high-ridership rapid transit routes, affording on-street transit a level of accommodation approaching that of transitways. On streets with two or more travel lanes in each direction, and especially streets with existing center-running streetcars, service can be substantively improved by dedicating the center travel lanes to transit and installing accessible boarding platforms. This combination provides many of the benefits of LRT or BRT in a core urban setting.

On this street, a center-running streetcar route has been retrofitted for longer LRVs and buses, with extended platforms and exclusive use of the center lanes, while using the existing tracks and catenaries. Lower-cost implementations focused on building simple, safe boarding islands can also succeed at a widespread system transformation.

RECOMMENDATIONS

1 Transit vehicles move in a straight line. At stops, parking is prohibited and the general traffic lane bends around the platforms to the right, as a curbside lane. A similar arrangement is used to create left-turn pockets where needed. Using a very low design speed results in short, space-saving transitions.

2 Stations are built on raised platforms in the roadway, staggered across the intersection as far-side stops to conserve street space.

3 Passengers are directed to crosswalks using station furnishings, such as lean bars, shelters, plantings, short vertical barriers, and both visual and tactile cues.

4 Left turns across the center transit lanes are either restricted or accommodated with separate phases to prevent direct conflicts with transit vehicles. Lagging left-turn phases allow transit and parallel pedestrians to cross before cars turn, improving safety by encouraging pedestrians to cross with the signal.

5 Refuge islands are used to channel the flow of traffic, "shadowing" the left turn lanes and shortening pedestrian crossing distances.

6 Transit signal heads are used at intersections to reduce driver confusion and the risk of turn conflicts, especially where TSP is used.

7 Sightlines between the station and the sidewalk are preserved to ensure the visibility and safety of waiting passengers.

8 Advance or adaptive transit signal priority detects transit vehicles as they progress through the corridor, allowing pedestrians safe crossing time while truncating red phases to allow transit to arrive on green phases. Spreading phase modifications through multiple intersections reduces impacts to general traffic flow (see *Turn Restrictions*, page 156).

Off-board fare collection at stations enables all-door boarding, reducing stop dwell time and travel time variability (see page 182).

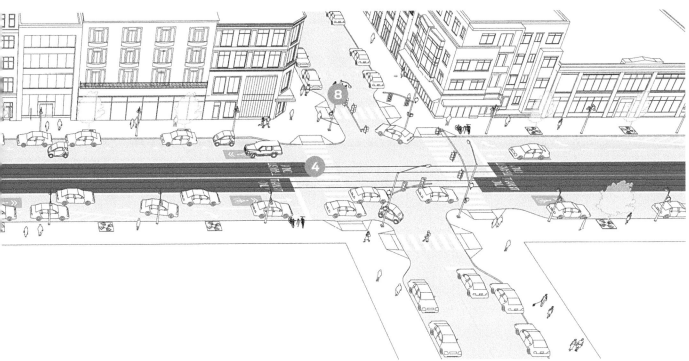

Two-way downtown street with center-running light rail (62 feet)

Case Study: sbX Green Line, San Bernardino, CA

In 2014, OmniTrans and the City of San Bernardino introduced the sbX Green Line, the city's first bus rapid transit line. The 16-mile route includes both median and side-running dedicated transit lanes, center median stations, and new articulated buses with both left- and right-side doors.

Critically, the sbX has protection from traffic delay where it is most needed, allowing the line to serve a high ridership on a dedicated rapid route. In downtown San Bernardino, sbX operates in center-running transit lanes, separated from general travel lanes by double stripes and raised pavement warnings. As buses leave downtown, they transition into side-running transit lanes or mixed-traffic lanes.

Corridor signalization was optimized for transit with active signal priority, and turns across transit lanes are either prohibited or permitted during protected turn phases. The transit lanes are controlled with transit signal heads, distinguishing bus flow from general traffic. Crosswalks and station access were enhanced with pedestrian refuges.

A major component of the sbX project was procurement of the new fleet: low-floor buses with doors on both sides to access both center- and side-boarding platforms. The project seized the chance to improve station quality with the new fleet, providing level boarding and off-board payment to ease accessible boarding and expedite stops. Stations are designed with transit curbs (see page 102) to allow buses to roll within 2 inches of the boarding platform. Buses and stations are configured to board wheelchairs and bikes in separate doors, increasing accessibility and ease of boarding. Finally, stations are designed for comfort, offering accessible ramps, high-quality seating, ticket vending machines, canopies and windscreens, public art, low-water vegetation, and WiFi.

The sbX Green Line has increased transit's mode share on the corridor, with weekly ridership growing 79% by the end of the first year of operations, passing 500,000 annual rides with expectations for further growth. With a new transit hub opening in 2015, the city expects to see up to a 30% increase in ridership on the route between 2015 and 2016. OmniTrans is planning a system of up to ten BRT routes on the model of the Green Line.

South E St., **SAN BERNARDINO, CA** (62 feet)

Downtown Median Transit Street

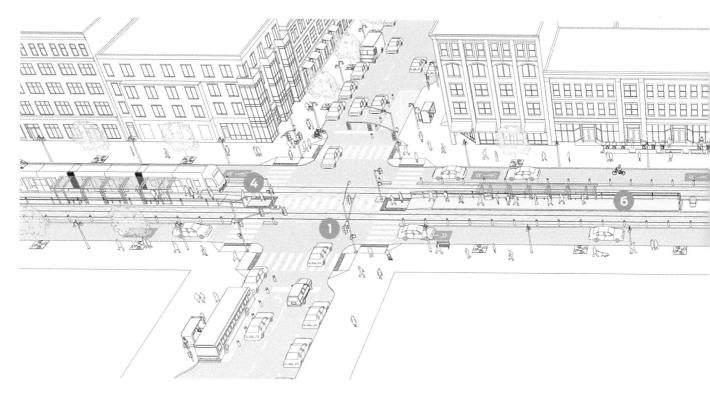

On a busy downtown street, creating a transitway along a central median provides a high-capacity transit facility with few conflicts, and can be used to create a series of linear plazas, transforming the character of the street.

The downtown median transitway preserves the priority of a long route such as a BRT or LRT line as it transitions from larger corridors or off-street rights-of-way; it can also serve a set of local routes that come together on a downtown street. This configuration, similar in size to many neighborhood main streets, fits well in moderately sized downtown streets, and other pedestrian-friendly places, with accommodation of private motor vehicles and bikes in a low-speed shared lane for local access by all modes. Traffic volumes can be further reduced by providing block-long plazas on alternating sides of the street, with opportunities for bicycle-only or bus and bike access in the side lane.

RECOMMENDATIONS

1 The transitway is separated through grade changes, textured pavement, curbs, or other barriers, so general traffic is either deterred or physically prevented from entering the transitway.

Stations promote the visibility and attractiveness of transit service, with the opportunity for high-quality amenities, passenger information, and streetscape beautification.

2 Median transitways can include green infrastructure and environmental enhancements within the transitway. Durable urban materials such as brick, stone, and unit pavers can be used on the transitway or across the entire right-of-way.

While curb and sidewalk reconstruction can introduce distinctive pavement materials and green infrastructure. A median transitway can often be implemented independently of a curb reconstruction, saving time and money.

3 At intersections, special attention is required. Use separate turn phases, prohibit left turns across the median transitway, or prohibit left turns when transit vehicles are present. Extend vertical elements to the intersection edge where turns are prohibited. Use transit signals and either active TSP or transit signal progressions (see Chapter 6, *Intersections*, on page 147)

4 Crosswalks from median to median enable safe and convenient pedestrian access to stations, and should be provided when turns across the transitway are prohibited.

5 Large refuge spaces accommodate groups of alighting passengers, and improve pedestrian safety and access by shortening crossing distances, and reducing the number and complexity of movements and potential vehicle conflicts that pedestrians are exposed to. Refuges allow slower pedestrians to break up their crossings, and allow more flexible signal timing plans.[6] Where pedestrian crossings traverse tracks and bus transitways, audible warnings ensure all pedestrians are aware of oncoming transit vehicles.

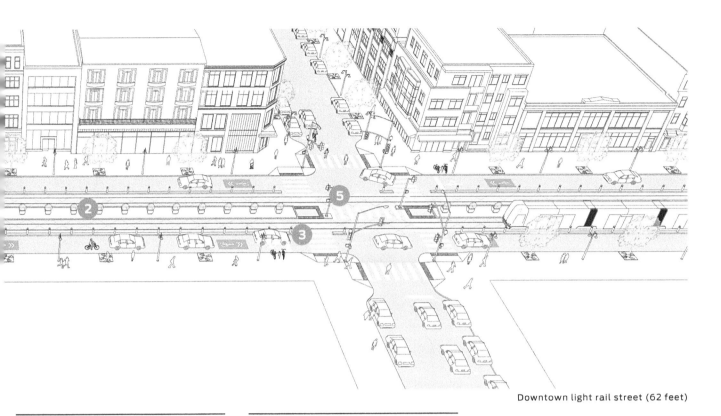

Downtown light rail street (62 feet)

Bicyclist volumes will likely be high due to the high density of destinations along the corridor. Where space exists, protected bike lanes are recommended. Bicycles may also be accommodated in shared travel lanes where speeds are low. Accommodate bicycle turns at right angles using two-stage turn queue boxes (see page 166). Where motor vehicle through-traffic is prohibited, consider providing a cycle track through the plaza.

6 One platform can serve both travel directions, or platforms can be staggered across an intersection or along a block. Staggered split platforms provide higher passenger capacity on relatively narrow medians (see *Median Stop, Left-Side Boarding* on page 86).

Washington Ave., **MINNEAPOLIS, MN** (54 feet)

Main St., **HOUSTON, TX** (62 feet)

Edgefront Transit Street

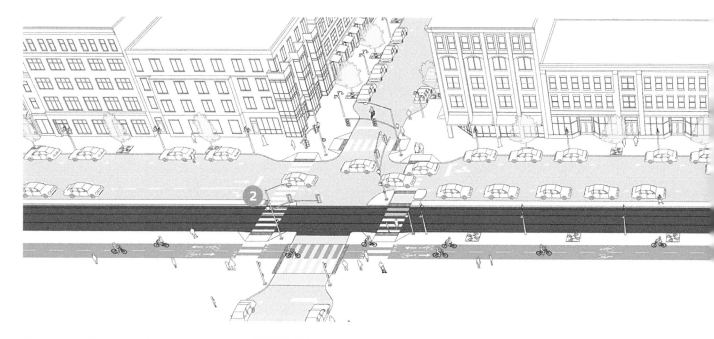

Along waterfronts, parks, campuses and other "edge conditions," where one side of a street has long stretches with limited vehicular crossings, streets can be configured for high-capacity transit with fewer conflicts. Edgefront transitway corridors use side transitways to create an expanded public realm by insulating people on foot from parallel vehicular traffic. These redesigns can dramatically transform the character of a disused waterfront street or a previously failing megablock, safely integrating multiple street users into a premier streetscape.

RECOMMENDATIONS

1 The configuration of edgefront transit streets—with a bi-directional side transitway located along one side of a street corridor with limited intersecting streets—allows unimpeded transit movement with easy access to the sidewalk (see *Side Transitway*, page 130, for additional guidance).

Since turns across the transitway are extremely limited, a bi-directional transitway can be placed adjacent to a parallel bi-directional bikeway or bi-directional or uni-directional general motor vehicle traffic without significantly increasing the risk of conflicts.

With sufficient turn management, edgefront transit streets can also succeed on a typical street grid.

If limited horizontal separation is available, use vertical separation elements to create a visually exclusive transitway adjacent to vehicle travel lanes (see page 136).

2 In the few places where streets cross the transitway, use signage in combination with small curb radii, distinctive materials, and other visual cues to ensure vehicles do not turn into the transitway. Restrict turns across the transitway or use separate turn phases across to avoid conflicts (see page 156).

For vehicles turning into travel lanes parallel to the transitway, extending turning lane pavement markings through the intersection helps to indicate the path of travel (MUTCD §3B-08).

Use transit signal heads for the transitway to avoid confusion among other street users.

3 In this example, stations accommodate right-side boarding, which can support use by multiple vehicle types, including buses running in an "open BRT" line (for platform design guidance, see *Stop Design Factors* on page 59).

If parking is provided next to the transitway, provide a walkway between the parking and transit lane to permit access to parked vehicles.

4 Stations are adjacent to the sidewalk on one side, providing easy pedestrian access. In a downtown or high-activity setting, pedestrian crossings should be provided at all signalized intersections, including T intersections where motor vehicles do not cross tracks. At pedestrian crossings over tracks, provide cues that can be perceived by touch, hearing, and sight. Use audible signals at signalized crossings.

Use street furniture or tactile cues to demarcate the edge of the pedestrian space next to the transit lane. Placing a bikeway between the far sidewalk and the transitway provides additional separation between people on foot and transit vehicles. Use grade separation to prevent bicycles from rolling into the transitway.

SW Moody Ave., **PORTLAND, OR** (80 feet)

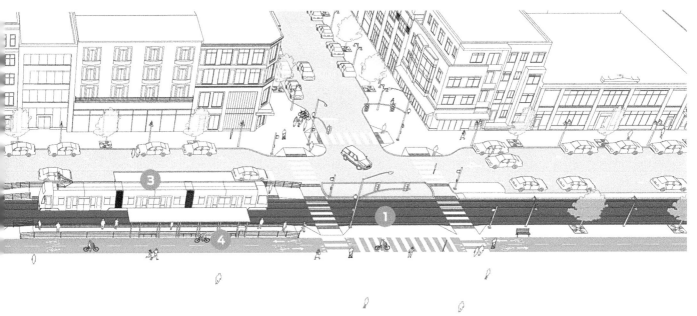

Edgefront transit street, with bi-directional transitway and bikeway (60 feet)

Case Study: Queens Quay, Toronto, ON

In June 2015, the City of Toronto completed the reconstruction of Queens Quay, transforming an underused waterfront street in downtown Toronto into a hallmark destination. The street, formerly configured as two roadbeds, was reconfigured from four lanes of vehicle traffic to two, shifting all private motor vehicle traffic to the former north roadbed. Free of vehicular traffic, the south side of Queens Quay now hosts a side transitway, a broad pedestrian promenade, and a new bi-directional bikeway which filled a gap in the Lake Ontario Waterfront Trail. The transitway carries streetcars in both directions, between vehicle traffic and the waterfront promenade. New landscaped sidewalks on the north side of the street with significant green infrastructure, including connected tree pits, encourage more on-street activity and are attracting new businesses to the street. Along with the installation of high-quality furniture, these design elements in a comprehensive reconstruction have transformed this important transit corridor into a marquee urban place.

Street design was focused on providing a space in which pedestrians, bicyclists, and transit have priority. Turns across the transitway are permitted only during protected phases from dedicated lanes. Where vehicle traffic crosses the transitway and pedestrian promenade, the intersection is raised to alert motorists that they are entering an active space, and must expect the presence of transit vehicles, people walking, and people bicycling. An optimized signal system was implemented at the same time as reconstruction, allowing active transit signal priority with extended green signal phases, pedestrian and bike signals, as well as audible warnings.

For motor vehicles, a primary source of delay before the project was curbside access and loading activity in travel lanes, now accommodated in periodic "lay-bys," or pull-out spaces for short-term stopping and loading. Dedicated turn lanes, coordinated signal timing, and freight management have also simplified traffic operations in the corridor.

Queen's Quay, **TORONTO, ON**

Offset Bus Lane Street

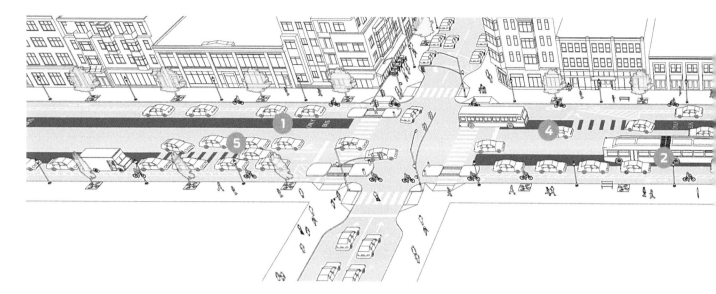

Offset transit lanes—running between a parallel parking lane and a general through-traffic lane—can be applied to a wide variety of streets. Often implemented through simple lane conversions, offset bus lanes are shown here on a wide two-way street characteristic of downtown thoroughfares and multi-modal corridors. Dedicated offset lanes are a core part of the transit toolbox for urban streets. Offset transit lanes provide priority space for frequent or high-volume transit service, a variety of curbside uses and turning movements, and a comfortable sidewalk environment.

On corridor streets, marked and camera-enforced lanes, enhanced station design, longer stop spacing, and prominent route and system branding can improve both travel time and legibility, drawing new passengers and supporting a higher frequency of service.

RECOMMENDATIONS

1 On this street, the right lane in both travel directions has been designated as a bus lane, reducing transit delays due to general queues and improving reliability, especially at peak periods.

2 Frequent, tiered service is provided on this street, with local and rapid service sharing the transit lanes. High transit volumes (up to about 20 buses per hour) are compatible with this street configuration. Somewhat higher volumes can be accommodated by prohibiting turns and increasing the number of local pull-out stops where rapid service can bypass the local route.

3 At rapid service stops, in-lane stops are provided. Rapid/local stops can be near- or far-side but should be on the same block where possible to provide legibility to passengers. If streetcars are used for local service, provide far-side in-lane stops, allowing a rapid bus to pass in the second lane. Tiered stops can provide pull-out bays for local service, allowing the rapid to pass the local (see *Tiered Stop* on page 72).

4 At intersections with high right-turn volume, and a far-side stop or no stop, the parking lane is converted to a right-turn pocket and the transit lane continues to the intersection. At intersections with a low right turn volume and a far-side stop or no stop, turns are permitted from the transit lane. A blank-out sign can be used to prohibit the right turn when a bus or streetcar is approaching.

Right turns are prohibited or managed where a near-side stop is provided.

5 At intersections where left turns are permitted but infrequent, and there is a far-side stop or no stop, the transit lane can be dropped at the approach to allow general traffic through movement in the right lane when no bus is present.

6 Providing dedicated bikeways improves the overall function of the street for transit, especially on neighborhood and corridor streets. On arterials where high traffic volume degrades transit service quality and creates safety challenges for active users, pairing transit lanes with protected bike lanes provides comfort, convenience, and safety for all modes.

Dedicated phases or turning restrictions for left- and right-turning movements across the bike and transit lanes reduce conflicts and improve through movement for transit and general traffic.

Two-way downtown street with offset bus lanes and parking-protected bike lanes (75 feet)

If block length and local stop spacing are similar, local stops can alternate near- and far-side to avoid double-stopping at red signals.

With high transit volumes and tiered service, a transit-supportive corridor signal progression rather than active TSP prioritizes most arriving transit vehicles.

At intersections with a high left-turn volume, the transit lane and adjacent traffic lane can be bent towards the sidewalk to create a left-turn pocket.

Curbside management improves the effectiveness of this offset lane conversion. Truck loading zones and priced parking reduce the incidence of double-parking, but high parking turnover can also result in transit delays. Providing other curbside uses along the corridor, including parklets and islands at stops and crosswalks, can reduce parking maneuver delays and improve pedestrian visibility by clearing the transit lane near intersections (refer to the *Urban Street Design Guide* for additional guidance on refuge islands, curb extensions, and parklets).

Lane enforcement, ideally automated enforcement, is indispensable in areas with high parking demand, as offset lanes are susceptible to blocking by double-parked vehicles and deliveries.

Case Study: Webster Avenue Select Bus Service, New York City, NY

As part of New York City's Select Bus Service program, NYC DOT and the MTA have partnered to upgrade targeted bus routes to provide frequent and high-quality rapid bus service. Significant upgrades were made to Webster Avenue in the Bronx as part of a package to improve the Bx41 bus route, including the installation of offset bus lanes in both travel directions along 4 miles of this major bus corridor.

In addition to dedicated bus lanes, the project included signal coordination, all-door boarding, the introduction of off-board fare payment, and new buses. Three critical intersections were substantially redesigned, using new signals and pedestrian crossings, left-turn prohibitions, and simplified intersection geometry with shorter pedestrian crossings. Refuge islands and related pedestrian safety improvements were installed along the corridor.

Prior to the project, the MTA operated a Local and a Limited service on the Bx41 route, with a total ridership of just under 20,000 passengers per day. Both Local and SBS service use the new dedicated lane, which may be entered by general traffic to permit turns and parking.

Comparing service from a year before installation to a year after, bus travel times through the corridor dropped 19% to 23% for rapid buses. A Bx41 SBS trip during the PM peak fell to 40 minutes, compared to 52 minutes on the previously operated Bx41 Limited. The local bus also saw benefits, with trip times reduced by 11 to 17%.

Ridership grew 25% on the Bx41 SBS route in the year following implementation, and a share of previous Bx41 local riders shifted to the Select bus, now reaching a combined 25,000 riders per day on both the local and SBS routes. Finally, general traffic volumes and travel speeds remained similar a year after implementation, with slightly shorter travel times in peak periods

The redesign of Webster Ave. demonstrates how organizing a multi-lane street, with an exclusive transit lane combined with operationally important design changes, can increase a street's person capacity, substantially reduce travel times, and improve walking conditions and network connectivity, without affecting the movement of private motor vehicles and freight.

Webster Ave., **NEW YORK CITY, NY** (68 feet)

Median Rapid Transit Corridor

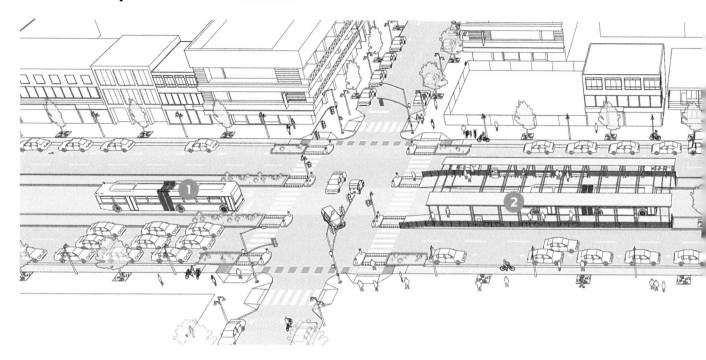

Wide highway-like arterial streets leading out from the city center, often with lower-density commercial development, are ideal routes for trunkline BRT or LRT lanes. With attention to the human environment and mixed-use zoning, these corridors can be transformed into active neighborhoods anchored by transit.

The central transitway creates significant capacity for high-frequency and high-ridership routes. Because of the level of investment, larger transit network master plans, neighborhood rezoning, or major redevelopment projects are prime opportunities to identify and implement median rapid transit corridors.

RECOMMENDATIONS

The median, left lanes, and left turn lanes of this formerly 7-lane street have been redesigned to serve an at-grade center busway, with right-boarding stations on the medians. Stations have been kept together to ease multi-directional transfers and reduce walking distances and crossings to access new buildings.

① A fully separated at-grade right-of-way provides for expedient transit service with few delays, even on the busiest streets.

② Stations are in the median, requiring careful planning around stop location and pedestrian access. Intersections without stations must also be designed for safe crossings, with the same low-speed turn radii and refuge areas that are provided at stations.

Median stations are designed with high platforms for fast boarding, with level boarding possible in LRT or closed BRT systems, where dedicated vehicles serve only stops on the transitway. Near-level boarding is possible in open BRT systems, where some buses use the transitway only for portions of their route.

Pedestrian safety and access have been substantially improved by cutting in half the maximum crossing distance between refuges and reducing top vehicle speeds to 25–30 mph. At station intersections, crossing distances are cut to a maximum of 24 feet by prohibiting left turns. Raised parking-protected cycle tracks, offset from right turns by refuge islands, provide a high-comfort, high-volume bicycle facility.

The configuration shown has right-boarding platforms, allowing the use of a wider range of buses. Open median boarding platforms can be uncomfortable for passengers if fast, high-volume traffic is present, especially where platform width is constrained, or where pedestrian crossings are distant. Large semi-enclosed stations, as well as mature trees where available, improve passenger waiting conditions and the attractiveness of transit.

③ Left turns are a primary operational concern on a street of this scale, and should be either prohibited or provided only during protected signal phases. Left-turn prohibitions are preferred at intersections with stations. If left turns must be accommodated at stations, right-side platforms can be staggered across intersections to create far-side stops with room for turn lanes near-side (see page 84).

Left-turn lanes are separated in time (with leading and lagging or split phases), and turning paths are guided by markings. Vehicles turning from cross streets are directed into the receiving lane with intersection markings, including red color at the transitway entrance.

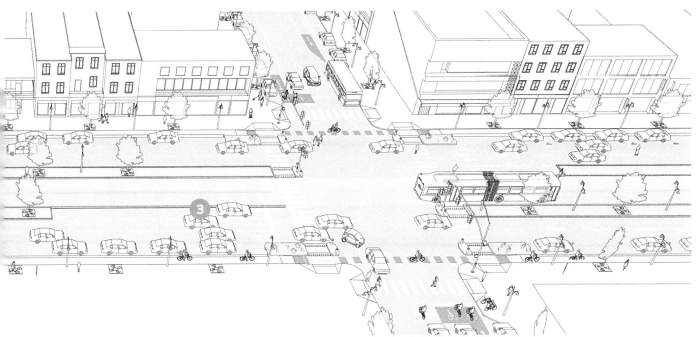

Major corridor with median rapid transit corridor (114 feet curb-to-curb, 140-foot right-of-way)

Implement this design along with active transit signal priority, or pre-time the signals along the corridor to account for typical dwell time.

Rezone adjoining blocks to allow mixed-use development at urban densities, prioritizing active ground floor uses such as retail and food service.

Require sidewalk improvements and reduce the number of driveways during redevelopment.

Case Study: Metroway BRT, Alexandria & Arlington, VA

Metroway in Alexandria and Arlington, VA opened in September 2014 as the Washington, D.C. region's first BRT line. In anticipation of redevelopment at the decommissioned Potomac Yards, Alexandria and Arlington worked with regional transit service provider WMATA and local developers to create a comfortable, high-capacity transit line that can support growing ridership.

Between Potomac and East Glebe stations, Metroway operates in an exclusive median transitway along Route 1. The transitway was constructed as a fully separated two-way 24-foot concrete bus running way, with planted medians on either side. Lanes narrow from 12 to 11 feet at stations to allow for wider platforms. Left turns across the transitway are managed in protected phases from dedicated lanes, using transit signals to distinguish the through bus phase from through motor vehicle phases. The mile-long center transitway was designed and implemented by the City of Alexandria, with a dedicated-lane extension planned by neighboring Arlington County.

Using right-boarding median stations, Metroway is an open BRT line, continuing in a right-side alignment and allowing the local bus route to use the center transitway. Station platforms are 10 inches high to allow fast near-level boarding, and are compatible with a new low-floor bus fleet and other buses. Off-board fare collection is planned.

An important element of the project was to design stops as places, creating high-quality stations along the transitway. The large shelters double as public art, with distinctive blue patterned glass; in Arlington, canopies completely shade the transitway. Station-area investments created an inviting walking environment around stations, with plantings and trees in wide medians, full median pedestrian refuges to break up crossings, distinctive concrete in the transitway, and much more visible crosswalks.

To reconstruct the street and procure new branded buses, the two jurisdictions shared funding responsibility, combined with FTA and TIGER funding. With a final project cost of under $8 million per mile, Metroway is a cost-effective investment, providing an established and visible transit service.

Ridership is up 23% compared with the pre-existing route, with six-minute headways during weekday peak periods. Metroway demonstrates the power of BRT, when linked with economic development, to create a lasting transit advantage for a growing place.

Metroway, **ALEXANDRIA, VA** (100 feet)

Transit Boulevard

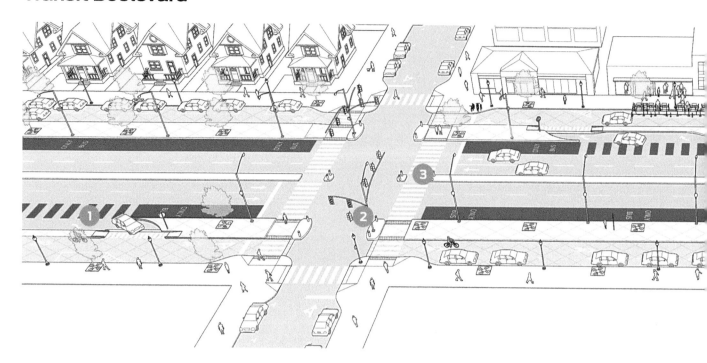

Among the largest streets in a city, boulevards with side medians provide a ready-made opportunity for right-boarding open BRT lines. The configuration of the street into a central roadway and side-running service lanes, separated by medians, provides right-boarding buses with separation from local vehicle access, bikes, parking, and loading. Dedicated transit lanes on the right side of the main roadway, along the service road medians, can provide a transitway-like level of capacity, and serve a high volume of buses.

On many existing boulevards, transit runs on the slower side roadway, which has sometimes been signalized to improve transit speeds. However, unmanaged turns create safety issues for all modes, while the large central roadway encourages high vehicle speeds. This configuration creates two very different street sections: one serving high-volume through movement, the other serving permeability and local access by all modes.

RECOMMENDATIONS

On this boulevard, the right lanes of the central roadway have been assigned as bus transit lanes. Rapid stops have been upgraded to stations located on the side medians between the side and central roadways.

Right turns from the central roadway are prohibited to prevent conflicts with through-moving buses and the side roadways. Turn lanes and protected turn phases can be provided for left turns, but lengthen signal cycles and increase delay for all crossing modes.

Where local and rapid service share the bus lane, queue jump signals can be used to allow the rapid to periodically pass a local bus stopped at a far-side stop. This configuration has potentially very high capacity, capable of accommodating very high bus volumes (up to 30–50 buses per hour) due to the absence of competing curbside uses.

1 Right turns are accommodated in mid-block slip lanes with a low-speed geometry and yield or stop controls to enter the side roadway. Slip lanes are long enough to avoid blocking the transit lane, and far enough from intersections to avoid being blocked by queues on the side roadway. Blank-out signs can be used to restrict right-side exits when the bus is approaching.

2 The side medians are extended as refuge islands to the intersection edge to reinforce the right-turn restriction from center lanes.

Left turns from boulevards are typically prohibited due to operational and geometric constraints; where a wide boulevard intersects a narrower street, the paths of left-turning vehicles from both directions come into conflict with one another.

3 Pedestrian clearance intervals are timed to allow a full crossing of the roadway at a standard walking speed. Refuge islands permit slower pedestrians to cross in multiple stages. If the service lanes are stop-controlled, pedestrian clearance time can be reduced to the time needed to cross from median to median, reducing the total length of the signal cycle and transit signal delay.

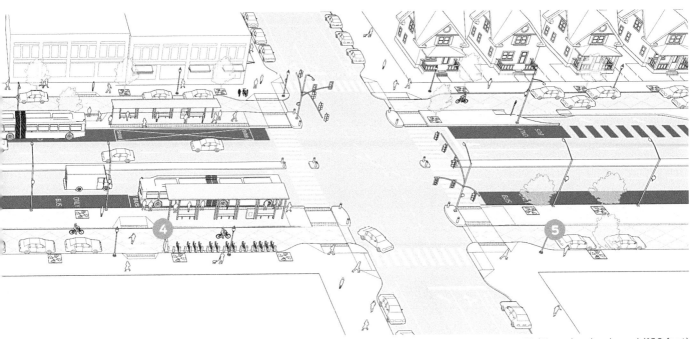

Multiway bus boulevard (130 feet)

K St. NW, **WASHINGTON, DC** (110 feet)

4 Side roadways are designed to prioritize pedestrians. Traffic calming measures reduce speeds, such as raising the service lane to mid-level or sidewalk level to create a shared street. Using high-quality paving, furnishings, and vegetation connects the sidewalk and median as a single public space.

5 Side roadways can function as low-stress bicycle routes in a variety of configurations, including a low-speed shared configuration. Reduce through-traffic further by forcing motor vehicle turns periodically. Where side medians are sufficiently wide, or where space can be reassigned from the service lane, bike lanes or cycle tracks can be provided, benefiting from the same turn management strategies as the transit lane.

Conventional bus fleets or streetcars can operate in the configuration shown. Rail or bus guideways can also be integrated at street level or raised to median height.

The largest boulevards can support center-running BRT or LRT, even if side medians are present, as shown in the *Median Rapid Transit Corridor* configuration (see page 38).

Second Avenue, **SEATTLE, WA**

One-Way Streets

One-way transit streets provide an opportunity to move large volumes of people in all modes with relatively simple intersections and few conflicts among modes and movements. Many existing one-way streets are overbuilt and disorganized, with more traffic capacity than needed. These streets present a potential site for transit lanes and transitways on the right side of the street, with private vehicles in the center and bikeways on the left.

One-way couplets with transit service are part of many downtown and corridor networks. Historically, one-way conversions were detrimental to transit, achieving high transit operating speeds at the expense of ridership. One-way streets increase walking distances to transit at one end of a trip or the other, since each stop is split between two streets. For spontaneous trips, split routes make it more difficult to find the opposing-direction service. Larger one-way streets can easily become uninviting for pedestrians and cyclists and must be designed carefully to prevent speeding and motor vehicle dominance of the street.

Shared Transit Street

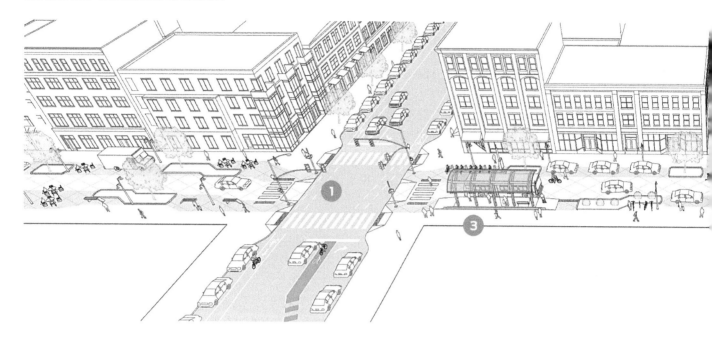

Shared street designs can transform small streets with inadequate walking space into excellent public spaces. On small downtown streets where local transit serves a high density of destinations, high pedestrian activity levels and low vehicle volumes often create shared conditions. Such under-performing rights-of-way can be transformed into an inviting plaza-like shared space while facilitating key transit connections.

Active ground floor land uses, such as small to medium-sized retail and food establishments, contribute to the streetscape and support transit demand throughout the day.

RECOMMENDATIONS

1 While shared streets are inherently flexible and can be used differently at peak travel times and peak business or activity periods, high traffic volumes erode pedestrian benefits. Reduce through-vehicle volumes by forcing non-transit vehicles to turn at key intersections. In most settings, the desired maximum vehicle volume will be roughly 1,000–1,500 vehicles per day. With very high pedestrian activity, it may be possible to accommodate 2,000–3,000 vehicles per day while preserving a strong pedestrian character.

2 Shared transit street right-of-way widths may vary, but the shared traveled way must be kept visually narrow and periodically constrained to strongly encourage low automobile speeds (10–15 mph or lower is desired). On shared streets with sufficient width for both a central traveled way and accessible pedestrian-only areas, street furniture, including bollards, benches, green infrastructure, street lights, and bicycle parking, may be sited to provide definition for a shared space, subtly delineating the shared traveled way from the pedestrian-only area.

While traffic speeds are considerably reduced on shared streets, average transit speeds are typically appropriate for short sections of local service. Shared streets have the potential to improve transit speed or reliability if general traffic volumes are reduced, or if intersection traffic controls can be eliminated as part of the shared street design.

All transit vehicle technologies can be used on shared streets. Low-emissions or no-emissions buses have a lower impact on the shared pedestrian environment than an internal-combustion fleet.

Transit frequency is a larger factor than vehicle type in shared street design. With high transit vehicle volume (such as 10–12 buses per hour), the pedestrian environment may degrade, eroding some of the public space benefits of the shared design. These benefits can be restored by further reducing the presence of mixed motor vehicle traffic. For very high transit volumes, a conventional transit mall design with large sidewalks is preferred.

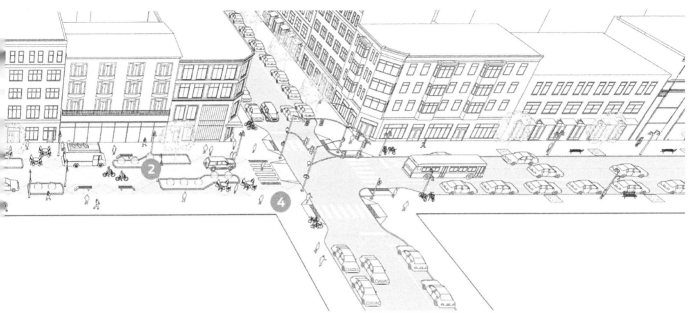

One-way shared transit street (42 feet, building-to-building)

Open sightlines, along with human-scale lighting, promote safety and comfort. Vegetation and planters mitigate the effects of vehicle noise.

3 At transit stops, small elevated platform areas can be developed alongside the shared traveled way to provide near-level or level boarding areas. Lifts, bridge plates, and ramps such as mini-high platforms can also be used to create accessible boarding (*ADA Std. 810.5.3*).

If a shared transit street is frequently closed to traffic to accommodate special events, plan alternate bus routes and evaluate rider impacts to determine whether permanent rerouting should be considered.

4 Sidewalks on crossing streets should cross the shared street at or near the level of the sidewalk. Detectable surfaces must be provided for pedestrian movements that cross the shared street at intersections.

See more guidance on shared streets in the *Urban Street Design Guide*.

Case Study: Bell Street, Seattle

Bell Street Park is Seattle's first shared street, designed with the goal of transforming an auto-oriented road into a vibrant, four-block shared street that improves mobility for all users while providing much needed open space.

Prior to reconstruction, Bell Street was a two-lane, one-way street with parking on both sides. This stretch was a critical corridor for buses: 300 pass through daily—with more than 100 of these during PM peak hours alone. As the city sought ways to reinvigorate the street while balancing modal needs, the shared street concept was introduced.

The project team developed the five design cues for the vision of Bell Street: *Reclaim, Elevate, Grid, Twist,* and *Meander.* These cues set forth ideas of how to best activate the space, both for mobility and community use.

The final design transformed Bell Street between 1st and 5th Avenues into a raised, 56,000-square-foot shared street with a single travel lane for pedestrians, buses, bicyclists, and autos. The travel lane is 10 feet wide, with light gray scored concrete, bordered by 4 feet of darker gray flexible space on either side to allow through-travel of wider vehicles, especially buses and emergency vehicles. The travel lane also shifts from side to side in a chicane-inspired treatment

to calm driving speeds, and provides intermittent parking and loading zones.

Textured pavement is flush across the street to prioritize pedestrian movement. Texture and color cues slow traffic while providing visual eddies to delineate meandering activity zones for seating, planters, and art installations. Signage is included at shared street entrance points to alert road users that they are entering a pedestrian priority zone.

Finally, while private vehicles are forced to turn off the street after a block, bus routes are still served by the shared street. Buses traverse Bell Street with 10–15 minute or better headways all day and late into the evening, 365 days per year—the same as the volume prior to reconstruction.

Bell Street, **SEATTLE, WA**
(65 feet building-to-building)

One-Way Streetcar Street

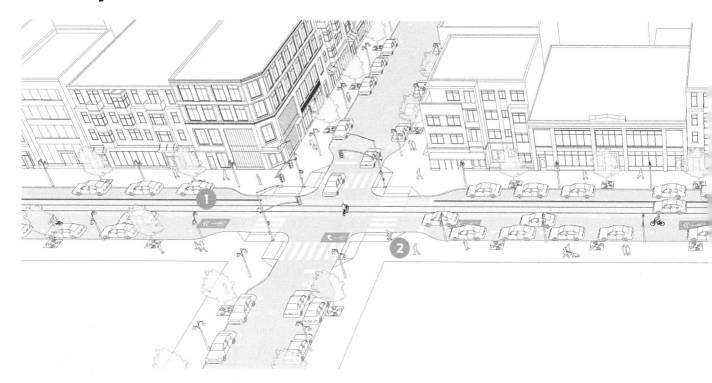

Small one-way streets operate in couplets in downtown or neighborhood main street contexts, often with short blocks, dense destinations, low traffic speeds, rich pedestrian activity, and frequent boarding activity. Streetcars enhance the sense of place, and often require retrofitted boarding platforms to provide basic accessibility.

Transformations enhance the pedestrian realm and rider queuing area, as well as signal timing and coordination strategies.

RECOMMENDATIONS

1 Motorists must be deterred from parking in, standing in, or otherwise blocking the streetcar lane. Use pavement patterns and markings, camera enforcement, and signage to deter obstructions (see page 134).

---

2 Transit service must be balanced with pedestrian volumes and movement. Curb extensions and streetscape enhancements benefit the pedestrian realm and create a pleasant experience walking to and waiting for transit.

In downtown networks where most streets operate one-way, time signals throughout the network to fixed low-speed progressions, which benefit transit operations, bicycling, and walking (see page 155 for additional guidance).[7]

---

3 Boarding bulbs provide create a comfortable waiting space, and eliminating the need to enter the street in order to board transit vehicles. Bulbs may need to be extended to meet the streetcar doors, and curb height and shape must be designed for compatibility with streetcar vehicles. Level or near-level boarding heights improve transit accessibility (see *Platform Height*, page 64).

On routes with significant bicycle traffic, streets should have separate bicycle lanes outside of the track zone. Alternatively, create high-quality parallel bicycle routes.

One-way street configuration can allow streetcars and bicyclists to operate on opposite sides of a street, reducing conflicts. If on the same side of the street, provide a sufficiently wide bikeway to avoid the risk of bicycle tires getting caught in flangeway gap or concrete seams.

---

4 Where necessary, direct bicycle turns and movements to cross tracks as near to 90 degrees as possible.

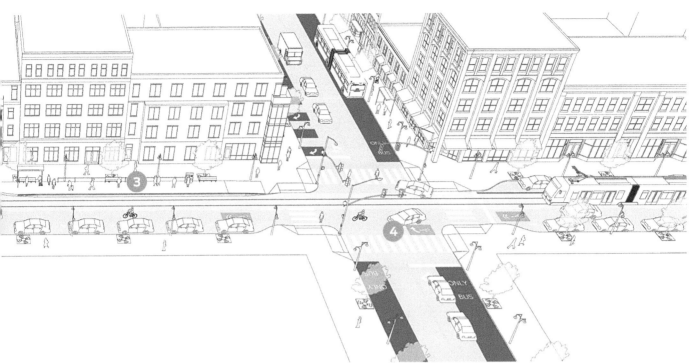

One-way streetcar corridor (38 feet)

NW 11th Ave., **PORTLAND, OR** (36 feet)

Where buses and streetcars use the same stop, the curb profile may change heights to serve accessible boardings across the transit fleet. **PORTLAND, OR**

Tiered Transit Street

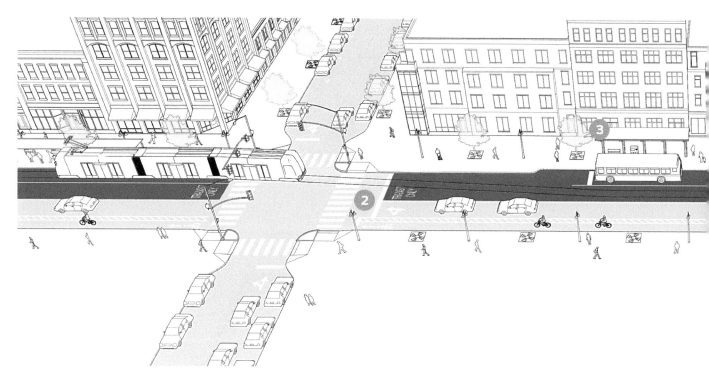

On one-way streets with very high transit ridership and a substantial volume of transit vehicles (typically with peak hour headways of 5 minutes or less)—especially on corridors serving multiple transit routes—double transit lanes can provide improved service and travel speed. Double transit lanes are generally only applicable on streets in dense districts with numerous transit routes. They may be especially helpful where many turning and weaving movements that hinder transit operation are observed.

RECOMMENDATIONS

1 Dual transit lanes allow buses to use the right lane for in-lane stops, and the left bus lane for travel and passing. Providing two transit lanes helps reduce transit vehicle delay from both general traffic and other transit vehicles. Configurations for both LRT and buses can serve stops on alternating blocks in a skip-stop arrangement.

The benefits of dedicated transit lanes are critical to creating service with high capacity, speed, frequency, and quality.

Dual transit lanes require strict enforcement. Automated camera enforcement can effectively deter drivers from entering restricted lanes.

Dual transit lanes must be curbside, as it is impractical for vehicles to access parking across two restricted lanes.

Dual transit lanes require turn restrictions during operation, as general traffic movements across dual lanes create multiple conflicts and hinder operations.

Lanes can be operated at all times, but are often enforced only during peak hours. Part-time operation may degrade the efficacy of dedicated lanes.

Demarcate transit lanes with solid white lines, and BUS ONLY or LRV ONLY lane markings (MUTCD §3D-01).

2 Restrict turns across double transit lanes to avoid conflicts between transit and turning vehicles.

3 At major transfer nodes, the on-street terminal stop configuration can provide more efficient operations and improved legibility for riders (see page 88). Stops and stations should be staggered in a skip-stop configuration, allowing through-moving transit vehicles to bypass dwelling vehicles and avoid delay. In downtown contexts, where pedestrian volumes are high, stops may be spaced closer together in order to distribute congestion caused by groups of passengers waiting on the sidewalk.

Dual transit lanes can be painted red to visually discourage drivers from entering and blocking the lanes (see page 134).

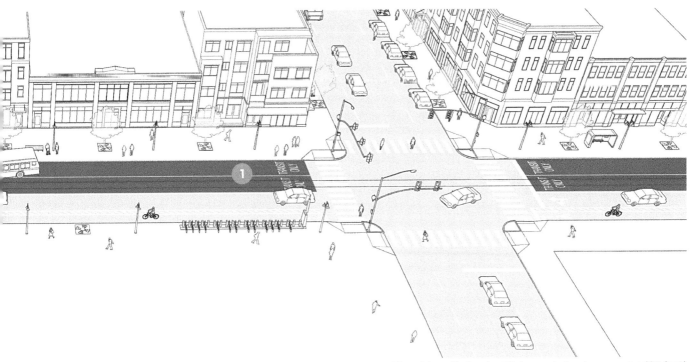

Tiered transit street, with bus and streetcar service (36 feet)

Raised separation elements can be employed in some configurations; where motorists turning from intersecting streets may mistakenly enter transit lanes, traversable barriers may be desirable (see page 136).

SW 5th St. transit mall, **PORTLAND, OR** (36 feet)

Madison Ave., **NEW YORK CITY, NY** (60 feet)

Parallel Paired Transitways

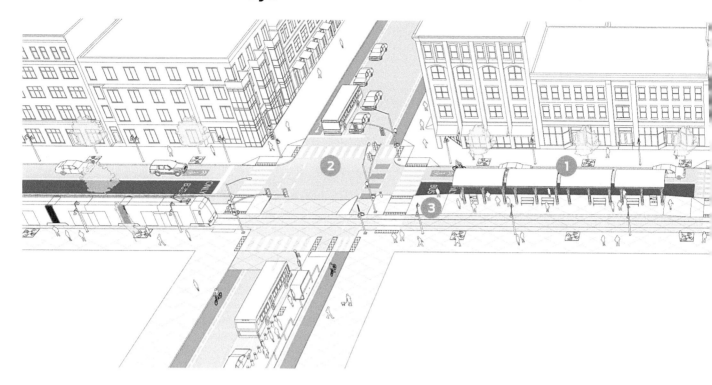

Paired transitways can be employed on major transit routes to provide dedicated space for bus, light rail, and streetcar service. Different modes or service types can be configured to run parallel to each other to create a transit priority corridor. Parallel transit lanes for each mode permit simplified cross-platform transfers.

Most frequently found in city centers, dual mode paired transitways are used on streets with heavy transit ridership on both bus and rail, or where transfers between modes are frequent.

RECOMMENDATIONS

Especially on street segments with frequent transit service, or in locations where a number of lines converge, dual-mode transitways can simplify transfers and bolster transit visibility and system identity.

1 Street and stop design must account for differences in vehicle design between different services and modes, including vehicle length, boarding height, and door location. Where these dimensions differ, separate platforms may be created, preferably adjacent to one another on the same block to ease transfers and reduce rider confusion.

2 Restrict turns across transitways to mitigate conflicts with transit vehicles; driver visibility may be poor.

Demarcate with solid white lines, and BUS ONLY or LRV ONLY lane markings (MUTCD §3D-01).

3 Clearly indicate transfer opportunities with signage showing routes and platform direction. Wayfinding and system information are essential to enabling passenger trip planning.

4 Transit signal heads can be used where confusion may emerge, such as where transit and vehicle traffic proceeds in separate phases.

High-quality paving materials, furnishings, and plantings improve the streetscape and invite activity, while also defining edges and ensuring pedestrians do not enter active transitways.

On this street, a rail transitway comfortably shares space with pedestrians, who freely use the full width of the sidewalk, transitway, and median, yielding when trains approach. Depending on bus and general traffic volumes and network role, the remainder of the street can also be designed as a shared transit street, creating a public space across the entire street.

Parallel paired transitway, with bus and light rail service (50 feet)

Light rail running at sidewalk level on 2nd St., **SAN JOSÉ, CA** (50 feet curbs/75 feet ROW)

Bus lane runs at street level. 1st St., **SAN JOSÉ, CA** (50 feet curbs/75 feet ROW)

One-Way Transit Corridor

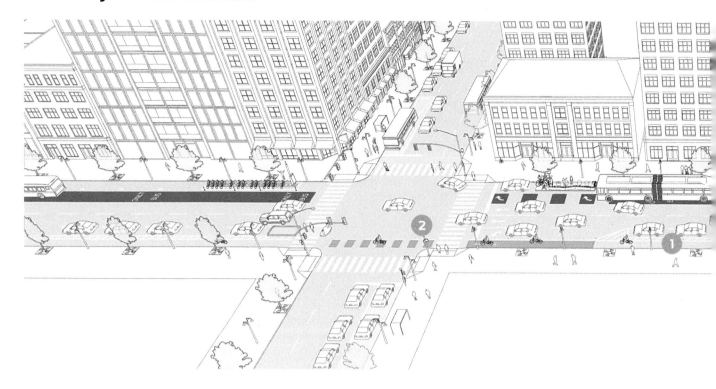

One-way corridor streets, which often have multiple travel lanes and significant daily throughput, and which connect multiple urban or activity centers, may be prime corridors to implement dedicated transit lanes. These may be trunkline transit routes where multiple bus lines converge and connect.

Implementing well-branded or high-capacity vehicles, robust stations and wayfinding, and dedicating on-street space improves on-time performance and rider experience, and increases the total person capacity of congested streets.

RECOMMENDATIONS

Transit lanes are typically most efficient on corridors with frequent service, generally more than six vehicles per hour.

1 To upgrade the street's role within the transit and bicycle networks, transit and bicycle lanes can be placed on opposite sides of the street, reducing bicyclist stress and bike-bus conflicts.

Allowing private vehicles to enter transit lanes degrades transit service and must be done strategically. Refer to Chapter 6: *Intersections* (page 147) for treatments accommodating turning movements through the transit lane, and Chapter 5: *Transit Lanes & Transitways* (page 109) for additional guidance on transit lane design.

2 Consider turning restrictions to mitigate conflicts by cars traversing transit lanes (see *Turn Restrictions*, page 156, for additional guidance and treatment selection).

Transit lanes can be enforced only at selected times, using methods such as dynamic signs to inform other road users of lane restrictions (see *Peak-Only Bus Lane*, page 120).

To gain the full benefit of transit lanes, integrate operational improvements to improve transit service reliability and comfort, including transit-friendly signal progressions, active TSP, all-door boarding, and extended or tiered stops.

If multiple routes operate along the same corridor, especially with heavy passenger loads or close stop spacing, evaluate skip-stop placement (see *On-Street Terminal*, page 88). Where possible, stops should be co-located to reduce pedestrian walking distance to make transfers.

Creating an easy-to-follow wayfinding system to direct passengers to the location of stops in both directions along a route is especially important for routes on one-way couplets.

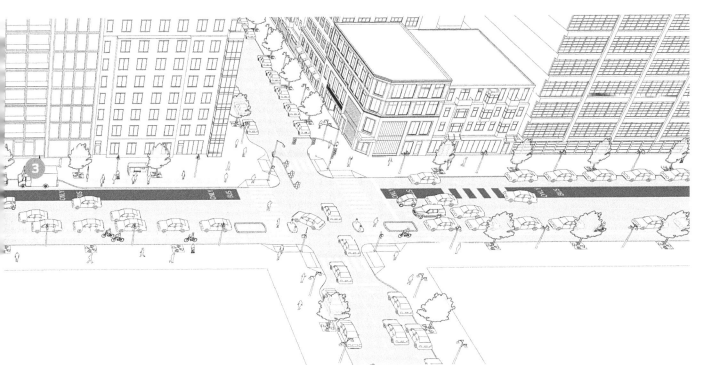

One-way transit corridor, with offset bus lane and protected bikeway (60 feet curbs)

3 Freight and taxi/livery vehicle standing may intrude on transit or bicycle lanes. Designate curbside loading zones, potentially with additional width or on the opposite side of the street, to accommodate frequent curbside activities without impacting transit operation.

First Ave., **NEW YORK CITY, NY** (72 feet curbs/95 feet ROW)

Dearborn St., **CHICAGO, IL** (50 feet curbs/85 feet ROW)

Contraflow Transit Street

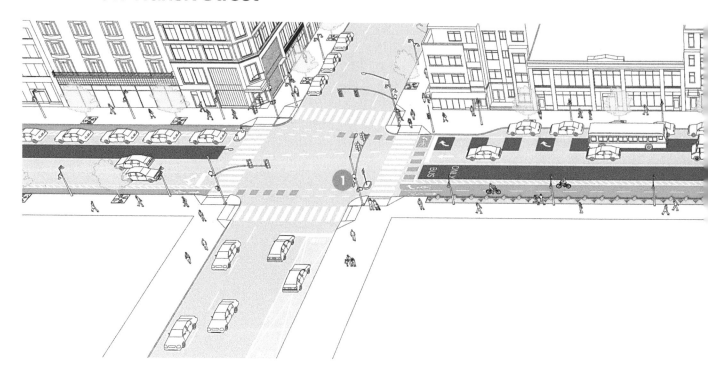

Contraflow transit streets are typically used to simplify transit routing in a complex one-way street network. The contraflow lane is typically configured to the left side of the street, and may operate for only a single block or for an entire corridor. Contraflow transit lanes can be a powerful tool for reducing travel times and improving route legibility, especially where suitable parallel routes do not exist, or where transit would be delayed making multiple or difficult turns.

Streets with left-side contraflow bus lanes operate like two-way streets but with general traffic prohibited in one direction. The use of color along the entire transit lane, optional vertical separation, and refuge islands all can alert people walking, biking and driving to the opposing travel direction of transit. With management or restrictions on left turns, these designs can be safer than two-way streets, and provide an opportunity for two-way protected bikeways along contraflow lanes.

RECOMMENDATIONS

1 Gateway treatments that clearly prohibit wrong-way or private vehicle entry at intersections—especially at the beginning of the contraflow segment—are essential to safe and functional operation of contraflow lanes. Forced turns may be marked through the intersection or guided with hard barriers. Wide cross streets provide smooth bus transitions.

Contraflow transit lanes are demarcated by solid double yellow lines (when hard barriers do not separate the lane from opposing traffic).

Multiple routes can be consolidated using a contraflow lane to move buses through congested corridors.

2 Contraflow bus lanes can employ TSP to activate the signal when approaching (see page 152).

Contraflow lanes should be painted red to discourage vehicles from entering and to alert pedestrians to the presence of a transit lane with vehicles coming from an unexpected direction (see page 124).

Prohibit or separate left turn phases at intersections, depending on bus and vehicle turning volumes (see page 156).

Give transit vehicles adequate space to operate safely: while curbside lanes can be as narrow as 11 feet, wider contraflow lanes may be desirable given widths of travel lanes in the opposing direction.

3 "Hard" barriers (e.g. concrete curb, median strips, bollards, or safe hit posts), or "soft" barriers (e.g. rumble strip or striped buffers) can be used to make the contraflow lane more legible.[8] Wider barriers can act as pedestrian refuge islands (see page 136).

4 When turning movements across contraflow lanes are restricted, an opportunity to provide a low-stress, bi-directional protected bike lane emerges. Refer to the *Urban Bikeway Design Guide* for additional design information.

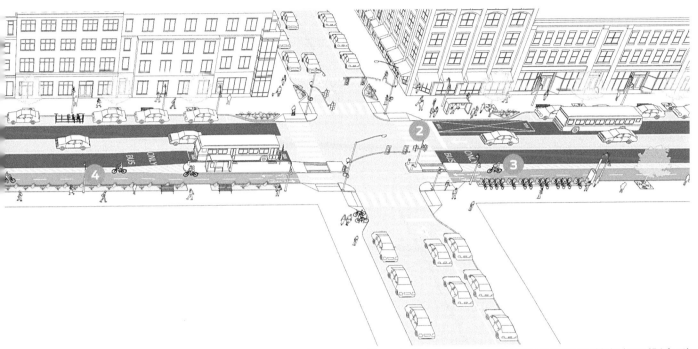

One-way transit street with contraflow lane and bi-directional protected bike lane (54 feet)

Buses can be re-routed onto a contraflow lane to eliminate the need to make sharp turns, especially through busy crosswalks with poor sight lines—one of the most significant safety conflicts for buses.

Carefully consider pedestrian behavior, enacting measures to discourage pedestrians from entering the roadway without looking, since buses may be coming from an unexpected direction. Pavement markings, audible warnings, and fencing (in limited instances) may improve pedestrian safety.

Contraflow lanes preclude inclusion of street parking or bus bulbs at the curbside in the contraflow direction.

Contraflow lanes must be operated 24 hours, or may generate confusion and conflicts.

Central (left-side) boarding station serving both directions, on one-way street with contraflow segment. Hilyard Station, E 11th Ave., **EUGENE, OR** (60 feet)

Haight St., **SAN FRANCISCO, CA** (45 feet curbs/65 feet ROW)

3. Stations & Stops

Transit stops are more than a place to wait. Investments in better stops are an opportunity to improve transit speeds and enhance the value of the street with green infrastructure and small public spaces. Passengers on all transit modes and service types can benefit from better stops.

Stops and stations fit into a larger geometric puzzle involving transit vehicles and intersection operations. While the location of a stop determines to a large extent how transit passengers gain access to transit service, the design and configuration of stops and stations impacts how everyone on the street interacts with the transit system. When designed with transit quality as the priority, stop configurations and location can be used to organize the interactions that occur at transit stops.

Station & Stop Principles

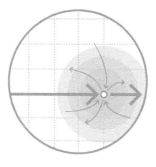

STATIONS ARE GATEWAYS

Design stops and stations as introductions to the transit system, paying special attention to how transit space interacts with the sidewalk and adjoining buildings. Comfortable stops with shade trees, shelter, places to sit or lean, and nearby business activity can anchor an improved local pedestrian realm and improve rider perceptions of transit service. Branding and distinctive stations serve to advertise frequent service, while clear information saves people time—and bolsters ridership.

FACILITATE MOVEMENT, EASE INTERACTIONS

Transit stops involve interactions among nearly everyone on the street, and the type and location of transit stops affect reliability and travel time. Stop location and design can support prompt transit and safe crossings by accounting for intersection operations, transfers to other routes, and local destinations. Cluster stops with bike share stations, car share, and for-hire-vehicle zones to create neighborhood mobility hubs, making the best use of station and sidewalk investments.

IN-LANE STOPS SAVE TIME

Use boarding islands and bulbs to allow transit vehicles to stop in their moving lane. Buses have long been expected to pull out of traffic to the curb, but this practice de-prioritizes transit, sometimes significantly on mixed-traffic streets. In-lane stops eliminate that delay, and provide an opportunity for near-level or level boarding. They also create shorter, safer pedestrian crossings, provide more walking space on the sidewalk, and make the street more predictable by sorting out bike-bus conflicts at stops.

UNIVERSAL DESIGN IS EQUITABLE DESIGN

Design streets so that people of all ages and abilities can safely reach transit stops and board comfortably. The elements that make transit more smoothly accessible can benefit all transit riders, regardless of physical or sensory ability. Thoughtful, human-centered design of transit infrastructure elevates the experience of riding transit, and can save both time and money.

DESIGN FOR SAFETY

Social safety and traffic safety at transit stops are critical for riders, and impact their decisions about where and when to take transit. Prioritizing walking access to transit stops, including direct routes and convenient, low-delay pedestrian crossings, is vital to achieving a safe system. Proximity to all-hours activity, human-scale lighting, and transparent shelters and structures all help provide riders with a secure place to wait.

INTEGRATE VEHICLE AND PLATFORM DESIGN

Transit vehicles, platforms and street surfaces work together as a system to achieve accessible and fast boarding. Design platforms that work flexibly with the range of transit vehicles already in use to ease boarding, and use fleet purchases and major street projects as opportunities to create level boarding.

Mission Street, SAN FRANCISCO, CA

Stop Design Factors

Transit stops are where transit passengers and transit vehicles meet and interact—and stop design factors like stop location or platform height and length define these interactions.

The success of a transit system depends in large part on how well on-street platforms respond to the design needs of people riding and operating transit, and how well they work with the design of transit vehicles themselves. They must accommodate accessible boardings and provide capacity for boarding, alighting, and waiting transit passengers without unnecessarily interrupting the flow of pedestrian traffic on nearby sidewalks. The location, height, length and configuration of on-street platforms are part of a vehicle-platform system, as relevant for buses as for rail. Each configuration presents its own opportunities, benefits, and challenges, interacting differently within street, passenger, and transit operations contexts.

Stop Placement & Intersection Configuration

FAR-SIDE, IN-LANE STOP

In-lane stops at the far side of an intersection confer the highest priority to transit operations at most signalized intersections.

Far-side in-lane stops are generally the preferred stop configuration where transit lanes or transitways are present.[1]

By allowing buses to move in a straight line, in-lane stops eliminate both pull-out time and traffic re-entry time, a source of delay and unreliable service. In-lane stops are especially valuable on streets operating at or near vehicle capacity, or on streets with long signal cycles, in which transit vehicles may experience long re-entry delays while waiting for traffic to clear.[2]

In-lane stops reduce wear on transit vehicles and street infrastructure by avoiding lane shifts during braking.

At signalized intersections, far-side stops allow transit vehicles to clear an intersection before stopping.

Far-side stops support the use of a broad array of active transit signal priority treatments with relatively simple infrastructure, since transit vehicle approaches can be anticipated based on typical approach speeds.

At intersections where transit vehicles turn, use far-side stops to simplify transit turns and allow pedestrians to better anticipate turning movements.

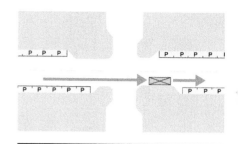

On single-lane streets where in-lane stops are most needed, far-side in-lane stops in mixed traffic may result in traffic behind the bus spilling back into the crosswalk and intersection. At these locations, provide a longer far-side stop that accommodates queued vehicles behind the stopped transit vehicle, or activate an early red phase after the transit vehicle clears the intersection.

Continue bike facilities behind the stop (see page 74).

NEAR-SIDE, IN-LANE STOP

Near-side stops at the approach to an intersection can facilitate in-lane stops in mixed-traffic lanes, where turning movements and queued vehicles behind transit vehicles do not block the intersection.

At stop-controlled locations with only one travel lane in each direction, near-side in-lane stops eliminate "double-stopping."

Where a high volume of vehicles turn onto the transit street, locating a stop near-side keeps the far side of the intersection clear to receive turns.

Where very high right turn volumes are present, an in-lane stop can be located on an island between the transit lane and right turn lane.[3]

Prohibit vehicles from entering opposing lanes to pass stopped transit vehicles. Place near-side stops close enough to the intersection that right-turning vehicles cannot merge in front of stopped transit vehicles.

Near-side stops may be employed with center-running transit lanes; center-boarding islands at near-side enable simpler pedestrian access at crosswalks.

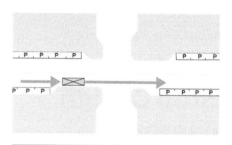

Continue bike facilities behind the stop (see page 74).

When applied with transit signal progressions, near-side and far-side stops can be alternated to reduce intersection delay.

MID-BLOCK, IN-LANE STOP

In-lane mid-block configurations use significantly less curb length than mid-block pull-out stops.

Signalized or traffic-calmed pedestrian crossings should be provided at mid-block stops.

Mid-block stops are applicable where large destinations justify high-volume access.

Continue bicycle facilities behind the stop (see page 74).

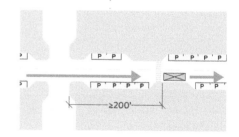

FAR-SIDE, PULL-OUT STOP

Far-side pull-out stops use intersection space efficiently, with little impact on general traffic if they are wide enough for a bus to pull completely out of traffic. Among pull-out configurations, far-side stops are preferred.

A far-side pull-out configuration shortens the transition distance needed along the stop platform. Buses can shift to the right while crossing the intersection.

A periodic pull-out stop on streets with primarily in-lane stops allows vehicles to pass while a bus is stopped.

Buses may be significantly delayed in re-entering the travel lane on high-volume streets. On routes where buses have difficulty merging back into traffic, buses often pull out of the travel lane only partially to avoid being blocked.[4]

Pull-out stops can be used for local stops adjacent to offset or curbside transit lanes to allow rapid services to pass local services.

Pull-out stops create additional space to receive left-turning transit vehicles and trucks.

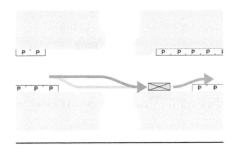

Far-side pull-out stops work well with queue jumps designed as bus-only approach lanes or shared right-turn lanes that advance transit vehicles into the stop.[5]

NEAR-SIDE, PULL-OUT STOP

Near-side pull-out stops favor motor vehicle traffic flow, and confer limited benefits to transit operations. At high traffic volume locations, the near-side stop functions as a right-turn lane when buses are not present.

When used as queue jump lanes with active transit signal priority, near-side stops can enhance operations at high-traffic-volume intersections.

Buses may have significant difficulty re-entering the traffic stream. Signal measures, such as upstream early red phases, can address this issue.

Near-side stops can be used to facilitate transfer between two intersecting routes.

A near-side pull-out stop should be set back from the crosswalk at least 15 feet. Stops located just before the crosswalk can block the visibility of pedestrians.

Except for transfer points, near-side pull-out stops are not generally preferred on multi-lane streets, but may be applied if a major near-side destination exists, or if problematic conditions such as driveways or missing sidewalks exist at the far-side location.[6]

In cities with yield-to-bus/yield-to-streetcar rules and high compliance, broader implementation of near-side pull-out stops is possible.

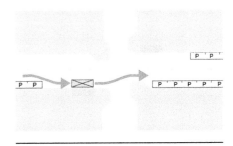

Place near-side stops close enough to the intersection that right-turning vehicles cannot merge in front of the bus.

Near-side stops present challenges at intersections with transit route turns. If buses are required to turn right from the curbside, provide a signal phase for the transit movement, or design the cross street to accommodate a vehicle sweeping across the second lane or the oncoming lane.

MID-BLOCK, PULL-OUT STOP

Mid-block pull-out stops are located more than 200 feet from intersections, and provide destination access on long blocks with mid-block crossings.

Use mid-block stops where traffic conditions at intersections would create safety issues for stopping buses or riders.

Mid-block pull-out stops may be applicable at heavy intermodal transfer points, or transit vehicle layover points.

Ensure that adequate curbside space exists to maneuver buses in and out of stops.

Signalized or traffic-calmed pedestrian crossings should be provided at mid-block stops.

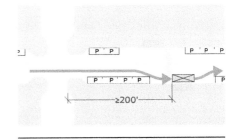

Where safe pedestrian crossings cannot be provided, mid-block stops are a last resort.

Platform Length: In-Lane Stops

Enabling transit vehicles to make in-lane stops confers a broad range of operational and accessibility benefits, and can often be accomplished with little to no adverse impact on general traffic flow.

Transit stops with in-lane boarding require significantly less curb length and do not occupy sidewalk space, freeing room for alternative uses, including expanded pedestrian capacity, green infrastructure, local business access and parking, or street furnishings.

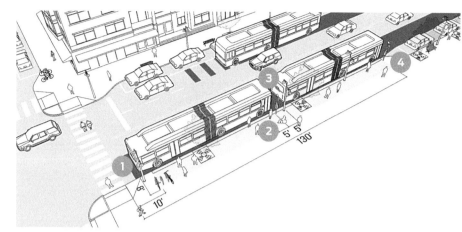

Far-side bulb stop with capacity for two articulated buses

Desired Minimum Platform Length by Vehicle Type (feet)[7]

Stop Position	40' Bus	60' Bus	2 x 40' Bus	2 x 60' Bus
Near-Side	35	55	80	115
Far-Side	45	65	90	130
Mid-Block	35	55	80	115

Dimensions are for standard buses. Streetcar and LRV specifications may vary.

DISCUSSION

Transit vehicles make in-lane stops using boarding bulbs, boarding islands, median platforms, or curbside sidewalk stops.

In-lane stops limit the curb length needed for efficient transit stops, preserving space for other curbside uses.

Boarding bulbs and islands minimize interruption of the sidewalk, providing comfortable space for waiting riders, and shortening crossing distances.

Stop platforms may serve a streetscape function as well, creating space for planters, bioswales, furniture, or bike parking.

Ensure platform length provides adequate space for waiting passengers at high-volume stops and routes.[8]

At low transit volumes, in-lane stops have little effect on street operations but reduce transit delay.

At high transit volumes, in-lane stops improve transit speed and provide room for more buses per block.

CRITICAL

Refer to the above table for preferred platform lengths with bus stops. Rail platform length will vary based on vehicle length, but should extend from the front door through the rear door.

1 Locate platform with at least 10 feet of clear distance from crosswalk or curb return. Measure to transit stop pole at near-side, or rear of transit vehicle at far-side.

2 While 5 feet is the minimum curb length for a receiving facility at each boarding door (*ADA Std. §810.2.2*), design platforms to be continuous through all doors, and consider additional elements to improve passenger comfort (see Chapter. 4: *Station & Stop Elements*, page 91).

3 Provide 5–10 feet of distance between each additional transit vehicle expected to be dwelling at the platform consistently throughout the day.[9]

4 Design boarding bulbs and islands to accommodate proper drainage and sweeping; tight radii may require maintenance agreements to ensure bulbs are properly cleaned and maintained.

Platform Length: Pull-Out Stops

With pull-out stops, buses shift out of the travel lane to service stops. While they have operational benefits for transit compared to in-lane stops in certain situations, they often provide benefits chiefly for through-traffic, while slowing bus operations due to the need to shift in and out of travel lanes.

Bus zones lengths at pull-out stops include transition or taper space in addition to platform length, resulting in a need for longer clear curb zones than with in-lane stops.

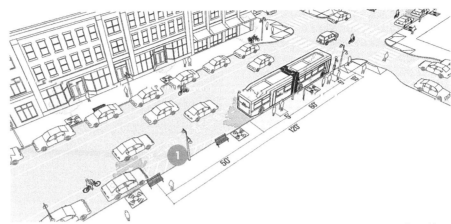

Near-side sidewalk stop for single 60-foot articulated bus

Desired Minimum Bus Zone Length by Vehicle Type (feet)

Stop Position	40' Bus	60' Bus	2 x 40' Bus	2 x 60' Bus
Near-Side	100	120	145	185
Far-Side	90	100	125	165
Far-Side, after right turn	140	160	140	230
Mid-Block	120	145	185	210

Dimensions are for standard buses. Streetcar and LRV specifications may vary.

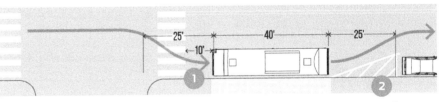

Example bus pull-out transition distances

DISCUSSION

Where buses are required to pull from traffic to make stops, longer bus zones are needed to accommodate transitions to and from traffic.

Short transition distances add delay to transit service and require sharper transitions to the curb, wearing transit vehicles and infrastructure more quickly.

Enforcement is required to keep pull-out stops clear; vehicles standing or parking in the stop zone constrain the operator's ability to pull completely to the platform.

Longer stops ease transitions into and out of stops, but require more curb length, reducing curbside parking spots.

At high-volume boarding locations, longer stops can be used to distribute queuing riders along the sidewalk and to ease pedestrian congestion.

Where buses make queue jump maneuvers, pull-out stops allow the bus to pull to the right of queued traffic and receive an advance green signal.

Where local and rapid/limited services are provided on the same route or corridor, local service may pull-out to stop at preferred transfer locations, allowing the rapid service to pass the local, and stop in-lane (see page 72).

CRITICAL

Pavement markings and NO PARKING: BUS STOP signs (MUTCD R7-107) must clearly delineate the edge of the stop zone to deter blockages.

Provide 5–10 feet of distance between each additional transit vehicle dwelling at the platform to allow a bus.

1 Locate stop zone with at least 10 feet of clear distance from crosswalk or curb return. Measure to transit stop pole at near-side, or rear of transit vehicle at far-side.

OPTIONAL

Bus-mounted cameras can enforce vehicles blocking the stop zone.

2 White diagonal hatch line markings may be striped to delineate the entry and exit tapers and discourage blocking.

Platform Height

Platform height affects ease of boarding; raised platforms enable easier, more accessible passenger boarding and alighting by decreasing step-down distance and gap between vehicle floor and platform. Level and near-level platform stops can also increase route efficiency, allowing vehicles to enter and exit stops more quickly.

Raised streetcar boarding platform, NW 10th Ave., **PORTLAND, OR**

Sidewalk/Curb Level

At sidewalk/curb level stops, passengers board from the sidewalk or curb level, often 4–6 inches.

Sidewalk/curb level boarding is commonly an "unimproved" condition, though it may be preferred where there is inadequate space to provide accessible slopes and ramps onto a higher platform.

Curb level boarding may be applied with boarding bulbs and, conditionally, with side boarding islands.

Platform edge or boarding positions should be indicated using markings or detectable warning strips (see page 67).

Street Level

At street level stops, passengers board and alight directly from the street level.

Applicable as a design condition on shared streets. Platforms should be provided for at least one door unless full-length ramps can be provided to street level.

May emerge as an unplanned condition when operators have difficulty pulling to the curb.

Street-level boarding is an existing condition at some rail stops.

The higher step for each passenger to board results in a longer cumulative boarding time.

Near-Level Boarding

Near-level platforms place the curb height at 0–11 inches.

Near-level platforms allow faster boarding, and are compatible with most existing transit fleets.

Allows an operator to either kneel the bus or deploy a short bridge plate or ramp. Short bridge plates, often used on streetcars, require far less space than a full-height bus ramp.[10]

Near-level platforms are suitable for side and center boarding islands, boarding bulbs, or sidewalk stops with sufficient width to provide a raised area. Provide ADA-compliant ramps to achieve desired height leading to the boarding pad. Ramps should not impede pedestrian paths or crossings [49 CFR §38.23(c), §38.83(c)].

Detectable warning strips must be installed along the edge of the boarding platform, except when part of an existing sidewalk.

Level Boarding

With level boarding, the platform height matches the floor height of transit vehicles (for on-street low-floor vehicles, typically 12–14 inches).

Can apply to light rail, streetcar, or retrofitted low-floor buses.[11]

Many agencies have transit vehicles that are incompatible with level boarding platforms: some vehicle design geometry may prevent them from pulling to the curb.

Transit vehicles must be able to pull in very close to the curb to eliminate the gap (see Transit Curbs, page 102).

Ramps are not deployed and vehicles do not kneel, reducing delay and adding convenience.

Detectable warning strips or another detectable surface must be installed along the edge of the boarding platform.

"Mini-High" Platform

The "Mini-High" platform is used as a retrofit for older streetcars and buses with high-floor boarding, using a small platform and ramp to permit accessible boarding to select vehicle doors.

Passengers requiring accessible boarding must board using the mini-high platform.

Railings and fall protection are required for the entire ramp length and top landing.[12]

Vehicle operators may have to service the ramp separately, or may have to deploy additional on-board ramps to give access, causing delay.

Detectable warning strips must be installed along the edge of the boarding platform.

Accessible Paths & Slopes

Designs that provide universal accessibility at stops and stations not only increase the equity of transit systems, but also reduce operational costs. Making fixed route transit service simpler, more comfortable, and more convenient for passengers using mobility devices can reduce the need for costly paratransit trips, reduce dwell time at stops, and, by substituting for ramp or lift deployment, eliminate or reduce the use of one of the most expensive subsystems on a transit vehicle.

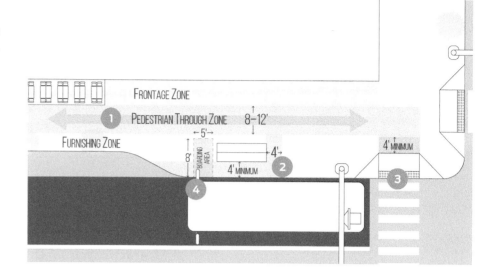

SIDEWALKS & CROSSINGS

1 For pedestrian travel paths, a clear width of 8–12 feet is preferred where transit is present, and may be wider based on pedestrian and transit rider capacity. Pinchpoints less than 6 feet wide create capacity and comfort issues and should be avoided.

A 4-foot clear width is acceptable around some design elements like shelters and seating,[13] and may be used especially where access is helpful but not essential, such as between a curb and the back of a building-facing shelter. Shelters and seating should be positioned so that all riders can comfortably wait, board, and alight without obstruction (see page 94).

2 Turns in travel paths must have a landing at least 4 feet deep (*ADAAG §403*), and a minimum 4-foot by 5-foot turning space is preferred (*PROWAG §304.2.1*).

3 Crosswalks must be accessible, with special attention to both people using wheelchairs and wheeled mobility devices and people with no or low vision. Curb ramps must be provided at all street crossings that involve a change in grade. Do not obstruct the top of the curb ramp.[14]

Curb ramps and other travel paths should be designed to prevent the accumulation of water and snow. Ramps may not have a slope exceeding 1:12. Ramps must have a landing for each 30 inches of rise (*ADAAG §405*).

Inclines and cross slopes of the street may impact other surfaces and should be accounted for in curb heights, sidewalks and boarding platforms, and drainage infrastructure. A 1 to 2% slope is often needed for proper drainage of sidewalks.

TRANSIT PLATFORMS

4 An accessible boarding area must be provided, typically measuring 5 feet long (parallel to the curb) by 8 feet wide (perpendicular to the curb). This includes 5 feet of width for a wheelchair waiting area, plus additional width to deploy a wheelchair ramp to serve the waiting area (typically 3 feet). Longer ramps may require additional length (see *ADAAG §810.2.2*).

To provide accessible boarding, the vertical step between a platform and a vehicle (or ramp) must not exceed 5/8 inch, with a maximum horizontal gap of 3 inches (*49 CFR §38.23*) (see *Transit Curbs*, page 102).

For near-level boarding, bridge plates used to enable accessible boarding should not rise more than 3 inches or exceed 1:8 slope, with shallower slopes preferred. The slope for a bridge plate depends on the height of the vehicle floor and ranges from 1:4 to 1:12 [*49 CFR §38.83(c)(5)*].

Transit platform surfaces, like sidewalks, must meet specific slope requirements. Cross slopes on most sidewalks should be between 0.5% and 2% to achieve both good drainage and accessibility. Landing areas should have less than 1% cross slope to facilitate the accessible boarding area (*ADAAG §403*).

Travel paths and ramps must comply with other accessibility requirements (see *ADA Std. Chapter 4: Accessible Routes* and *PROWAG Ch. R3: Technical Requirements* for additional regulations and guidance).

Automatically deploying bridge plates can be used to close the gap between a transit vehicle and the platform. **EUGENE, OR**

Universal Design Elements

Universal design features are critical throughout the transportation network, making it possible for any street user to comfortably and conveniently reach every transit stop. Universal street design facilitates station access, system equity, and ease of movement for all users, especially people using wheelchairs or mobility devices, the elderly, people with children and strollers, and people carrying groceries or packages.

Employ tactile, visual, and audible design elements together to guide people of all abilities through the street environment. Consistently using detectable surfaces, color contrast, and audible warnings assists all users, enhancing safety and accessibility.

TACTILE CUES

Detectable warning strips must be at least 24 inches deep, and must be applied at all curb ramps for their entire width, or at any location where pedestrians cross into another modal zone (i.e. bike lanes or vehicle lanes) along a flush transition (*DOT 504 §406.8*).[15]

Where the boarding platform is higher than a typical curb height, including near-level or level boarding platforms, 24-inch deep detectable warning strips must be applied the entire length of the platform edge (*PROWAG §R208*).[16]

Where passengers using wheelchairs are directed to specified doors, ensure the accessible doors are clearly communicated throughout the boarding platform using signs and markings.

At sidewalk-level stops, detectable warning strips may be used to indicate door locations.[17]

COLOR

Use color consistently to delineate modal zones and edges; for instance, transit lanes may be red/terra cotta, and bike zones or crossings may be green. Color repetition reinforces legibility, and should be employed at conflict zones, flush crossings, or likely sites for encroachment. Color-coded detectable warning strips can draw attention to conflict points.

Detectable warning strips should visually contrast with adjacent surfaces to alert pedestrians that they are crossing into a new modal zone (such as a transitway, bikeway, or vehicle traveled way).

Distinctly colored pavements and detectable warnings between pedestrian and bicycle zones. **PORTLAND, OR**

LIGHTING

Pedestrian-scale lighting, typically including lamps less than 25 feet high, increases comfort and safety around stops.[18]

Higher illumination around transit stops should be gradual rather than sudden to avoid creation of virtual shadows as driver and bicyclist eyes adjust.

AUDIBLE CUES

Signalized crossings may include accessible pedestrian signals (APS), which utilize audible cues to inform pedestrians of signal phases, including announcements or rapid percussive tones. If audible cues rely upon push-button activation, the button should be located near the curb ramp for each crossing direction, and far enough apart to distinguish from other ramps.

Stops and stations with real-time arrival information should include audible announcement capabilities (refer to *Passenger Information & Wayfinding* on page 100).

Washington Street, CHICAGO, IL

Stop Configurations

While stop location determines to a large extent how transit vehicles approach stops and interact with traffic, the physical configuration of stops and stations impact how riders interact with the transit system. Transit stops play a significant role in the urban street puzzle, and can be used not only to provide comfortable and accessible transit access, but also to organize traffic interactions and manage curbside activity.

The manner in which the transit stop is integrated into the streetscape determines its ability to bolster transit operations, serve street users, and activate underutilized space.

Boarding Bulb Stop

Boarding bulb stops use curb extensions that align the transit stop with the parking lane, creating an in-lane stop. Boarding bulbs enable side-running transit vehicles to stop without making large lateral shifts. Boarding bulbs improve speed and reliability, decreasing the amount of time lost when merging in and out of traffic.

Boarding bulb stops can become a focal point for improved public space along the street, creating space for waiting passengers, furnishings, bike parking, and other pedestrian amenities and community facilities without encroaching on the pedestrian through zone.

Boarding bulb stop on 34th St., **NEW YORK CITY, NY**

APPLICATION

Boarding bulb stops are applicable in both dedicated and mixed-traffic conditions, wherever transit vehicles operate in offset lanes without right-side bike facilities. Boarding bulbs can be installed at near-side, far-side, and mid-block stops, at both signalized and unsignalized locations.

Boarding bulb stops are especially applicable where merging into traffic from pull-out stops creates operational delays.

Use where transit passenger volumes require a larger dedicated waiting area than is available on the sidewalk.

BENEFITS

Boarding bulb stops allow transit vehicles to make in-lane stops, reducing dwell time and transit delay.[1]

Boarding bulb stops provide more space for transit passenger amenities while maintaining a clear pedestrian path on the sidewalk.[2]

When placed at intersections, boarding bulb stops also act as curb extensions to shorten pedestrian crossings.

In-lane stops can reduce bus and pavement wear and tear, reducing maintenance costs.

Boarding bulb stops shorten stop length, eliminating transition distance required to leave and merge back into traffic at pull-out stops. Space can be re-purposed to provide streetscape improvements such as parklets, bioswales, or additional bike and vehicle parking.

CONSIDERATIONS

Coordination between design and transit operations staff is needed to create effective, accessible boarding bulb stops (*ADA Std.* 403.5.1).

Designers should work with transit providers to determine the clear width necessary to create fully accessible boarding, which may vary based on vehicle type.

Overhang into the travel lane is often needed to create small enough clearances for rail vehicles. If buses operate in the same lane, driver training may be necessary.

Bulb stops often require drainage modifications; if catch basins cannot be moved, use trench drains covered by walkable grates along the length of the boarding bulb. Additional width may be needed to accommodate the trench drain.

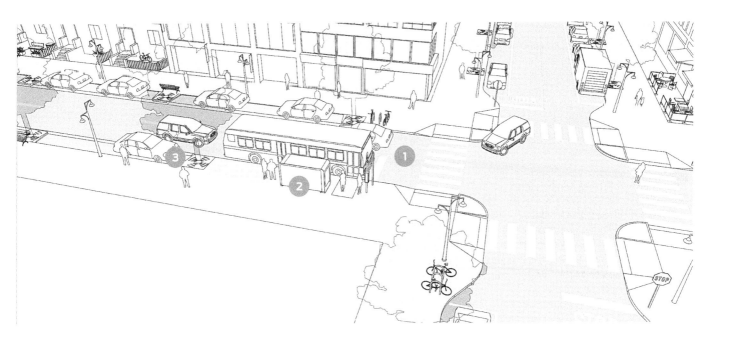

CRITICAL

Boarding bulb width must meet accessibility requirements (*ADA Std. 810.2.2*). With most ramp technology, boarding areas at each accessible door must be 5 by 8 feet, along with 4-foot clear paths to reach each accessible door (*ADA Std.* 403.5.1) (see page 67). Shelters, seating, trash bins, plantings, vending machines, and utility boxes must be placed clear of accessible paths.

Cross slopes no greater than 2% should be provided along the accessible paths and landing area.

Coordinate to ensure placement of accessible boarding areas is compatible across all vehicles in the transit fleet serving the stop.

1 At stops adjacent to crosswalks, provide at least 10 feet of clear sidewalk space, ahead of transit vehicle at near-side stops and behind the transit vehicle at far-side stops.

2 If shelters are placed on boarding bulbs, they must be placed clear of front- and back-door boarding areas.

RECOMMENDED

Boarding bulb length is determined by the boarding area required for the expected number of buses dwelling at a given moment (see page 62), but should be at least long enough to serve all doors of at least one design vehicle.

Boarding bulb stops should include passenger features like shelters, seating, wayfinding, and route information.

At bus stops, extend the bulb to within 2 feet of the edge of the travel lane; bulbs typically extend 6–8 feet from the existing curbline, and require minimal lateral movement for bus access.

OPTIONAL

Extend the boarding bulb at far-side stops to provide room for cars to queue behind a dwelling bus. Signs and markings should communicate to drivers not to "block the box."

3 Include green features like bioswales or planters to improve streetscape and stormwater recapture.

Where traffic buildup behind transit vehicles is of concern (i.e. where a street has one travel lane in each direction), periodic pull-out stops may be used to allow vehicles to pass buses. Priority treatments to allow buses to re-enter traffic should be provided.

Boarding bulb, N 45th St., **SEATTLE, WA**

Modular rubber platforms create an interim boarding bulb

Boarding Bulb Stop *(continued)*

TIERED STOP

Where local and rapid/limited service serve the same corridor or route, rapid stops may provide a combined pull-out/in-lane stop—where rapid service stops in-lane, local buses pull-out.

1 Pull-out stop is located before the bulb stop and serves the local service. Each stop should include its own "pole and sign," as well as legible rider and route information. Distinguishing between local and rapid service stop locations is critical for trip planning.

2 Rapid/limited bus service is accommodated by the boarding bulb. Regardless of arrival order, rapid buses are able to jump local buses in the queue and allow transfer between services. Curb radii at the back of the bulb must be great enough to accommodate the local bus's transition back into the travel lane.

3 Stop amenities (e.g. shelters, seating, wayfinding, and trash bins) can be placed on the bulb to preserve capacity and throughput of the sidewalk. For rapid service, stop shelter and amenities should be more robustly designed, including expanded capacity and seating, maps and real-time arrival information, and wayfinding.

4 Concrete bus pads are "S" shaped and continuous through the stop, conforming to the shape of the curb.

LEVEL BOARDING BULB AT STREETCAR STOP

1 Where boarding bulbs involve a height change, they must provide an accessible ramp to sidewalk grade (*ADA Std. §405*) (see page 66).

2 Steps may be used to provide non-accessible entries and exits to create multiple access points.

On platforms serving buses and LRVs, concave transit curbs can be used to enable buses to pull within 2 inches of the platform edge. Curbs may have an inset lip to allow the streetcar body to slightly overhang the platform while still allowing buses to gain close access (see page 102).

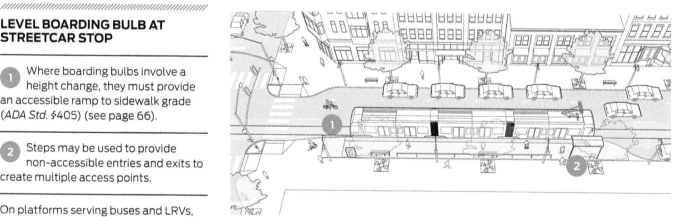

Side Boarding Island Stop

Side boarding islands, like boarding bulbs, are dedicated waiting and boarding areas for passengers that streamline transit service and improve accessibility by enabling in-lane stops.

Side boarding islands are separated from the sidewalk by a bike channel, eliminating conflicts between transit vehicles and bikes at stops. For both streetcars and buses, boarding islands allow the creation of accessible in-lane stops with near-level or level boarding.

Boarding island with bike channel on Dexter Ave., **SEATTLE, WA**

APPLICATION

Streets with moderate to high transit frequency, transit ridership, pedestrian volume, or bicycling volume can utilize boarding islands to maintain in-lane stops and provide separation to more users.

If bicycle facilities exist or are planned, island stops maintain continuity of the bike lanes.

If in-lane stops are desirable, especially adjacent to offset transit lanes, boarding islands can be accommodated in existing street width.

Platforms can be configured for level or near-level boarding.

If sidewalk width permits, boarding islands may be applied to streets with curbside transit operations and a bike facility.

BENEFITS

In-lane stop style reduces transit vehicle dwell times; on busy streets, in-lane stops may reduce stop delay between 5 and 20 seconds per location. Delay reductions are amplified as traffic congestion increases.[3]

Boarding islands eliminate bus-bike "leapfrogging" conflict at stops, in which buses merge across the bicycle travel path at stops, causing bicycles to merge into general traffic to pass the stopped bus, only to be passed again as the bus accelerates. At boarding islands, both buses and bicycles can move straight at the stop, in their own dedicated space.

Islands provide more space for transit passengers and amenities while maintaining a clear pedestrian path on the sidewalk. Operators are able to deploy ramps or bridge plates, as needed, onto the island without disrupting pedestrian flow.

CONSIDERATIONS

Boarding islands usually require less complex drainage modifications than boarding bulbs.

At high-volume stops, it may be necessary to require people on bikes to yield to people accessing the island directly from the sidewalk. Markings, color, and signage must reinforce appropriate yield behavior.

Lateral alignment with streetcars may require realignment of general traffic lanes or bike lane.

Bicycle signals can enhance the clarity of intersection movements. Consider using bike signals with far-side boarding islands to provide a dedicated bike and pedestrian through phase, especially if high turn volumes or a right-turn pocket is present. Bike signals are also applicable at near-side boarding islands where turns are prohibited and bicycles move concurrently with other through-traffic.

Side Boarding Island Stop (continued)

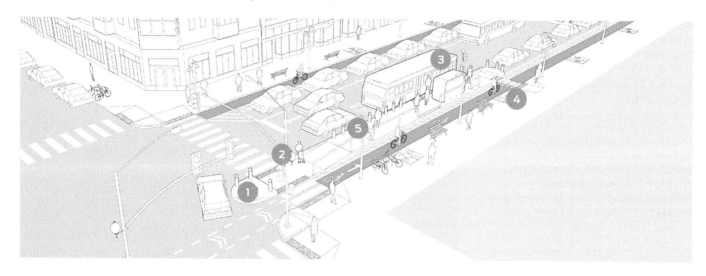

CRITICAL

Boarding islands must be designed to permit accessible boarding. For low-floor vehicles using bridge plates, near-level boarding can usually be achieved with a 9.5- to 12-inch platform. Higher (14-inch) platforms typically require that all doors be configured for level boarding, and may be incompatible with some buses.

An accessible boarding area, typically 8 feet wide by 5 feet long, must be provided to permit boarding maneuvers by a person using a wheelchair (*ADA Std.* 810.2.2) (see page 67).

Where the bike lane or cycle track requires bicyclists to yield at a crosswalk from the sidewalk onto the island, the BIKES YIELD TO PEDESTRIANS sign (MUTCD R9-6) and yield triangle markings must be installed.

Platform must be aligned to streetcar tracks with appropriate lateral clearance for level boarding; may require 9-foot moving lane or other track or lane realignment in cases with right-lane mixed-traffic operations.

Platform access ramp may have a maximum slope of 1:12 at a crosswalk or other crossing point, at the sidewalk and onto the platform (*ADA Std.* 405.2).

① Use reflective signage or other visible raised element on the leading (back left) corner of the island. KEEP LEFT or KEEP RIGHT (MUTCD R4-8) or object marker (OM-3) signs may be used.

Detectable warning strips must be placed on both sides of every crossing over the bike lane.

RECOMMENDED

② An accessible ramp should be placed at the intersection end of the island entering the crosswalk. If there is no crosswalk at the intersection, install one, with a refuge island tip to protect pedestrians (at least 6 feet wide).

For mid-block stops, include raised crosswalks across bike channel to encourage people on bikes to yield to people accessing the island.

③ Boarding island stops should include shelters, seating, wayfinding, and passenger information when feasible.

④ Shelters should be located at least 10 feet from crosswalks over the bike lane to allow visibility between people on bicycles and people exiting the island. Leaning rails may be located along this gap.

OPTIONAL

⑤ Install leaning rails along the edge of the island along the bike channel on portions of the island without a shelter or accessible boarding area. If leaning rails or fence are installed along the accessible boarding area, the total island width usually must be increased to 9 feet. Boarding islands can be extended to include bike parking, additional seating, parklets, or other community facilities.

In locations with wide sidewalks and no parking, the bike lane or cycle track may be bent in to the sidewalk to create a boarding island. In this case, raised crossings are an option to encourage yielding to people accessing the island, and to reduce bicycle speeds at the stop. Bike lanes should not generally be bent into the sidewalk to create pull-out bus stops on streets with parking lanes.

A YIELD stencil marking may be marked in the bike channel prior to the crosswalk to reinforce the requirement to yield.

Duboce Ave., **SAN FRANCISCO, CA**

NEAR-SIDE STOP WITH BIKE CHANNEL AT SIDEWALK LEVEL

1 The boarding platform must at minimum span from the front door to the rear door, and may be extended to meet capacity demands.

2 The bicycle lane behind the floating boarding island can be at street grade or may be raised. Where the bike lane changes grade, bicycle ramps should not exceed a 1:8 slope.[4] If raised, delineate bike and pedestrian realms using colored paint or paving materials.

Bike lanes may be narrowed to slow bicycle traffic and reduce conflicts, with a minimum 5-foot width.

3 Mark pedestrian crossings through bike lane. Yield teeth and other markings and signs such as YIELD stencils and BIKES YIELD TO PEDESTRIANS (MUTCD R9-6) signs inform bicyclists of the requirement to yield to pedestrians.

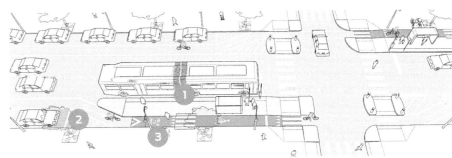

Near-side in-lane stop with conventional bike lane

Where a near-side island is combined with a right-turn restriction, extend the refuge island into the intersection and reduce the curb radius to self-enforce the turn restriction and provide additional pedestrian space.

Continuing the bike lane in a protected configuration through the intersection simplifies interactions with pedestrians and provides right-turning vehicles with a place to wait as they approach the conflict zone.[5]

Two-way cycle track at sidewalk level, Moody St., **PORTLAND, OR**

FAR-SIDE STOP WITH BIKE CHANNEL AT STREET LEVEL

1 If high turn volumes are present, include a rear storage area so cars are less likely to queue into the intersection while the bus dwells. More storage space may be necessary on streets with only one lane per direction.

2 Accessible ramps should be paired with crosswalks to direct users to safe crossings. If the bike channel stays at street grade, ensure that ramps, landings, and detectable warnings are provided whenever pedestrians cross into another "modal zone" (i.e. bikeway or travel lane).

3 At high passenger volumes, channelize pedestrian movements on and off the platform to reduce conflicts.

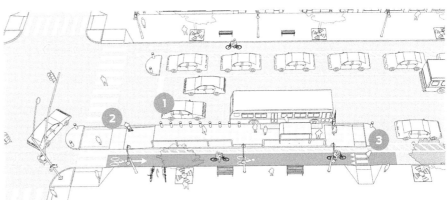

Far-side in-lane with protected bike lane

If a lean bar or railing is installed continuously along the back of the platform, the island must be at least 9 feet wide to accommodate the 8-foot deep accessible landing. If the accessible landing opens directly to an accessible crossing (either flush or raised), the island may be 8 feet wide.

A crossing over the bike channel may be raised to provide a flush path to the sidewalk. Install yield teeth and "YIELD TO PEDESTRIANS" signs. Bicycle ramps should not exceed a 1:8 slope.

Shared Cycle Track Stop

Shared cycle track stops are an important retrofit option for constrained transit streets with in-lane stops, especially of streetcars, if a boarding island configuration does not fit in either the street or the sidewalk.

In shared cycle track stops, a bike lane or protected bike lane rises and runs along the boarding area, along the extended curb, rather than wrapping behind the boarding area. Bicyclists can ride through the boarding area when no transit vehicles are present, but must yield the space to boarding and alighting passengers when a bus or streetcar stops.

Shared cycle track stop, Sherbourne St., **TORONTO, ON**

APPLICATION & CONTEXT

Used where limited right-of-way precludes boarding islands, including on streets with standard bicycle lanes, or where level boarding buses or LRVs are used.

Generally occurs in a curbside condition; if street parking exists in the cross section, space may be available for a boarding island or bulb.

Bicycle lanes ramp up to platform height before the stop, and then ramp down after. Bicyclists should be at street grade at intersections.

BENEFITS

On streets with light rail, allows bicyclists to stay out of the track zone when passing boarding areas.

Provides more space for transit passengers and amenities while maintaining a clear pedestrian path on the sidewalk.

Space within bike lane can be used to partially satisfy accessible boarding zone requirements.

Can facilitate level or near-level boarding.

CONSIDERATIONS

Measures must be taken to ensure bicyclists yield to boarding and alighting transit passengers; compliance is critical to providing safe and comfortable conditions.

CRITICAL

1. Place detectable warning strips along the edge of the sidewalk where passengers step into the shared raised boarding area, and along the boarding area curb where passengers board the transit vehicle. Use shark's teeth yield markings near the top of the bicycle ramp leading to the platform.

2. The whole width of shared cycle track area can be used as the accessible boarding area for wheelchair lifts. However, wheelchair users must have a waiting area provided that is accessible to allow maneuvers to the space, and must be located outside of conflict areas.

3. Ensure cycle track is wide enough for compatibility with maintenance equipment (sweepers or plows), or enact maintenance agreements.

Slope of bicycle ramp shall not exceed 1:8.

Shared boarding locations require comprehensive multi-sense information to guide visually disabled passengers. Provide audible announcements that a transit vehicle is arriving, including the route name if multiple routes are present.

Curbside activities that will conflict with bike movements and visibility (such as lay-bys or parking bays) must be prohibited at minimum 20 feet from either direction of the bike ramps.

RECOMMENDED

4. Where transit shelter is closer than 3 feet to bike lane, it should open to the building side to maintain accessible paths and to avoid pedestrian conflicts with passing bicycles.

Shelter should be transparent to allow waiting passengers and bus operators to see each other.

5. Ensure bicyclists are well positioned in view of turning traffic. Terminate the boarding platform at least 10 feet from the crosswalk to allow bicyclists to queue in front of transit vehicles.

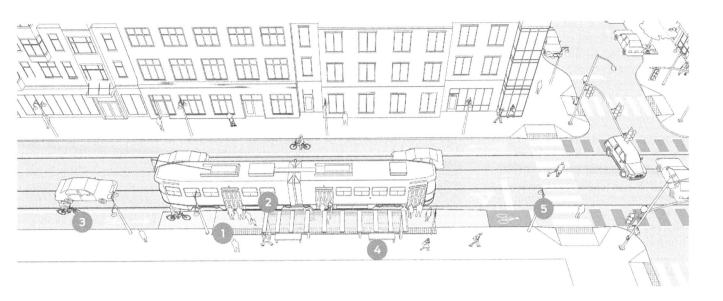

Case Study: Roncesvalles Avenue & Sherbourne Street, Toronto

As part of an effort to balance bicycling and transit accommodations, the City of Toronto has introduced innovative stop designs on two constrained streets: Roncesvalles Avenue is a neighborhood streetcar street, and Sherbourne Street is an important bus corridor leading downtown.

The city first reconstructed Roncesvalles Avenue, which includes a legacy streetcar line. Many bicyclists use the street to access its density of destinations, though there is not width available for dedicated bicycling infrastructure. However, to facilitate safe bicycling movements at stops while providing accessible boarding for transit riders, the city tested a shared boarding/bike lane—the bicycle lane rises to curb level at stops, which bulb out into the parking lane shadow. When the streetcar arrives, bicyclists must yield to boarding or alighting transit passengers. At all other times, bicyclists may cross the bulb without having to cross the streetcar tracks, eliminating a significant hazard.

Key to the success of the Roncesvalles Avenue treatment is a strong culture of compliance, and existing regulations requiring all other road users to yield to transit.

Learning from Roncesvalles, the city applied the treatment to Sherbourne Street, another key but narrow corridor, where a protected bike lane was slated to be installed. Because the constrained right-of-way precluded installation of boarding islands, the raised boarding bike lane was installed at stop locations, allowing transit riders to gain accessible boarding to the bus, while accommodating bicyclists in a high-quality, low-stress facility along the 1.5-mile corridor.

One key lesson from the Roncesvalles Avenue facility was applied to Sherbourne Street—on the boarding lane, a detectable warning strip was applied at two locations on the platform. First, as bikes entered the platform, yellow detectable strip was installed at the top of the ramp to warn bicyclists of the yield expectation. Along the length of the platform at the back edge (between platform and sidewalk), a detectable strip is used to warn pedestrians they are entering a shared facility. When the bus arrives, transit riders have priority; at all other times, bicyclists have priority through the facility. In addition to the grade change, the bike lane also narrows slightly through the platform to slow bicyclists as they move through.

Finally, the city is able to sweep and plow the cycle track all seasons using mini-sweep vehicles.

Roncesvalles Ave., **TORONTO, ON** (42 feet)

Sherbourne St., **TORONTO, ON** (45 feet)

Curbside Pull-Out Stop

Curbside pull-out stops are a low-cost option for bus stops on streets with curbside parking. While bus transition time is longer than for in-lane designs, it is relatively easy to make these stops accessible, provided sidewalks are sufficiently wide.

Since pull-out stops prioritize through-traffic, including through-moving transit, they are most useful where flow is a priority or where in-lane stops would be problematic. These include local stops along a route with rapid or express service, time-point stops, and other stops with long dwell times. Managing bus-bike conflicts and providing sufficient sidewalk width are specific needs when using this stop configuration.

Pull-out stop on street with bus lane on Webster Ave., **NEW YORK CITY, NY**

APPLICATION & CONTEXT

At queue jumps and queue bypasses, buses use the curbside lane to progress through congested intersections and service stops on the sidewalk.

At time points or end-of-route layovers, pull-out stops create space for the bus to wait out of traffic flow. Layovers are occasionally used for streetcars.

On streets with low-frequency bus service, high target speeds (≥35 mph), or where in-lane stops are not geometrically feasible, sidewalk stops provide a safe boarding space with limited expense.

CONSIDERATIONS

Pull-out stops consume somewhat more time than in-lane stops, since buses exit the travel lane completely, pull to the curb for passenger boarding and alighting, and then merge back into the flow of traffic.

Sidewalk stops may create conflicts between through-moving pedestrians and alighting passengers when the bus is dwelling.[6]

Shelters, seating, and other stop furnishings should be provided in the street furniture or curb zone of the sidewalk, leaving a wide enough clear path to accommodate pedestrian through-traffic. The through zone should be 8–12 feet wide in most downtown or commercial streets; see the *Urban Street Design Guide* for sidewalk guidance.

When curbside stops are partially blocked by illegal loading or parking, transit vehicles may have insufficient space to transition, increasing the likelihood that passengers will be forced to board from street level and that the through-traffic lane will be blocked.

Even when provided with entry and exit tapers, buses may not be able to pull close to curb, making boarding more difficult.

CRITICAL

An accessible boarding area, typically 5 feet long (parallel to the curb) by 8 feet wide, must be provided to permit boarding maneuvers by a person using a wheelchair (*ADA Std.* 810.2.2) (see page 67). 10 feet of width is preferred.

RECOMMENDED

To accommodate smooth transitions, sidewalk pull-out stops are typically 90 feet long when located near-side, and 100 feet when located far-side.

Buses can be equipped with enforcement cameras to discourage lanes from being blocked.

"Lay-by" configurations, where transit bays are carved out of the sidewalk, should be avoided on most streets, and applied only with very wide sidewalks (typically over 30 feet), or if the rest of the sidewalk has been widened but in-lane stops are not feasible.

OPTIONAL

When the pull-out stop is configured as a queue jump, install either a transit signal head to facilitate the queue jump, or a green signal with an extended hood, shielding it from the view of general traffic.[7]

NEAR-SIDE PULL-OUT STOP

This configuration is applicable where a neighborhood street crosses a larger street that may or may not be stop-controlled. If two similarly sized streets intersect with moderate to high traffic volumes, traffic signals with low-speed progressions may confer greater benefit to users.

1 At signal-controlled locations, the near-side pull-out stop may be implemented as a queue jump—the bus pulls into the stop, completes boardings, and then receives an advance or extended green phase through the intersection, while general traffic is held.

In stop-controlled configurations, the bus may pull into a near-side stop, allowing traffic behind to pull forward to the stop line and proceed while the bus is dwelling. When the bus completes boarding, it pulls forward and proceeds.

Where a small neighborhood street intersects a larger corridor or destination street and high transfer volume between intersecting routes is expected, the near-side stop can be paired with an adjacent far-side stop on the cross street, facilitating easy and safe transfer.

Locate the bus stop at least 10 feet from the crosswalk to ensure pedestrians and drivers have adequate sightlines.

Bus stop zone must be wide enough to ensure buses do not extend into adjacent lanes.

FAR-SIDE PULL-OUT WITH BIKE LANE

Appropriate at intersections with high traffic volumes, where traffic is heavier on the near side, complex intersections with multi-phase signals, or where traffic conditions may cause delays by locating near-side.[8]

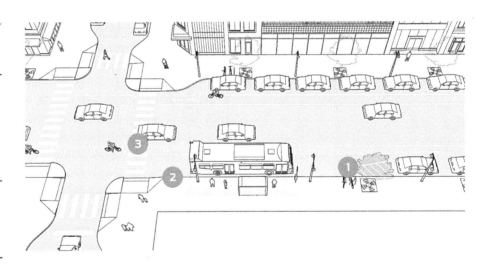

1 Exit taper is typically 25–30 feet. Enforcement should ensure stop areas remain unblocked by parking or loading.

2 Platform length includes length of the bus plus 10 feet of clearance from back of vehicle to crosswalk.

Through-traffic, including bicycles, is directed straight, to the left of the bus zone, while buses transition across the bike lane to the right.

The bus stop lane must be wide enough to ensure buses do not extend into the bike lane.

3 Use conflict-zone markings to position bicyclists to the left of the bus zone. Mark the bike lane to the left of the bus stop; place the seam of the concrete bus pad to either side of the bike zone, as seams and cracks pose a hazard to bike wheels. The bike zone should be at minimum 4 feet wide (refer to the *Urban Bikeway Design Guide*).

At signalized intersections, a leading bicycle interval allows bicyclists to continue ahead of buses pulling over to the stop, but may add transit delay.

In-Lane Sidewalk Stop

Where transit vehicles run adjacent to the curb, passengers board and alight directly from the sidewalk.

Curbside stops are also often observed in dedicated transit lanes, where pulling out of traffic is unnecessary.

APPLICATION & CONTEXT

Along curbside running ways in either mixed traffic or in dedicated transit lanes.

On mixed-traffic streets with low or moderate transit frequency, and with posted speeds at 30 mph or lower.

With dedicated curbside transit lanes, including dual and contraflow transit lanes.

BENEFITS

Sidewalk stops on the existing curb are typically the lowest-cost treatment, requiring only signage and an ADA boarding area to receive transit passengers on the existing curb. Along curbside running ways, the curbside sidewalk stop may be the only option.

Where pull-out bus bays (or "lay-bys") can be filled in to create in-lane curbside stops, buses save time and reduce wear, while improving pedestrian space.

CONSIDERATIONS

Where transit is not provided with a dedicated lane, making stops may cause traffic following the transit vehicle to queue behind it.

On two-lane, two-way streets where overtaking a stopped bus may create hazards, consider measures to prevent vehicles from passing.

CRITICAL

Stop zone must be 10 feet clear of the crosswalk or curb return whether near- or far-side.

Stop length must equal the length of the bus, and curbside boarding area should include both the front and back doors.

Ensure stop amenities do not block accessible boarding area or travel path.

RECOMMENDED

Red transit lanes enhance motorist and pedestrian awareness of curbside transit lanes and transit vehicles.

Shelters, even narrow shelters, improve passenger experience and establish the stop as a place for transit.[9] Consider omitting shelters on narrow sidewalks where pedestrian flow would be impeded.

34th St., **NEW YORK CITY, NY**

CHARLOTTE, NC

FAR-SIDE IN-LANE STOP WITH SHARED BUS-BIKE LANE

In constrained conditions where width prevents dedicated bike and transit facilities from being provided separately (13 feet or less).

Mark advisory bike lane to the left of the bus stop; place the seam of the concrete bus pad to either side of the advisory lane, as seams and cracks pose a hazard to bicycle wheels.

Position shared-lane markings to the left side of the bus-bike lane.

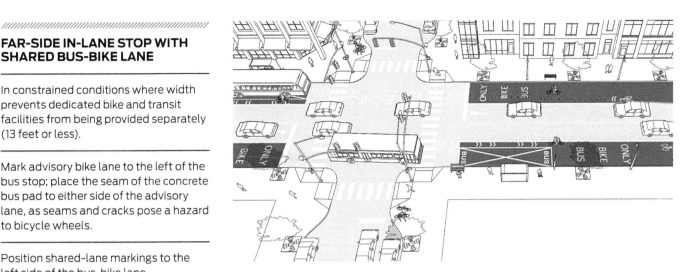

In-Street Boarding Island Stop

Located between center-running transit lanes and general traffic lanes to the right, in-street boarding islands create in-lane stops, giving streetcars and buses priority within the street while allocating space for through-moving vehicles.

In-street boarding islands call for careful management of pedestrian interactions to access the boarding platform.

In-street boarding island on left side of one-way street, 4th Ave. South, **SEATTLE, WA**

APPLICATION & CONTEXT

In-street boarding island stops are applicable on streets with center-running transit where in-lane stops are desirable. Especially on streets with high transit ridership or service frequency, center-boarding islands greatly enhance service for bus or rail.

Platforms can be configured for level or near-level boarding with a variety of transit vehicles, including streetcars and buses.

Appropriate for a wide variety of service types, from streetcar to bus to light rail, operating local or rapid services.

Island stops must be placed at controlled (with stop signs or signals) intersections, where a crosswalk facilitates safe pedestrian access to the island.

BENEFITS

In-street boarding island stops enable the use of center-running transit on relatively small streets where full-scale stations are not feasible or necessary.

In-lane stop location reduces transit vehicle dwell times.

Boarding island stops provide dedicated space for transit passengers and amenities while maintaining a clear pedestrian path on the sidewalk.

Island stops provide a refuge area for pedestrians crossing the street in addition to transit passengers.

In-street island on K St. NW, **WASHINGTON, DC**

CONSIDERATIONS

Designs should provide adequate pedestrian crossing opportunities to and from the island, accounting for potentially high pedestrian volumes. Insufficient crossing width and long pedestrian wait times may increase the incentive for pedestrians to cross traffic lanes unsafely.

When applied to near-side stops, consider turn management strategies. Near-side applications may be most effective at intersections without the conflicts presented by left-turn movements.

In-street boarding island on Market St., **SAN FRANCISCO, CA**

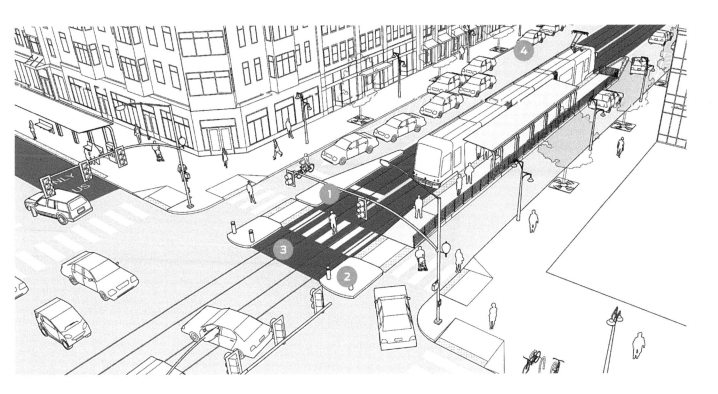

CRITICAL

Platform must be aligned to streetcar tracks with appropriate lateral clearance for level boarding. Stops for rail vehicles may require a 9-foot moving lane next to the island, or other track or lane realignment to bring vehicles close to the platform.

Center island platforms must be either level or near-level boarding. 24-inch wide detectable warning strips should be placed along the entire boarding edge of the platform to indicate vehicle position.

Detectable warning strips must be placed on both sides of every flush pedestrian crossing.

1 Platform access ramp may have a maximum slope of 1:12 at a crosswalk or other crossing point, at the sidewalk and onto the platform (*ADA Std.* 405.2, 810.2.2).

An accessible boarding area, typically 8 feet wide by 5 feet long, must be provided to permit boarding maneuvers by a person using a wheelchair (*ADA Std.* 810.2.2) (see page 67), generally requiring islands to be at minimum 8 feet wide. Islands with railings along the rear side will require an extra foot of space, making the total width 9 feet.

2 Reflective signage or other visible raised element on the leading corner (back left corner) of the island. KEEP LEFT or KEEP RIGHT (MUTCD R4-8) or object marker (OM-3) signs may be used.

Ensure that pedestrian refuge islands crossing transitways are wide enough to allow groups of people to wait, particularly near stations. Discourage pedestrians from waiting in unsafe locations in the roadway, especially near railways. Where spacing between parallel tracks provides no clear zone between passing LRVs, clearly indicate the danger area and discourage pedestrians from waiting in this area.

RECOMMENDED

Railings shall be installed along the through lane to the right of the island to control pedestrian access and discourage dangerous crossings. Channelize pedestrian movements to platform entrances with enhanced crossing treatments. Railings must not impede accessible width, usually extending the island width to at least 9 feet.

For center-boarding islands serving both bus and rail, near-level height (8–12 inches) is preferred, as buses are not typically able to access 14-inch level boarding heights.

3 At intersections, install refuge island tips at least 6 feet wide to provide pedestrians protection in the crosswalk.

OPTIONAL

4 Boarding island extensions can be used for green infrastructure, including rain gardens and other stormwater retention facilities.

Median Stop, Right-Side Boarding

Where transit runs along a wide median separating travel directions, center-median stops highlight and give brand identity to transit service.

Often located on historically or culturally significant routes like vintage streetcar lines, the median stop often provides a wide and comfortable queuing space.

Passengers may board from the edge of the median, with separate platforms for each direction.

Streetcar running way and stop in center median, Saint Charles St., **NEW ORLEANS, LA**

APPLICATION & CONTEXT

Where transit runs along a wide median separating travel directions, including light rail, streetcar, or BRT routes.

On multiway boulevards, median stops may be provided on the island between the primary and service roads.

Where transit service is faster along longer routes, stations are spaced further apart (typically ½–1 mile), with a greater amount of investment in quality and comfort.[10]

BENEFITS

Stations enjoy many of the benefits of center-boarding islands, but with increased separation from travel lanes and passenger comfort.

The center median stop provides ample space for passengers boarding and alighting.

Continuous median provides space for plantings and other streetscape elements.

CONSIDERATIONS

Stations should provide high-quality physical space and passenger amenities, including shelters, seating, system information, trash receptacles, and fare machines.

Especially on existing streetcar lines, median stops offer challenges to universal access. Upgrades to stops should include accessible ramps to reach the platform. Accessibility may also be challenging where existing islands are narrow. Vehicle solutions, such as using bridge plates instead of foldout ramps, can reduce the necessary width of the island.

Left-turn restrictions or phase separation should be incorporated, especially near stations. Left-turning vehicles present common conflicts with pedestrians and transit vehicles.

As passengers are required to cross travel lanes when entering and exiting stops, intersection design and signalization must prioritize pedestrian movements to eliminate turn conflicts.

Consider treatments to address the safety concerns presented when passengers run across travel lanes to catch an approaching train.

Track crossings may demand special treatments to guide pedestrians through stations with limited sightlines, including signage and markings or active warning systems to draw attention. Treatments like Z-crossings and barriers that disrupt pedestrian paths should be limited to locations where safety is a demonstrable concern.[11]

CRITICAL

1 Platform length must be sufficient to serve the expected number of buses or railcars at the station consistently throughout the day (see *In-Lane Stop Length,* page 62).

Platforms must provide at least 8 feet of width plus any width required for shelter or railing installation. Clear landing areas must be provided at all doors, with 4-foot paths for the length of the platform.

2 24-inch deep detectable warning strips are required where pedestrians cross into vehicle or bike lanes across flush surfaces, and along the entire boarding direction of platforms higher than a typical curb height (4–6 inches).

Ensure that pedestrian refuge islands crossing transitways are wide enough to allow groups of people to wait, particularly near stations. Discourage pedestrians from waiting in unsafe locations in the roadway, especially near railways. Where spacing between parallel tracks provides no clear zone between passing LRVs, clearly indicate the danger area and employ designs which discourage pedestrians from waiting in this area.

RECOMMENDED

Platform height should aim for level or near-level, or low-floor boarding (10–14 inches). "Mini-high" platforms may be used as a retrofit treatment to provide accessible access at select doors on vintage or historic streetcars.[12]

3 Transit curbs allow transit vehicles to pull within 2 inches of the platform (see page 102).

Where right-of-way width allows, both stations can be located on the same side of the intersection (as shown in the illustration above). Median side-boarding stations can also be staggered along a block or offset across intersections. This may be advantageous where width is constrained, or to enable active transit signal priority, or to provide signalized left turns.

Left-turn restrictions or phase separation should be used if median stations are near a left-turn movement to address conflicts with mixed traffic, both for transit vehicles and for passengers entering and leaving stations (see page 156).

Where stations are staggered along a block, provide refuge islands and signalized crossings at desire lines, such as between the platforms or at a mid-block point.

4 Robust shelters provide climate-appropriate protection from rain, wind, and sun. Shelter roofs should overhang transit vehicles.

Median right-boarding station, **ALEXANDRIA, VA**

Median Stop, Left-Side Boarding

Center-median stops and stations offer the highest level of comfort and visibility for high-frequency and high-volume transit routes.

Combined platforms that service both travel directions deliver efficient service, clear boarding procedure, and excellent passenger amenities to enhance brand identity and service efficacy.

Passengers board from the center of the median through doors on the left side of transit vehicles.

Health Line BRT station on boarding island, Euclid Ave. at E 13th St., **CLEVELAND, OH**

APPLICATION & CONTEXT

On streets with center-running transit lanes or a separated transitway, right-of-way width may be conserved by providing left-boarding platforms.

Left-boarding platforms may be combined, serving bi-directional service, or staggered, serving inbound and outbound stops opposite an intersection.

In downtown and corridor street contexts, where transit routes require high-capacity stops.

BENEFITS

The center median stop provides dedicated space for passengers boarding and alighting.

This space may be more comfortable for waiting passengers, as it is buffered from travel lanes by the transitway.

Median stops unlock streetscape improvement opportunities, including installation of green space, furniture, or public art within or in the shadow of the station.

Bi-directional platforms can reduce confusion in finding the correct platform for the desired travel direction.

CONSIDERATIONS

Passengers are required to cross travel lanes when entering and exiting stops—provide pedestrian improvements through design and signal strategies that reduce vehicle conflicts.

Left-turn restrictions or phase separation should be incorporated, especially near stations. Left-turning vehicles present common conflicts with pedestrians and transit vehicles.

Central platforms require left-boarding vehicles or special design consideration; left-boarding or dual-side boarding buses can be more difficult to procure.

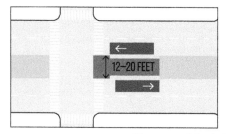
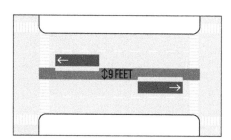
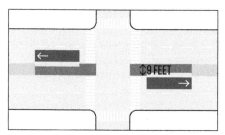

Three possible station and intersection configurations for median left-side stops, with minimum platform widths

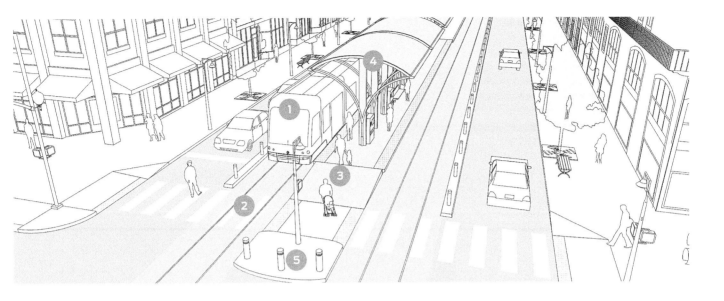

CRITICAL

① Left-side boarding platforms require compatible vehicles, either LRVs, streetcars, or custom buses.

Level or near-level boarding must be provided on median platforms. Center boarding stops are good candidates for fully level boarding, since route-specific vehicles are deployed in most cases.

On bi-directional platforms, 24-inch detectable warning strip must extend the length of the platform on both sides.

② Signage and pavement treatments, including markings or color, warn pedestrians to clear from unsafe waiting spaces.

If proof-of-payment fare payment is used, platforms may be open. Turnstile-controlled stations should be partially enclosed to control entry onto the platform, with openings located in alignment with vehicle doors (see *Fares & Boarding*, page 182).

RECOMMENDED

③ While the minimum accessible platform width is typically 8 feet, platforms serving both travel directions require wider platforms, especially at busier stations. 12 feet is the preferred minimum width (10 feet in constrained conditions), expanding as capacity increases. Platforms serving only one direction may be a minimum of 9 feet wide (including space for a railing along the rear of the platform).

④ Provide high-quality amenities like shelter, seating, schedules, real-time arrival, wayfinding, system information, and maps to nearby destinations.

Utilizing proof-of-payment systems and all-door boarding can improve on-time performance on high-traffic routes.

⑤ A refuge island tip should be installed to provide pedestrians protection from vehicles. The pedestrian landing or refuge area must be large enough to accommodate peak passenger alighting volumes. Wider crosswalks (longer refuge areas) are the simplest way to achieve higher capacity. Provide bollards to prevent automobile use of this space for illegal movements.

OPTIONAL

In cold or rainy climates, stations may be enclosed to provide comfortable waiting space.

Integrate bicycling into transit access; provide bike parking within 50 feet of the platform entrance (see page 105).

If bicycles are allowed on transit vehicles utilize signage and markings to direct bicycles to preferred doors. Separate bicycles from wheelchair areas on transit vehicles where possible.

Left-boarding LRT station with uni-directional boarding island, Main St., **HOUSTON, TX**

On-Street Terminal

On-street terminals serving many routes can increase capacity and reduce transit vehicle congestion where multiple routes converge. By grouping routes and spacing stops in a skip-stop configuration, passenger boardings can be dispersed using skip-stop configurations and enhanced boarding platforms for heavy passenger volumes.

Buses, streetcars, and light rail vehicles can be accommodated in mixed-traffic lanes, or may have dedicated lanes to manage high transit volumes.

On-Street Terminal on Marquette Ave., **MINNEAPOLIS, MN**

APPLICATION & CONTEXT

Downtown areas served by a robust transit network can see streets clogged with buses competing for space among other users, including large numbers of waiting passengers. They also may see large volumes of transfers. On-street terminals can improve operations along high-volume transit corridors with dedicated lanes, skip-stop siting, and enhanced boarding areas.

BENEFITS

Reduces conflicts between transit vehicles in corridors with heavy transit volumes along multiple routes.[13]

Skip-stop placement allows high-frequency bus corridors to serve different routes at groups of bus stops, and distributes waiting passengers along a corridor.

CONSIDERATIONS

Terminal stops facilitate high-volume transfers, so branding and signage are critical to legibility and passenger understanding. Information should be clear, concise, and visible whether it is posted as simple displays or as dynamic real-time information.

If bike lanes are present, place them on the opposite side of the street from transit lanes to reduce conflicts from frequent transit movements on one-way streets, or provide high-quality bike facilities on a nearby parallel street.

Terminal stops may need additional space to allow vehicles to lay over between runs.

Analyze the need for active warning systems, especially if multiple transit modes share space.

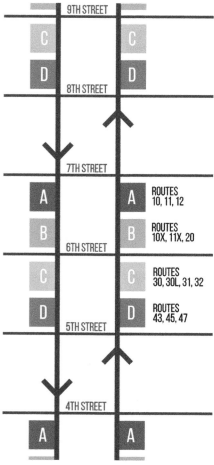

Sample skip-stop placement on downtown street grid with one-way couplet.

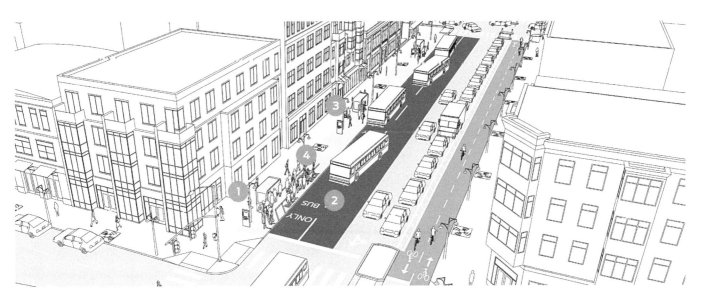

CRITICAL

(1) Transit stop signs must clearly communicate which routes are served at which locations.

(2) The on-street terminal must always operate in the curbside lane; to ensure stops remain unobstructed, all other curbside activities must be prohibited on the terminal side of the street.

Stop length must meet the criteria of a pull-out stop, though transition lengths may be shared between stops—one stop's exit taper may act as the next stop's entry (see page 62). Transit vehicles make stops in the curbside lane, and travel in the offset lane.

RECOMMENDED

Stopping patterns should be consistent to aid rider recognition. Signage and maps use letter or color motifs to communicate and reinforce stopping patterns, with each route consistently making stops in the same block location.

(3) Strip maps, system maps, and wayfinding infrastructure should be consistently and prominently displayed to assist riders in finding correct stop locations.

Real-time arrival information should be prominently displayed.

OPTIONAL

(4) For high-boarding stops with either all-door boarding or multiple lines, managed passenger queues may be implemented at the stop to speed boarding, sort passengers into distinct queues, and maintain a clear pedestrian zone on the sidewalk (see page 106).

Stop identifier signs on SW 5th Ave. transit mall, **PORTLAND, OR**

Bus stop on SW 5th Ave. transit mall, **PORTLAND, OR**

Marquette Ave. on-street terminal/bus lanes, **MINNEAPOLIS, MN**

4. Station & Stop Elements

Improving on-street transit stops accomplishes a dual mission of making transit more attractive and highlighting the agency brand, while bringing immense benefits to accessibility and performance. Stops and stations are often where existing and potential riders first interact with a transit service; stops provide essential information and frame the level of comfort and satisfaction riders have with transit service.

Stops can be upgraded using interim design measures, but incorporating high-quality transit stop design and amenities into capital projects can expand pedestrian capacity and promote transit streets as a desirable place in the urban environment. Creating a simple, legible, and pleasant experience at the transit stop grows the capacity of the whole system, and can help transform transit from a basic coverage service to a desirable mobility option.

Folsom Street, **SAN FRANCISCO, CA**

Stop Elements

Stops are tools to attract riders, improve operational efficiency, build the brand identity of a system, and foster local economic development.

Transit stops exist on a continuum, from minimal sign-and-pole stops to fully enclosed stations. While financial constraints often limit the provision of stop elements on existing routes, investing in high-quality stops can change both the perception and reality of transit service. The design, prominence, and comfort of a transit stop is the first indication that people receive about their own potential experience as passengers. Stop elements and design have a bearing on all the key decision points in a transit trip, affecting whether a trip is taken by transit or a competing mode, and even whether to make a specific trip at a specific time of day or in uncertain weather. Platforms enable faster boarding, good maps and signage make trips easier, and integrating stops with adjacent buildings or green infrastructure can dramatically enhance the streetscape.

Small Transit Shelter

The provision of shelters should be prioritized with the goal of improving comfort for the most passengers. In addition to stops with a moderate number of boardings, shelters should be provided at transfer points, at stops in weather-exposed locations or without nearby potential sheltering locations, and at stops with a relatively high use by senior and child passengers.

At low-volume stops where service is less frequent or only basic coverage service is provided, basic shelters can provide passengers with comfortable seating and vital information. Provision of comfortable shelter and seating can significantly improve perception of wait time and rider satisfaction.[1]

Basic shelters are ideal for the passenger volumes and context of a neighborhood transit street.

COMFORT

1 Ensure the waiting passengers can be seen from outside by using glass or open design for the back wall. Include lighting in the shelter, or locate shelters in a well-lit area.

Social safety is a primary consideration at shelters. Use transparent materials to enhance visibility of waiting passengers.[2]

Shelters must be cleaned and maintained. Advertising revenue, or concessions that require the installation of shelters in exchange for revenue, can fund shelter maintenance in full or in part.

Shelter design should respond to climate and location in providing comfort to passengers. Consider the micro-climate of a specific stop in choosing a shelter design. Observe conditions at specific stops. Stops may be more or less affected by sun, wind, or rainfall depending on the arrangement of nearby buildings and trees.

Include trash bins, especially at high-volume stops. Ensure maintenance plan is in place.

Advertisements on shelters must not block sight lines between vehicle operators and waiting passengers.

Shelters should include space to rest, either a bench or leaning rail, and space for a wheelchair user next to the bench.

Two-sided shelters provide good protection from precipitation and some protection from wind, with open sightlines to approaching vehicles.

On narrow sidewalks, placing the shelter ahead of the front door loading zone allows the shelter to be very close to the curb, as the path from the shelter to the front door is not blocked by a shelter wall. A 4-foot deep shelter may be placed as close as a foot from the curb.

Three-sided shelters offer protection from wind and more intense storms, but usually require an opening in the rear side of the shelter or a large space between the shelter and curb, to provide an accessible path.

Four-sided shelters, usually with an entrance at both the sidewalk and curb side, can enhance comfort in extreme winter climates. They must be at least 5 feet deep to provide an accessible path inside the shelter, and be set back from the curbside, and must have an opening at least 32 inches wide.

Shelters open at both back and front, including cantilevered shelters or post shelters, are easy to place, and provide protection from sun and light rain but little wind blockage.

INFORMATION & WAYFINDING

2 Pole and bus stop signs must indicate critical information including the stop name, route number, stop number, direction or destination, and system logo.

Shelter should include stop name and further system information.

Bus stop signs should be given their own exclusive pole, as opposed to being affixed to existing sign poles.

Small Transit Shelter *(continued)*

CAPACITY

Small shelters are used for stops where a relatively small number of people wait at a given time, including stops with high turnover and frequent arriving transit.

Use stop ridership data and observed stop usage conditions, as well as factors such as climate and nearby destinations, to determine level of coverage and capacity needed.

PLACEMENT

Shelters can be oriented open to curb (typical); with its back towards the curb; at the building-side of the sidewalk; or integrated into a building facade.

1 An 8- to 12-foot wide pedestrian through-zone on the sidewalk, behind or in front of the shelter, is preferred in commercial and high-use settings. Maintain a minimum 5-foot sidewalk clear zone, which may be wider than the ADA standard (*PROWAG §R302*) in some cases.

2 A 4-foot wide clear path must be provided for access to any elements such as shelters or informational displays, and any interactive elements such as push buttons.

3 While the minimum unobstructed boarding area must be 5 feet long parallel to the curb, 8–12 feet of length is preferred to allow for variation in door location in operation. Account for different door locations across the transit fleet.

4 Trees and other green elements can be integrated into the stop area in line with shelters and outside of clear paths and accessible landing areas, providing shade and a more comfortable waiting environment.

Passengers waiting in shelters must be able to easily see arriving transit vehicles and must be readily visible to operators if transit vehicles stop only on demand.

ALL DIMENSIONS SHOWN ARE MINIMUMS

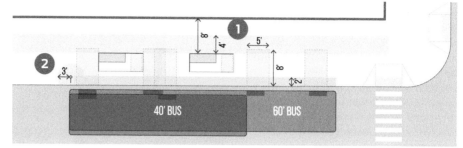

Bus stop on 15-foot sidewalk

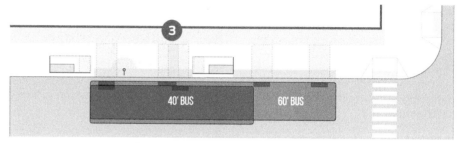

Bus stop on 12-foot sidewalk with shelters open towards building

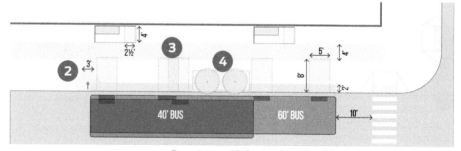

Bus stop on 15-foot sidewalk with shelters at building line

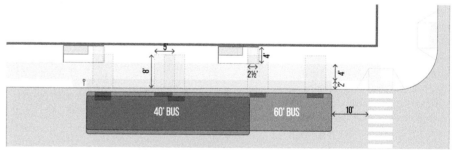

Bus stop on 10-foot sidewalk with shelters at building line

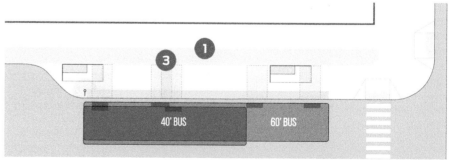

Bus stop on 8-foot boarding bulb

Placement of the shelter and supporting posts or walls must not conflict with accessible travel paths, boarding areas, and transit vehicle door zones.

Shelters with seating must provide a minimum 2.5- by 4-foot clear space for wheelchair users located entirely within the shelter space. Clear zone must not overlap with the seating area, consisting of seat and a seating zone extending 1.5 feet in front of the seat (*ADAAG §R308, 404*).

Accessible boarding areas and clear paths may be fully or partially under the shelter canopy, as long as shelter supports or other stop elements do not obstruct them.

Shelters are typically 4 feet deep, though they may be as narrow as 2 feet in constrained conditions. Narrow shelters typically have only enough space for a covered standing/leaning area and information displays.

Branded rapid service transit stop, **SEATTLE, WA**

Shelter on boarding bulb with landscaping features, **SAN FRANCISCO, CA**

Shelter illuminated at night, **SAN FRANCISCO, CA**

Branded rapid service shelter on constrained sidewalk, **SEATTLE, WA**

Partially enclosed shelter, **TORONTO, ON**

Shelter on side-boarding island, **CAMBRIDGE, MA**

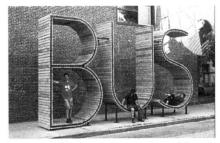
Shelter as interactive public art, **BALTIMORE, MD**

Large Transit Shelter

Larger shelters with signature design features like easy-to-understand information, enhanced seating or waiting areas, or landscaping elements improve perceived wait times and general passenger satisfaction.

Shelters can give the transit stop a more substantial physical presence in the streetscape, calling attention to the quality of service available.

On higher-frequency transit streets, shelter dimensions and amenities should be expanded to meet increased demand.

Large transit shelter on boarding island

PLACEMENT

Large shelters are used on higher-frequency or higher-capacity routes, especially stops serving articulated vehicles or multiple vehicles simultaneously, as well as on transit corridors and destination streets, especially where transit placemaking is desired.

May serve one or both travel directions, depending on placement.

Permeability to the sidewalk is important with longer shelters; consider open designs. On boarding islands, carefully consider pedestrian crossings.

Placement of shelters' supporting posts or walls must not conflict with accessible travel paths, boarding areas, or transit vehicle door zones.

Shelter placement must allow a minimum of 4 feet through-path around all sides when at the level of the sidewalk, and around the front (street) side if elevated on a platform.

CAPACITY

Use stop ridership data and observed conditions, such as weather, nearby destinations and land uses (e.g. senior centers) to determine level of coverage and capacity.

Off-board fare collection and proof-of-payment can be implemented to speed boarding at high-capacity stops, which can reduce per passenger dwell time by half.[3] Ticket vending can be integrated into stop/shelter space.

Land use characteristics and nearby destinations inform stop design; if significant trip generators are within a quarter-mile, high-amenity shelters are desired.

As daily boardings increase, observe queuing volumes to determine length, capacity, and amenities provided at shelters.

INFORMATION & WAYFINDING

Real-time displays, either simple LED or full color, communicate multiple routes and up-to-date wait times. Real-time arrival information increases rider satisfaction.

Should include highly-visible signage identifying the station and travel direction(s).

System logo and branding should be prominent, reinforcing network presence.

Passengers waiting in the shelter must be able to easily see arriving transit vehicles, and passengers must be readily visible to operators if transit vehicles stop only on demand.

Include lighting in the shelter, or locate shelters in a well-lit area. Ensure the shelter can be seen from outside by using glass or open design for the back wall.

COMFORT

Typically physically separated from pedestrian through paths, usually on boarding islands with raised platforms.

Shelters can be oriented open to curb (typical); back towards the curb; at the building-side of the sidewalk; or integrated into a building facade.

The pitch and location of shelter roofs must account for precipitation, preventing the roof drip line from falling onto passengers between the shelter and the transit vehicle. Roofs may be extended slightly over a transitway to prevent rainfall at the door.

Social safety is a primary consideration at shelters. Use transparent materials to enhance visibility of waiting passengers.

Include trash bins, especially at high-volume stops. Ensure a maintenance plan is in place.[4]

Consider climate in both design and materials selection; metals should be covered in a hot climate. In cold, snowy, or harsh climates, enclosed shelters provide additional weather protection.

Provide opportunities for placemaking, especially by integrating public art or amenities.

ENCLOSURES

At stops or stations with high ridership or long queues, larger station enclosures with more seating provide a higher level of passenger comfort and indicate the importance of the station.

Due to limited sightlines, enclosed shelters should only be used on routes where transit vehicles make all stops.

Heating or lighting may be provided within enclosures to increase comfort.

Enclosures may be provided in collaboration with abutting buildings and structures, such as retail or commercial facilities.

Environmental controls within transit shelters shall be proximity-actuated. *(ADA Std. §R308.2).*

Riders must purchase a ticket or tap an RFID fare card before passing cordon into paid fare area indicated by sign, **SEATTLE, WA**

Health Line BRT station on Euclid Ave., **CLEVELAND, OH**

Large canopy transit shelter on LoopLink BRT route, **CHICAGO, IL**

Large Select Bus Service shelter, **NEW YORK CITY, NY**

Seating

Seating is one of the most basic features at transit stops. Seats are an opportunity to incorporate attractive design and durable materials into a transit stop. Seats should be designed or selected on the basis of comfort relative to expected wait time and boarding demand at a stop.

Providing comfortable seating at or near transit stops dramatically improves the comfort of the passenger experience. Comfortable seating can provide valuable resting places whether or not a transit trip is involved.

Branded rapid service bus shelter with bench and leaning rail, **SEATTLE, WA**

BENCHES

The provision of seating at transit stops should be prioritized with the goal of improving comfort for the greatest number of passengers. Stops with a moderate or high number of boardings should be furnished with seating, as should stops with long wait times and stops with relatively high use by senior and child passengers. Observe peak hour queues at stops and stations to determine the adequate number of seats to install.

Seating shall not conflict with paths, leaving 4 feet of clear distance on all sides where pedestrians are expected (3 feet minimum, *ADAAG §403*).

Benches may be contained by or affixed to shelters.

Benches shall be at least 43 inches long, and 20–24 inches wide, with the seat 17–19 inches above ground level (*ADAAG §903*).

Ensure benches are designed to prevent accumulation of water.

In hot, sunny climates, avoid materials that retain heat (i.e. metal in direct sunlight).

At small stops, provide several individual seats or a bench with raised separation between seats.

At stops with high boardings, provide other opportunities for resting, including lean bars. Shallow benches wrapped around shelter elements can also provide seating for a large number of waiting passengers.

LEANING RAIL

The most minimal accommodation, a leaning rail, rises 30–38 inches and allows passengers to rest while waiting.

Can be used to channelize pedestrian movements to and from boarding platforms when placed at the back of the boarding area.

Should be offset 6 inches from the non-boarding edge of boarding islands, and 1 foot from the edge of bike channels.

Leaning rail, **NEW YORK CITY, NY**

Fare Vending

Ticket machines allow riders to purchase single fares, add value to fare cards, or generate proof-of-payment (PoP) tickets from passes.

Off-board fare collection and PoP systems may require fare machines to be placed on stop and station platforms.

Select Bus Service ticket machine, 34th St., **NEW YORK CITY, NY**

APPLICATION

Ticket machines enable off-board fare payment and all-door boarding.

BENEFITS

Riders can use a number of payment methods to ride transit, including credit and debit cards, cash, and mobile payment systems.

Riders can purchase multiple fare types, and can integrate regional fare systems when agencies collaborate.

CONSIDERATIONS

Curbside fare machines are costly to install and maintain; use on high-frequency or high-volume corridors where reduced dwell time is a priority.

Accessibility is key; fare payment purchase instructions should be clear, simple, and well communicated, potentially in multiple languages. Machines should also include raised lettering or audible instructions, unless alternatives are available for visually-impaired passengers.

Cities are beginning to leverage mobile technology for ticketing, including system apps for off-board fare and pass purchases. The need for off-board fare payment may be reduced or eliminated where passengers are widely able to pay by app, substantially reducing the need for on-board fare payment.

CRITICAL

Vending machines must not block accessible path and boarding areas, or bus door zones.

Install an adequate number of machines to handle the expected number of passengers purchasing tickets during peak hours, especially if all riders must collect PoP tickets to board. Assess how many tickets can be purchased per machine per hour, and ensure fare machines can accommodate peak hour boardings.

Operable parts (including buttons or touch screens) must be placed at a height between 34 and 48 inches to accommodate users in wheelchairs (ADA Std. $308).

Passenger Information & Wayfinding

Every transit stop must include information about routes served at the stop in a clear, legible manner.

Providing clear and simple information like route and system maps, schedules, expected travel times, real-time arrival times, and ridership procedures makes the system more attractive and simpler to use, and improves rider satisfaction.

Additionally, good information can enhance the transit stop as a gateway to its surrounding neighborhood or destinations.

Illuminated map and information display, **LOS ANGELES, CA**

APPLICATION

Maps, routes, and other wayfinding should be prominent at stations and stops, especially high-volume, high-activity, or transfer stops.

System information may include strip maps of single routes, fixed schedules or frequencies, full system maps, and pertinent transfer maps or schedules.

Information can be shown on hanging signs or signage integrated into the shelter. Temporary posted information should be protected from weather behind placards.

At busy transfer nodes, wayfinding guides riders promptly to connecting routes.

Outside of stations, wayfinding materials guide rider decision making and transit access.

Where bus routes run on one-way streets, or where the location of the stop in the opposite direction is not obvious, wayfinding signage should indicate its location.

BENEFITS

Providing route information that is clear, understandable, and accurate makes it easier for passengers to understand their travel options.

Wayfinding signage makes it easier to find bus stops, especially where stops for opposing travel directions are not located immediately nearby each other.

Alerting riders about nearby, transit-accessible destinations enables them to make more informed decisions about their travel options.

Schedule and real-time arrival information reduce uncertainty and improve rider satisfaction.[5]

Stops and stations are gateways to their destinations, and wayfinding can highlight key destinations.

Concise signage and tactile cues can assist transit users in navigating unfamiliar surroundings or novel transit use conditions.

CONSIDERATIONS

Level of detail for information displayed must be carefully considered to provide clarity and avoid confusion. Avoid over-signing, or cluttering the station area with too much information which may be ignored or contribute to information overload.

Listing key information about route frequency, running times throughout the week, and accessible destinations allows riders to make well-informed decisions about travel and routes.

Simple network structures and rider procedures can be inherently easier to understand and may require less instruction.

Apply universal design principles to passenger information and wayfinding elements, including audible and tactile resources (see page 67).

CRITICAL

Each stop shall include a stop name or identifier (destination/cross street, or numbered/lettered identifier); route identification; network and route map; schedule and route information; and clear indication of stop location and position. Bus route identification signs must comply with accessibility requirements.[6]

For riders with visual disabilities, provide an alternative to visual display boards; audible announcements are preferred over braille and other methods that require finding the display. Consider station/street noise and environmental characteristics during implementation.

If at an intersection, signs identifying stop location must be visible from all corners with either a recognizable system logo or standard transit stop marker.

Use wayfinding signage and materials that are consistent with regional or agency brand; consistent use of logos, colors, and fonts reinforces visibility.

Place wayfinding in predictable locations, such as overhead or at eye-level, and at regular intervals.

Place wayfinding elements at progressive intervals, and disclose necessary information at decision points.

Name stops, stations, and destinations to reinforce brand and recognizability.

Where multiple stops are located in close proximity to each other, mark stops with letters or numbers to ease stop identification and facilitate transfers (see *On-Street Terminal*, page 88).

Signs identifying a stop name, location, or identifier must be prominent enough to be seen by passengers riding inside a transit vehicle, to aid in stop identification.

RECOMMENDED

Real-time arrival displays with mobile app integration improve rider satisfaction and can increase ridership. Real-time displays can range from simple one-color LED text to full-resolution screens, and should be accompanied by audible announcements.

Integrate route and real-time arrival information into mobile applications, with emphasis on applications usable by people with visual disabilities. Providing information in these formats can strongly complement the written, visual and audio information present at a stop.

Include relevant transportation connections and services, including regional routes and bike share stations, to expand rider options.

To direct riders to from stations to destinations in the station area, indicate travel direction and times in easily understood units, such as approximate walking time.

Paving materials may indicate direction to subtly guide users through transit facilities.

Platforms may indicate door boarding areas with detectable surfaces, on-platform markings, or signage (i.e. "Wait Here," "Step Aside," etc.).

Real-time bus arrival and wayfinding sign, **NEW YORK CITY, NY**

In-station wayfinding signage, **RICHMOND HILL, ON**

Audible bus arrivals announcement is activated by push-button, **WASHINGTON, DC**

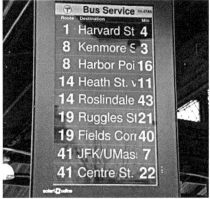

Real-time bus arrival sign, **BOSTON, MA**

Transit Curbs

Designing a curb with transit vehicles in mind can allow vehicles to pull close to the platform and to "dock," reducing the gap between the vehicle and the platform, and helping to facilitate level or near-level boarding.

Types of transit curbs applicable to streets include concave-shaped concrete, as well as standard rectangular-section curbs with hard rubber, plastic or other polymer bumpers.

Civic Center sbX station with a concave curb, **SAN BERNARDINO, CA**

APPLICATION

At locations with level or near-level platforms with low-floor vehicles, transit curbs should be considered.

Transit curbs allow drivers to pull the bus within 2 inches of the curb without scraping the vehicle wheels or lugnuts.

For curbs to be effective, vehicles must enter the stop straight-on, making in-lane stops best suited for transit curbs. Pull-out stops must provide sufficient straightening distance (see page 63).

The curb can be designed with a slope or concave shape—the curb's shape positions the bus as the driver pulls in, allowing the bus to stop within 2 inches of the platform.

Variations similar to the Kassel Curb and Dresden Combibord can be applied with streetcars or trams. A small recess at the platform level allows the rail vehicle to hang over the curb and reduce the gap between platform and vehicle floor.

CONSIDERATIONS

Pedestrians may not expect the shape or height of the curb. Use pavers, paint, or railings to alert and guide pedestrian footfalls. High-contrast color or materials also support visibility.

Use only where buses have little lateral movement entering the stop, and the boarding area extends the entire length of the bus.[7]

CRITICAL

Curb height must be greater than 6 inches.

Taper curb at platform entry and exit.[8]

Install detectable warning strips to warn pedestrians of curb location, especially on flat surfaces where platform height is greater than 6 inches.

Entry taper on a Kassel-type transit curb.

A 3-inch thick rubber rail allows buses to hug a near-level curb, **SEATTLE, WA**

BRT station with plastic bumper applied to curb, **EUGENE, OR**

Bus Pads

Bus pads are highly durable areas of the roadway surface at bus stops, usually constructed in concrete, addressing the common issue of asphalt distortion at bus stops.

Conventional asphalt pavement is flexible, and can be moved by the force and heat generated by braking buses and trucks, leading to wave-shaped hills or hummocks along the length of a bus stop. This issue is pronounced at high-volume stops where dwelling buses further heat the roadway surface, as well as near-side stops in mixed-traffic lanes where trucks may be adding to wear.

Transit shelter with checkered-colored concrete bus pad, NE 83rd St., **REDMOND, WA**

APPLICATION

At bus stops, especially at high-volume stops where asphalt pavement deforms under the weight of buses.

CRITICAL

Pavement at bus stops must be kept smooth at crosswalks to maintain accessibility.

Along bus stops with through bicycle traffic, such as in-lane stops, smooth pavement must be provided.

RECOMMENDED

Bus pads should be at least 8.5 feet wide to accommodate both wheels of a bus, but should be wider at locations without precision loading, to provide a consistent surface when the bus does not pull fully to the curb.

At in-lane stops, the bus pad should extend across the full width of the lane, and end on the lane line.

At pull-out stops where the bus crosses a bike lane, the concrete bus pad should end at either the right edge of the bike lane or the left edge of the bike lane (including its full width), to prevent the creation of a longitudinal seam within the bike lane. Where bikes pass stopped buses, as on shared bus-bike lanes, bus pads should be provided across the full width of the lane to provide a level surface to both buses and bikes.

At curbside pull-out stops, bus pads should be provided for the full length of the clear curb zone, ending before reaching the crosswalk.

At in-lane stops, bus pad length should be determined based on the length of the full bus zone. The ideal length of a comparable pull-out stop (with the same bus vehicle length and number of berths) can be used to determine the length of the bus pad.

Bus pads should end before the crosswalk to prevent lateral or longitudinal pavement seams in the crosswalk. If a bus pad must be extended into the crosswalk, it should extend across the full width of the crosswalk to prevent wheelchairs from encountering seams between concrete and asphalt.

Green Infrastructure

Incorporating green infrastructure into transit street design can improve water quality, detain stormwater flows, reduce the volume of stormwater runoff, and relieve burden on municipal water treatment systems.

Green infrastructure can complement transit by calming traffic, enhancing comfort while waiting for transit,[9] and creating opportunities for safer pedestrian crossing at bus bulbs and curb extensions with green infrastructure.

Plantings at an S Line streetcar stop, **SALT LAKE CITY, UT**

APPLICATION

Integrate green infrastructure into sidewalks, medians, curbs, and other features, including bioswales, flow-through planters, or pervious strips.

At stations and terminals, an enhanced landscape can improve aesthetic appearance, user comfort, and ecological performance.

BENEFITS

A tree canopy and green features can improve transit experience for waiting riders, increasing comfort and reducing perceived wait time.

Green infrastructure improves the natural ecosystem and reduces harmful pollutants. Where vehicles leave oil and other pollutants on the road surface, a bioswale facility can prevent large amounts of pollution from entering the watershed.

CONSIDERATIONS

Select appropriate plantings; in dry climates, drought-resistant landscaping (xeriscaping) reduces water and maintenance requirements.

Choose green infrastructure based on pedestrian volume and the intensity of use on a sidewalk

RECOMMENDED

As required, install a perforated pipe at the base of the facility to collect the treated runoff.

Bioswales have a slight longitudinal slope that moves water along the surface to allow sediments and pollutants to settle out. In-place infiltration then allows localized groundwater to recharge. Ideal side slopes are 4:1, with a maximum slope of 3:1. Use a maximum 2% gentle side slope to direct water flow into the facility. Use appropriate media composition for soil construction. The engineered soil mixture should consist of 5% maximum clay content.

The planter should drain within 24 hours; this is especially critical near transit stops where pooling can degrade transit access.

Ensure that infiltration rates meet their minimum and maximum criteria. The engineered soil mixture should be designed to pass 5–10 inches of rain water per hour.

Where a near-side boarding bulb is combined with a turn restriction, design the curb to self-enforce the turn restriction and monitor closely to ensure that transit vehicles are not suffering from delays.

Refer to the *Urban Street Design Guide* for more detailed guidance.

Bus stop with bioswale on N. Denver Ave.,
PORTLAND, OR

Bike Parking

Bike parking can supplement transit ridership both in bustling urban corridors and at regional stops and stations, and can replace time- and space-consuming on-bus bicycle racks.

Bike parking elements can expand transit sheds, enhancing access to stop-adjacent destinations, and boosting intermodal connectivity.

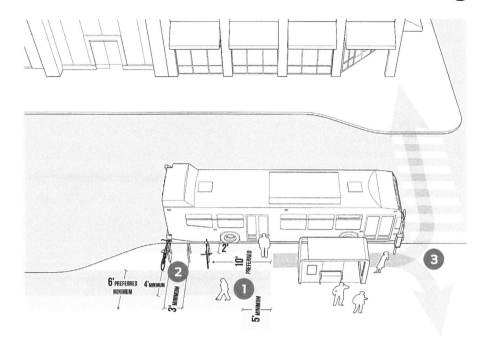

Bike parking may be sited on bus stops with accessible paths.

APPLICATION

Provide short- and long-term bike parking options where demand exists or is expected.

BENEFITS

Short- and long-term bicycle parking enables first- and last-mile connections, as well as access to destinations, and should be considered near all stations and stops.

Adequate bike parking deters unintended locking, including chaining bikes to trees, sign poles, or seating elements.

CONSIDERATIONS

Parked bicycles must not impede access paths to and from transit vehicles or along walking routes. Consider the distance available between parked bicycles and other elements.

CRITICAL

1 Provide a clear zone around bicycle parking to avoid impeding traffic, including near transit vehicle doors, on adjacent sidewalks, and through long-term storage facilities.

2 If multiple bicycle racks are installed, place them at least 3 feet apart to allow convenient, uncluttered access.

Locate parking in well-lit areas in full view of sidewalks and pedestrian paths.

RECOMMENDED

3 Short-term bike parking should be located within 50 feet of stop or station entrance, as well as major destinations.

OPTIONAL

At feeders and terminals, long-term bicycle storage, including bike lockers or cages, provides enhanced security and protection from weather, enabling first- and last-mile trips. These facilities should be installed close to the entrances to major stations.

Covered bike parking, **PORTLAND, OR**

Bicycle station, **WASHINGTON, DC**

Bicycle storage, **BOULDER, CO**

Passenger Queue Management

A major source of delay on high-volume transit routes occurs where large numbers of passengers board and alight in constrained space, especially curbside bus and BRT stops.

Managed boarding procedures can reduce interference and conflict with pedestrian movement adjacent to the transit stop, and make the boarding process itself more efficient.

Managed queue at Broadway Station for 99 B-line, **VANCOUVER, BC**

APPLICATION

Where transit passengers are observed blocking the sidewalk, especially at high-volume stops (≥100 boardings per hour at peak), queue management may be valuable.

On boarding platforms serving large transit vehicles with multi-door boarding, queue management shows waiting passengers how to evenly distribute themselves.

BENEFITS

Queue management markings organize waiting passengers at busy transit stops and preserves a pedestrian through-zone.

Where all-door boarding applies, well-marked queuing space disperses riders along the entire platform, speeding the boarding process.

CONSIDERATIONS

Alighting passengers must be able to exit before boarding passengers enter; ensure markings and signs communicate this requirement and make room for alighting riders.

Stops serving multiple routes must provide a separate boarding and queuing area for each route.

CRITICAL

Mark queue lines for each door of the transit vehicle, with pathways directed clear of the pedestrian through-zone.

Use wayfinding principles of progressive information; alert passengers of the route number and which door to board through markings and signs.

RECOMMENDED

Lean bars may be provided at long queues.

5. Transit Lanes & Transitways

Transit street design elements are an investment—often the dense, constrained downtown and urban centers where transit has the highest potential ridership are also the places with the slowest and least predictable traffic speeds. In these contexts, where congestion is high and private parking is limited, transit has the greatest potential to efficiently move more people through fixed right-of-way. Allocating on-street transit facilities can boost reliability, travel speed, capacity, and modal balance, increasing the total performance of the street.

Transit lanes and transitways must communicate to all users how street width is allocated in time and space. Transit lanes delineate space within the roadbed as exclusive, either full- or part-time, and can generate transit benefits with relatively low implementation costs. Transitways physically separate a portion of the street for transit's exclusive use, providing high-quality running way at all times.

SW Morrison Street, **PORTLAND, OR**

Transit Lanes

Transit lanes are a portion of the street designated by signs and markings for the preferential or exclusive use of transit vehicles, sometimes permitting limited use by other vehicles. Transit lanes, unlike on-street transitways, are not physically separated from other traffic. This section focuses on the selection, design, and operational or management requirements of specific transit lane varieties, based on vehicle type and street position.

Transit Lanes

Example of street with center transit lanes and in-street island stop

DISCUSSION

On busy urban streets, transit lanes are the building blocks to provide reliable and robust transit service. Continuous running ways yield the greatest benefit to transit operations, and can often be implemented with little impact, or even positive impact, on general traffic flow.

Transit lanes are implemented by repurposing general traffic lanes or parking lanes and are usually implemented on streets that also accommodate private motor vehicles in at least one direction.

Transit lanes are flexible. They can be dedicated at all times, or only during peak times or daylight hours. Full-time lanes better serve transit performance and visibility, but peak-period lanes may be appropriate in specific contexts.

APPLICATION

Transit lanes are broadly applicable on downtown and corridor streets where transit is delayed by congestion and curbside activities.

Streets with high motor vehicle traffic volume and congestion are good candidates for dedicated lanes, which organize traffic flow and improve on-time performance and transit efficiency.

Smaller streets may be converted to transit-priority or other shared transit streets.

CONSIDERATIONS

The decision to dedicate a lane to transit on a multilane street should be based on a combination of factors, with special emphasis on transit volume and demand, including future demand, and the potential to reduce total person delay or to limit increases to average travel time over both short and long term analysis periods.

While motor vehicle traffic capacity or travel time is one of many supporting considerations, dedicating lanes to transit should not be ruled out on the basis of any single factor. Vehicle level of service is not an acceptable planning factor when viewed in isolation, and its use should be limited to understanding queue lengths and other changes with potential network impacts.

It is essential to manage turns across transit facilities, sometimes accommodating turns in ways that reduce transit delays, and sometimes prohibiting them or otherwise managing their impacts. As on other multi-lane urban streets, turning movements typically involve conflicts with people walking and biking and with other traffic flows, and require special consideration.

Transit travel time variability and reliability over the day are a good indicator of the potential benefits of transit lanes, especially if boardings are consistent throughout.

Markings, signage, and enforcement maintain the integrity of transit lanes. Automated electronic enforcement, including license-plate readers or video, is preferable to labor-intensive patrols.

Offset Transit Lane

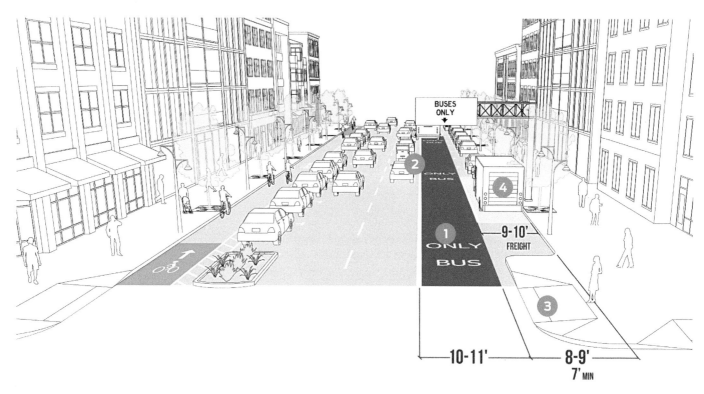

When adjacent to offset transit lanes, curbside access lanes must be adequately wide to not obstruct the transit lane

Also known as "floating" or "parking-adjacent" lanes, offset transit lanes place transit vehicles in the right-most moving lane, but are offset from the curb by street parking, curb extensions, or raised cycle tracks.

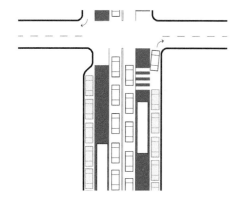

APPLICATION

On multi-lane streets with on-street parking, loading, parklets, and other curbside uses, especially streets with retail.

Where existing bulb-outs or other geometric considerations preclude the use of curbside parking lanes for transit.

Streets with in-lane stops in the form of bus bulbs, islands, and other significant stop amenities.

BENEFITS

Offset transit lanes accommodate high transit vehicle volumes and improve both reliability and travel times on streets operating near or beyond their motor vehicle traffic capacity.

Offset transit lanes reduce delays due to congestion.

Offset transit lanes raise the visibility of high-quality services, especially rapid service.

Offset transit lanes maintain space for other curbside uses, such as parking, loading, bulb-outs, or parklets.[1]

CONSIDERATIONS

Implementation is relatively easy; reconstruction of curbs is less likely to be necessary than for curbside transit lanes.

In commercial areas, lanes are prone to encroachment due to double-parking, deliveries, and taxicabs; enforcement is critical.[2]

Turns can be accommodated in short facilities near the intersection, including right-turn pockets, shared transit/bike/right-turn lanes, or dropped transit lanes (see page 158). Each of these facilities may reduce vehicle delay within the complete operation of the street, but can also degrade transit service, and must be applied carefully.

Vertical separation elements between the bus and mixed-traffic lane are usually not feasible, since parking is preserved.

CRITICAL

1 Designate lanes using BUS ONLY markings and signs (MUTCD 3D-01 or similar markings).

2 Dedicated transit lanes must be separated from other traffic using solid single stripes or double white stripes. A solid single white line conveys that crossing into the transit lane is discouraged, and typically indicates that using the transit lane to pass is prohibited, whereas a double solid white line means that encroachment is legally prohibited (MUTCD 3B.04)

Enforcement is critical to maintaining the lane's integrity. Vehicle-mounted photo/video enforcement has been demonstrated to be effective in improving transit lane compliance.[3]

RECOMMENDED

Bus lane width should be determined within the overall assemblage of a street, taking into consideration adjacent lane uses, with a desired width of 10–11 feet. (Refer to page 142 for additional guidance on lane widths and buffer distance). At stops, bus lane may narrow to 9 feet.

Red color treatments are effective in reinforcing lane designation (see *Pavement Markings & Color*, page 134). Apply red color along the entire lane.

3 Bus bulbs should be installed at stops to enable in-lane stops, and provide space for other stop and sidewalk amenities. Curb extensions may be installed at non-stop intersections to increase pedestrian space and shorten crossing distance— interim treatments and materials such as paint, planters, and bollards can be implemented at low cost.

4 It may be desirable to assign additional space to a buffer or to a parking lane rather than to the bus lane, especially when large vehicles use the parking lane for loading. A 10-foot bus lane provides a predictable operating environment when adjacent to a buffer or bicycle lane on at least one side.

Bus lanes may be wider to calm traffic in other lanes and reduce risk of mirror damage and minor collisions. Since mixed-traffic lanes should not be wider than 11 feet in urban conditions, extra width may be assigned to the transit lane or to a marked buffer if 2 or more feet are available.[4] If adjacent to a buffer or a bike lane, a 10- or 11-foot bus lane should be provided.

To keep bus lanes unobstructed, parking lanes adjacent to an offset bus lane should be 8–9 feet wide in most cases, or up to 10 feet when truck loading zones are designated or curbside deliveries are frequent. 7-foot parking lanes may be used next to 11-foot bus lanes if compliance is high and wider vehicles are not permitted to park.

OPTIONAL

Provide shared right-turn lanes or right-turn pockets at intersections with moderate to heavy turn volumes. Offset transit lanes can allow other users, including taxis, for-hire vehicles, and bicycles. Use markings and signs to indicate permitted users.

34th St., **NEW YORK CITY, NY**

O'Farrell St., **SAN FRANCISCO, CA**

Curbside Transit Lane

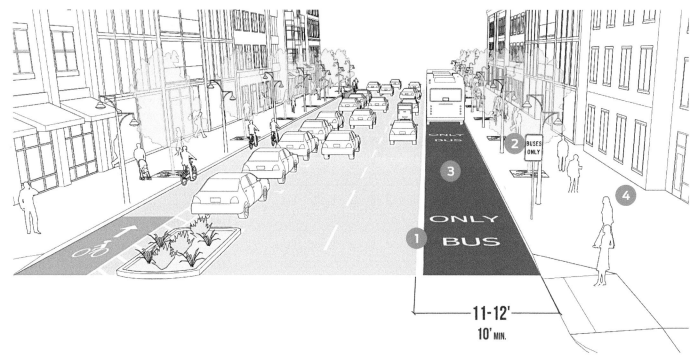

Curbside transit lanes should be 11 to 12 feet wide, but may be designed at the 10-foot minimum in constrained conditions

The lane adjacent to the curb can be dedicated to transit vehicles, especially on through corridors where parking is either not provided or not well utilized.

Curbside transit lanes can be implemented with varying levels of separation, increasing service capacity and allowing riders to board directly from the curb.

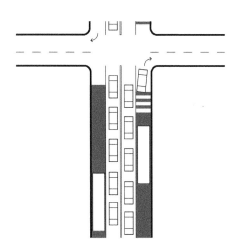

APPLICATION

Where no space for center transitway boarding islands or offset transit lane boarding bulbs exists.

On streets with no curbside parking, or where curbside parking removal is acceptable.

On streets with in-lane sidewalk stops (see page 80).

On streets with wide sidewalks and furnishing zones that provide space for shelters and strong lateral separation between passing buses and pedestrians in the sidewalk through-zone.

BENEFITS

Transit vehicles are not delayed by interactions with parking or loading vehicles if well enforced.

A curbside transit lane can have differing, flexible uses throughout the day, such as parking or a shared bus-bike use (see page 120). However, full-time lane dedication improves integrity in some conditions.

CONSIDERATIONS

Special design attention must be given to right turns from streets with curbside transit lanes (see page 158).

Lanes are prone to encroachment by loading, deliveries, and taxicabs. Enforcement is needed.

Where rain pooling is an issue, gutters and drainage in bus lanes next to the curb must be kept clear to avoid splashing onto the sidewalk. Concrete gutters or lanes may be preferable for curbside bus lanes.

Where snow is a consideration, lanes must be cleared in such a way that plowed snow does not block the lane for transit vehicles. Stop locations must also be kept completely clear of snow at boarding areas.

Because bus stops are typically located directly on the adjacent sidewalk, stops must leave enough room for waiting passengers and passing pedestrian traffic.

CRITICAL

1 Designate lanes using a single or double solid white line, as well as a stenciled "BUS ONLY" marking (refer to MUTCD 3D.01). In some jurisdictions, markings may be required for each permitted user (e.g. "TAXI, LRT, BUS ONLY").

2 Signage must designate the transit lane as restricted. Place signs either on the curbside or overhead (MUTCD 2B.20).

RECOMMENDED

3 Mark the transit lane with red color. Red color treatments are effective in reinforcing lane designation (see *Pavement Markings & Color,* page 134).

Enforcement is critical to the lane's integrity. Vehicle-mounted video enforcement has demonstrated efficacy in improving transit lane compliance.

The desired width of a curbside bus lane next to a mixed-traffic lane is 10–12 feet, including a gutterpan if present. Bus-only lanes should not typically exceed 12 feet in width. If target operating speeds between stops are low, typically below 25 mph, 11-foot lanes are preferable to 12-foot lanes. If buses operate in an adjacent lane, a 12-foot curbside lane is desired.

Provision for curbside loading can improve compliance, such as timed freight parking on the other side of the street or around the corner from loading destinations.

At intersections with a high volume of turning movements, the curbside lane may need to drop to maintain traffic flow; refer to page 158 for intersection treatment guidance.

Curbside bus lane and stop, **SANTA MONICA, CA**

OPTIONAL

If 13 feet of width is available, full-time curbside bus lanes may be separated with left-side, traversable barriers, such as rumble strips. Separation is not appropriate in all contexts, and must be developed with special care for its impact on walking and bicycling access. If curbing or other hard separation is used, including mountable curbs, bus lanes should be designed to allow passing at selected points. The impact on snowplowing operations should be evaluated when considering the use of curbs to separate the bus lane from other traffic, in climates where snow is a possibility.

4 Wider sidewalks, especially those buffered with plantings or furnishings, increase pedestrian safety and comfort adjacent to curbside transit lanes.

Curbside lanes may be separated with hard barriers (e.g. concrete curbs), which may be intermittent or continuous (see *Transitways,* page 126). Where nearly continuous, curbs should at least be omitted for short segments to allow buses to pass, or to allow buses to pass break-downs or incursions.

On very high frequency corridors where bus traffic is significant enough to create congestion, double transit lanes can be implemented curbside. The second bus lane should be designed as an offset transit lane.

First Ave., **NEW YORK CITY, NY**

Rail Lane, Side Running

Streetcar and light rail lines can be configured in the right-most travel lane, either curbside or offset by parking. Streetcars and downtown light rail lines in many cities are served by side-running rail.

Whether in dedicated or mixed-traffic lanes, rail paths must be kept clear from all but the briefest obstructions. Streetcars and light rail vehicles (LRVs) have their own geometric needs that may differ from buses. While curbside rail lines are often furnished with a separated guideway, more flexible streetcar lanes may be desired to accommodate turning movements or off-peak traffic flow.

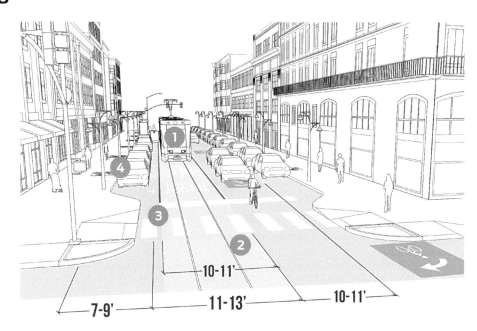

Side-running rail lanes assign buffer width to lane edges where obstructions are likely to occur; parking lanes should be marked as narrowly as possible to deter obstruction

APPLICATION

On two-way streets, offset streetcar and light rail lines operate in the right-most motorized lane, adjacent to a curbside parking lane. This operation allows boarding bulbs or islands at stations, and can accommodate loading, parking, and right turns to the right of the streetcar.

On one-way streets with parking, offset rail lines operate in the left-most or right-most lane.

A dedicated lane is preferable to mixed-traffic operation for curbside and offset rail, except in cases where even peak period traffic does not inhibit transit operations.

Where streetcars or LRVs operate in a curbside lane, a protected curbside transitway is preferred to physically prevent or discourage incursion by other vehicles.

BENEFITS

Dedicated streetcar or light rail lanes preserve on-time service, which is particularly important given the inherent inflexibility of streetcar routes.

Streetcars can provide a well-branded service with a higher capacity and a smoother ride.

Offset streetcar lanes create room for pedestrian realm enhancements such as boarding bulbs and islands, curb extensions, bioswales, planting strips, and parklets, while leaving space for on-street parking that is accessed by crossing the transit lane.

CONSIDERATIONS

Offset streetcar lanes must be clear of overhanging mirrors or other parts of parked cars. Lanes should be assigned the full width needed by the streetcar, with clear demarcation of the edge of the parking lane.

Catenary wire typically hangs 17–20 feet above street level; coordinate overhead elements with street trees and traffic signals.

Plan streetcar and bicycle routes concurrently so that bicyclists are fully accommodated within the network. Crossing tracks unexpectedly or at smaller angles presents danger for bicyclists. Curbside rail lanes can be designed to be suitable for bicycling but require more width and typically require designs that let bicycles pass to the right of the streetcar at stops. Local access by bicycle is a component of nearly all urban streets; where possible, bicycle traffic should be positioned on a different section of the street. Parallel, high-comfort routes should also be provided.

Streetcars typically have larger turning radii than buses. Where a streetcar makes turns, care must be taken to clear the entire swept path (see *Intersection Turn Radii,* page 170, and *Recessed Stop Bars,* page 172).

Rail lanes may sometimes need to be shared between streetcars and buses, or lane design may need to be interoperable to accommodate bus replacement of rail service. Rail lanes may be narrowed at platforms.

Where dedicated lanes cannot be provided, a combination of signal priority and short dedicated sections can be used to create a virtual transit lane (see page 165).

Bicyclists should be directed to portions of the street that are out of the way of tracks, especially where tracks cross the bicycle's path of travel at an angle. Embedded rails, switches, and seams are dangerous for cyclists and should cross bike paths at 90 degrees or as near as possible (minimum 60 degrees).[5]

CRITICAL

1 The streetcar lane must remain free of obstructions. On both shared and dedicated lanes, parking and standing must be prohibited and strictly enforced, preferably with camera enforcement. In low-compliance areas, no-stopping tow-away zones must be implemented. Curbside streetcar lanes must be designated using LRT ONLY markings and appropriate signs including LRT LANE (MUTCD R15-4a), RIGHT TURN PROHIBITION (R3-1), and NO STANDING (R7-4).

Lanes should be 11 feet wide in most configurations, though they may be wider to accommodate the dynamic vehicle envelope at turns. Lanes may narrow to 9 feet at station platforms.

2 Use appropriate paving material, such as concrete or large block pavers, to support rails and delineate the streetcar lane. The paved surface or markings should cover the swept path of streetcars (including mirrors), clearly indicating this clear zone to other drivers. Streetcar clear zones may be designated with a red stripe to reinforce visibility of the clear zone adjacent to parking, especially in narrow parking lanes where large vehicles may intrude into the streetcar zone.

3 Ensure transitions between asphalt, curb ramps, and streetcar paving material do not create accessibility issues. Do not place concrete seams in bike paths, and ensure there are no lips between pedestrian path and streetcar pad.

RECOMMENDED

4 Parking lanes adjacent to a streetcar lane should be at least 8 feet wide, and 9–10 feet where truck loading must be accommodated. Any overhang into the streetcar path will interrupt service.

On corridors with loading or commercial activities, manage freight loading zones to ensure streetcar lane remains clear. Use pricing and time limits to promote conditions in which one truck loading spot remains available within a short distance of each store. For curbside rail and on smaller streets, promote loading at low traffic volume periods, when a general traffic lane can be used for loading.

Wherever possible, provide freight loading on the side of the street opposite a streetcar track, or around the corner.

Implement transit signal priority techniques to reduce total travel time.

Especially in destination areas where high walking activity results in long potential queue blockages, turns across the streetcar track should be managed or prohibited.

Sign shows parked cars must be clear of offset rail lanes, **SEATTLE, WA**

PORTLAND, OR

SEATTLE, WA

Center Transit Lane

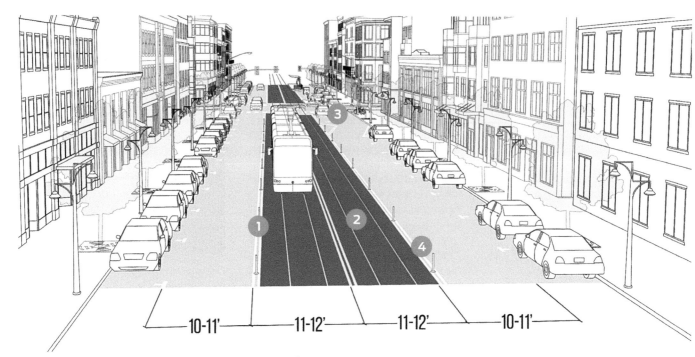

—10-11'— —11-12'— —11-12'— —10-11'—

Center transit lanes may be wider to reduce friction and risk of sideswipe crashes

Center transit lanes are typically used on major routes with frequent headways, and where traffic congestion may significantly affect reliability. They also reduce the chance of conflicts with parked vehicles. Center transit lanes can play a key role in creating high-quality transit service. While traditionally found on streetcar streets, center transit lanes can be used with buses as well.

With left turn restrictions and minimal separation, center transit lanes can be effectively converted to transitways.

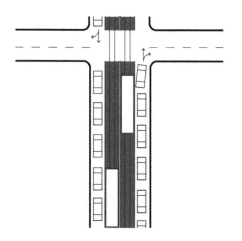

APPLICATION

Dedicated center transit lanes are highly applicable to center-running streetcars and light rail lines, including both new and existing rail lines.

Center transit lanes can be applied as part of the implementation of a BRT line or other bus improvements, on any bus routes with suitable stations.

Center transit lanes can be applied to both bus and rail lines where traffic congestion affects reliability, and are often more effective than right-side lanes.

BENEFITS

Center-running lanes serve buses and streetcars at potentially very high capacity and volume, while improving the pedestrian and passenger experience of the street.

Center transit lanes eliminate conflicts with drop-offs, deliveries, or illegal parking along the roadway edge, as well as with bicyclists and some turning movements. Combined with left turn restrictions or leading transit intervals, and all-door boarding, center transit lanes address a wide variety of sources of transit delay.

Center transit lanes can have an impact similar to that of a transitway, but does not require as much investment, time, or space to implement.

Existing center-running streetcar routes can achieve safety and travel time benefits from dedicated infrastructure.

Complementary treatments include stop consolidation, all-door boarding, and transit signal priority.

CONSIDERATIONS

Intersections require turning provisions to avoid conflicts with the through movements of transit vehicles. A combination of self-enforcing design and enforcement, ideally automated, is necessary to ensure the effectiveness of dedicated center bus lanes.

Stops for center lanes may need more street space than curbside lanes, since boarding islands must be placed in the street. Generally a minimum width of 28 feet is needed for transit lanes and stations at stop locations, and 22–24 feet in other sections.

Platform configuration must be compatible with transit vehicle characteristics—left-side boarding buses may be more expensive to procure.

Center platforms may reduce overall space occupied by stations, though side-boarding islands can have space benefits when stations are split across an intersection.

Right-boarding BRT stations allow the use of typical rolling stock, which often run on streets without dedicated lanes at the beginning or ends of their routes.

CRITICAL

1 Solid white lines or double white lines must be striped along the right side of the transit lane, along with BUS ONLY or LRT ONLY pavement markings (MUTCD 3D-01).

Boarding islands must be used for most transit vehicle types to create accessible boarding conditions.

RECOMMENDED

2 Center-running lanes should be designated using red/terra cotta color to emphasize the lane and deter drivers from entering it.

A center bus or streetcar lane should be 11–12 feet wide when placed adjacent to an opposing transit lane.

3 To avoid conflicts with center-running transit vehicles, left turns should be prohibited, or accommodated using left-turn lanes and dedicated signal phases. Left turns from the center bus lane add significant safety and operational issues for high-frequency bus service, but left turns may be permitted at times of day with longer headways.

Designs should anticipate transit vehicles operating at 25 mph, with higher design speeds only if local speed limits permit them. Curves may be regulated for much lower speeds, typically 10–15 mph, permitting vehicles to proceed safely within the same lane width as provided on straight sections of the bus lane. However, it is desirable for horizontal transitions of the transit lane to be designed with gradual transitions, consistent with general operating speeds on the corridor.

If additional space is available, a buffer should be marked or vertical delineation placed between the bus lane and the adjacent mixed-traffic lane to provide additional clearance and permit eventual construction of vertical elements.

OPTIONAL

Separation with soft (e.g. rumble strips) or hard (e.g. concrete curbs) barriers may be used to reduce encroachment from general traffic. Install reflective vertical elements to enhance visibility at night.

The mixed-traffic lane may transition to the right before a stop and to the left after a stop, creating room for parking and a turn lane.

Complement center transit lanes with all-door boarding and related fare collection strategies, as well as transit signal strategies.

Church St., **SAN FRANCISCO, CA**

Peak-Only Bus Lane

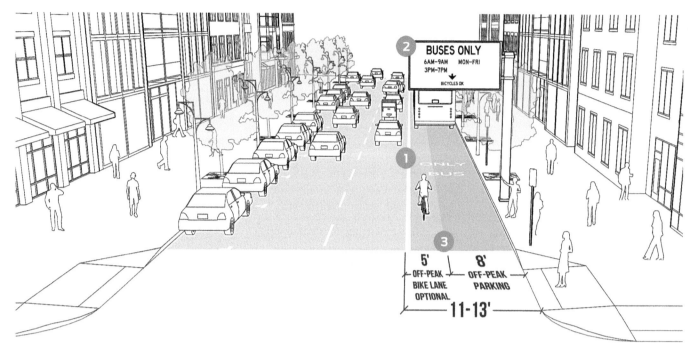

BUSES ONLY
6AM–9AM   MON–FRI
3PM–7PM
↓
BICYCLES OK

5'
OFF-PEAK
BIKE LANE
OPTIONAL

8'
OFF-PEAK
PARKING

11–13'

During off-peak hours, peak-only bus lanes can permit general traffic or curbside access for activities like loading and parking.

Many streets with a trunkline role in the bus network have high demand at peak commute periods, but a rich array of goods movement and social life at other times. A peak-only bus lane allows transit to take precedence over parking and curbside access at peak hours when it most benefits bus operations.

A peak-only bus lane can operate as a dedicated bus lane at peak travel periods and provide general curbside uses at other times. Wider lanes can enable an effective bicycle lane off-peak adjacent to parking. Peak-only transit lanes may also be exclusive to streetcars or buses at peak times, while permitting mixed traffic at other times.

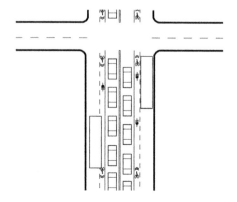

APPLICATION

Streets with predictable bus delay due to peak-period motor vehicle traffic, particularly due to queuing.

Streets with high peak-period bus frequency and generally high traffic volumes.

Streets with curbside loading, vending, high-turnover parking, or other important but physically flexible activities that can be relocated at some times.

Streets where offset lanes are not desired, such as where significant curbside transit stop improvements have been made.

Curbside peak-only lanes are most important on streets with one lane in each direction and parking. On commercial streets with more than one lane and parking, the assignment of a full-time or part-time offset bus lane with in-lane stop infrastructure may provide an advantage for both transit operations and local business and public life activity.

Peak-only lanes are not preferred on streets with narrow sidewalks and no sidewalk furnishing zone, as the absence of parking may place pedestrians uncomfortably close to traffic.

BENEFITS

Peak-only bus lanes provide a large boost to transit capacity at critical times, substantially improving both reliability and transit travel times on streets where congestion at peak causes transit delays.

Peak-only bus lanes allow stationary uses such as metered parking, freight loading, and street vending during non-peak periods.

Peak-only bus lanes are conducive to active transit signal priority treatments (see page 152).

Wider lanes can accommodate off-peak bicycle lanes adjacent to curbside parking, and shared bus-bike lanes during peak periods.

CONSIDERATIONS

Curbside peak-only bus lanes involve a trade-off between faster peak travel times and slower off-peak bus travel times, with slower pull-out stops during off-peak times. Corridors without heavily peaked traffic volumes may be better off with bus bulbs, which have moderate benefits 24 hours a day, than with peak-hour bus lanes, which have larger benefits for two to six hours per day.

Curbside bus lanes typically preclude installation of curb extensions.

Because bus stops are typically located directly on the adjacent sidewalk, enough room must be available for waiting passengers, stop amenities, and passing pedestrian traffic.

Peak curbside lanes typically replace peak-period parking, and have neutral traffic impact or may even increase traffic capacity.

CRITICAL

1 Pavement markings must indicate that the lane is dedicated to transit, including a solid white line and "BUS ONLY" stencil. Skip-lines may be applied where vehicles are permitted to cross, such as at intersections and turn pockets (see *Intersection Design for Transit*, page 158).

2 Signage must clearly indicate the lane restriction, as well as hours of enforcement and any turn allocations.

If the lane permits parking during non-operational hours, signage should clearly communicate times of parking prohibition (e.g. "No Parking, 7–9 AM") as well as any other parking regulations (e.g. "30 Minute Parking, 9 AM–4 PM").

RECOMMENDED

Camera enforcement combined with tow-away service is usually needed to operate a successful peak-only curbside bus lane.

OPTIONAL

3 During non-operational hours, the curbside portion of the lane may become a parking lane. A 12- or 13-foot wide lane can accommodate curbside parking with a bike lane during non-peak hours, and operate as a shared bus-bike lane during peak hours. Signage must communicate that bicycling is permitted at all times. Local regulation may need to be modified to permit bicycling in transit lanes.

Bicycle shared lane markings (MUTCD §9C-9) may be placed along the left edge of the bus lane to demarcate the bicycle space, and should be positioned along the roadway as they would be in other shared lanes (see the *Urban Bikeway Design Guide* for details).

A broken (dashed) line may be marked 7–9 feet from the curb, particularly at bus stops, to create an advisory bike lane designating the right edge of the bike operating space.

Sign for peak-only bus lane from which turns are also permitted, **SAN FRANCISCO, CA**

Peak-only bus lanes are supported by targeted enforcement and education campaigns, **SEATTLE, WA**

Shared Bus-Bike Lane

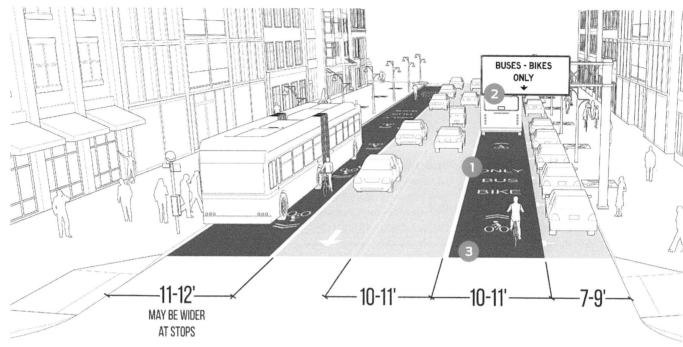

A shared bus-bike lane can fill in bicycle network gaps and provide destination access in constrained conditions

The shared bus-bike lane is not a high-comfort bike facility, nor is it appropriate at very high bus volumes. However, buses and bicycles often compete for the same space near the curb. On streets without dedicated bicycle infrastructure, curbside bus lanes frequently attract bicycle traffic, prompting some cities to permit bicycles in bus lanes.

Shared bus-bike lanes can accommodate both modes at low speeds and moderate bus headways, where buses are discouraged from passing, and bicyclists pass buses only at stops. In appropriate conditions, bus-bike lanes are an option on streets where dedicated bus and separate high-comfort bicycle facilities cannot be provided.

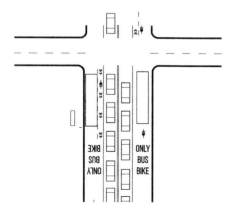

APPLICATION

Shared bus-bike lanes are most commonly applied on two-way streets with curbside or offset bus lanes, and no existing or planned bicycle facility.

Contraflow bus lanes with high bicycle demand and no other bicycle facilities in the contraflow direction may be regulated as shared bus-bike lanes.

Shared bus-bike lanes can be applied where parking is in place at off-peak times (see page 120).

Applications should generally be limited to bus lanes with operating speeds of 20 mph or less, and transit headways of 4 minutes or longer.

Lanes may be placed directly adjacent to the curb or offset from the curb by a parking lane.

BENEFITS

Curbside shared bus-bike lanes provide basic bicycle access on transit streets when no space is available for dedicated bikeways.

Shared bus-bike lanes provide increased space and visibility for active street users while improving transit service reliability.

CONSIDERATIONS

Dedicated bus and bicycle facilities are preferred over shared bus-bike lanes. Bus-bike lanes are not high-comfort bicycle facilities, and are not a substitute for dedicated bikeways, particularly at peak periods and on high-volume bus routes.

Special care must be taken not to require bicycle and bus traffic to mix at high speeds. As bus operational speeds and volumes increase, the number of passing events increases, eroding the comfort and, potentially, the safety of the facility for bicyclists.

CRITICAL

As on other streets with shared bicycle lanes, bicycle operation must be permitted across the entire road surface. Jurisdictions with "as far right as practicable" rules for bikes must explicitly permit flexible operation on streets with bus-bike lanes.

1 Pavement markings must indicate that the lane is dedicated to transit, including a solid white line and BIKE BUS ONLY or similar marking.

Buses must operate on the right side of the lane and pull to the curb at stops when possible. Coordination with transit operator instruction is key to the success of a bus-bike lane.

2 Install signs permitting buses and bicycles, and excluding other traffic. BUSES-BIKES ONLY signs may be used. Overhead signs are preferred.

RECOMMENDED

The width of a full-time bus-bike lane is 10–11 feet for offset lanes, and up to 12 feet for curbside lanes.

Lanes 13–15 feet wide should be avoided in most cases to limit unsafe passing movements. If 15–16 feet of width is available, consider providing a marked conventional bike lane on the left or right side of the bus lane, marked and signed as a green-colored bicycle lane to enhance visibility (see the *Urban Bikeway Design Guide*). If 13–14 feet of width is available, a marked buffer can be added on the left side of the bus-bike lane so that buses are guided to the right, allowing any passing bicycle traffic to use the buffer area at stops.

Particular attention should be paid to how buses and bicycles interact at bus stops. A bus-bike lane may be wider to allow bikes to pass stopped buses on the left. In these cases, a dashed line should be marked 9 feet from the curb to indicate to bicyclists where to pass. It may be appropriate to narrow adjacent general traffic lanes at bus stops to accommodate a bike passing zone.

3 Bicycle shared lane markings (MUTCD §9C-9) should be placed in the center or left side of the lane. At stops, place markings at the left side of the lane.

The typical width of a part-time bus-bike lane that permits parking during non-peak times, creating an off-peak bike lane, is 12–13 feet (see *Peak-Only Bus Lane*, page 120). If more space is available, mark a left-side buffer to create an off-peak buffered bike lane.

No vertical separation or significant pavement changes should be installed between bus-bike lanes and mixed-traffic lanes. Any means of separation, such as markings, should be easily traversable by bicycles.

OPTIONAL

Where space is available, creating a short bike channel wrapping behind transit stops can mitigate conflicts between transit vehicles and bicycles at stops, while also limiting pedestrian-bicyclist conflicts.

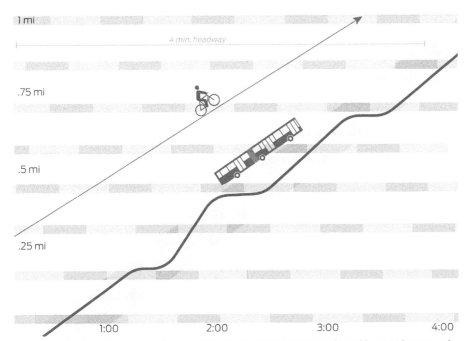

On transit streets where buses and bikes operate in a shared lane at low speeds, conflicts are limited due to their similar average travel speeds. Low-speed signal progressions accommodate bicycle-friendly speeds.

Washington St., **BOSTON, MA**

Chestnut St., **PHILADELPHIA, PA**

Contraflow Transit Lane

Contraflow lanes enable connectivity and shorten travel times for bus routes. Contraflow lanes are typically applied to transit routes to create strategic, efficient connections, but may also be applied to longer corridors in some types of street networks.

The contraflow lane can be thought of as a conventional two-way street, but with non-transit vehicles prohibited in the contraflow direction.

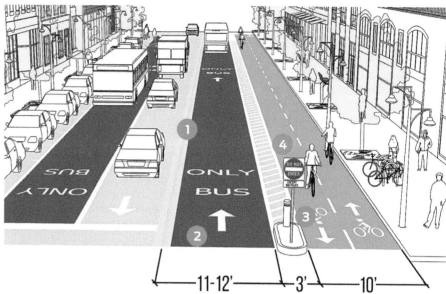

A contraflow transit lane is designed to prevent or discourage incursions, while reducing friction with adjacent traffic. Dimensions shown are recommended unless otherwise noted.

APPLICATION & CONTEXT

Used on streets where general traffic is limited to one-way, but transit operations benefit from bi-directional transit routing.

BENEFITS

Contraflow operation allows more efficient transit service where a one-way street network would otherwise involve route deviations or additional turns.

Running both directions of transit traffic on a street, instead of using a couplet of nearby parallel one-way streets, improves route legibility for passengers and better serves key destinations.

CRITICAL

1 A double-yellow centerline marking (MUTCD §3D-02) must be applied to separate contraflow traffic from opposing traffic.

2 BUS ONLY or LRT ONLY markings must be applied to demarcate the lane and deter drivers from using it (MUTCD §3D-01). Arrow pavement markings (MUTCD §3B-24) should be used to indicate direction of travel.

3 Gateway treatments that clearly prohibit wrong-way or private vehicle entry are essential to safe and functional operation. Use DO NOT ENTER and BUS ONLY (MUTCD §3D-01) or LRT ONLY signs for contraflow lanes; use ONE WAY EXCEPT BUSES signs (MUTCD §2G-03) for general traffic lanes.

At signalized intersections, install transit-only signals and bicycle signals facing the contraflow direction. Calculate clearance intervals using bike- and transit-specific speeds to provide safe movement across intersections.

RECOMMENDED

Contraflow lanes should be 11–12 feet wide. A buffer should be applied when additional space is available.

Red color should be applied to emphasize the lane and to deter drivers from using it.

Traffic signal coordination should be updated to reflect the two-way flow of buses.

Intersection turn management improves the safety and operation of a contraflow lane, and enables the addition of bikeways adjacent to the lane.

OPTIONAL

Where space is inadequate for a dedicated bike facility (either cycle track or contraflow bike lane), bicycle traffic may be allowed to use the contraflow bus lane, as long as the lane is wide enough to allow safe passing at stops (refer to *Shared Bus-Bike Lanes*, page 122). Where bicycle traffic is permitted, ONE WAY, DO NOT ENTER, and turn prohibition signs should be supplemented with an "EXCEPT BUSES AND BICYCLES" plaque.

Hard separation, such as curbs or bollards, or soft traversable separation, such as rumble strips, may be applied in the buffer or centerline to deter vehicles from encroaching. Access to the curb must be maintained for emergency vehicles. If bicycle travel is anticipated on the contraflow lane, it is critical that any soft separation is safely traversable by bicycles.

4 A contraflow configuration that includes a bikeway, pedestrian refuge islands, and/or left-turn lanes creates conditions suitable for longer contraflow routes.

Multiple contraflow lanes may be implemented on a street, accommodating very high transit volumes.

Metroway ALEXANDRIA, VA

Transitways

Transitways are running ways dedicated to the exclusive use of transit vehicles, protected from incursion by physical separation. Transitways often involve a higher level of investment than transit lanes, but they provide the highest level of transit reliability, speed, and comfort available on streets. This section focuses on contextual guidance and critical design criteria for exclusive transit facilities.

Transitways

DISCUSSION

Transitways are the most robust running way available on streets, providing continuous and exclusive facilities for transit. By physically deterring the entry of other vehicles into the exclusive transit facility, a transitway has the greatest potential to reduce transit delays related to traffic interference.

APPLICATION

Streets with consistently low transit travel speeds and high transit volume are candidates for more separation of transit from other traffic through physical design measures.

Transitways are equally applicable to buses and rail transit. The use of buses on protected right-of-way allows the creation of a flexible open BRT system. Streetcars can be used on transitways to similar affect.

Because transitways usually involve larger capital investments, they often involve vehicle procurements, and can be used as an opportunity to provide branded service, which can attract new riders.

BENEFITS

Transitways eliminate delays due to stopped or slow traffic, and provide a predictable environment for traffic operations that strongly complements improved boarding strategies that reduce dwell time.

Since turning movements must be managed, transitways eliminate most turn-based delay.

Since transitways are truly exclusive of other traffic, they are easy to coordinate with active signal priority in a wide variety of operational conditions, even when short blocks, high transit volume, or other challenges are present.

Transitways save operational costs on high-volume routes by accommodating long transit vehicles, such as multi-unit rail or bi-articulated buses.

Transitways give bus and rail modes a prominent place within the streetscape, promoting the quality of the transit line and system and reinforcing the service or system brand.

CONSIDERATIONS

Transitways support better transit performance than transit lanes, which in turn perform better than mixed traffic operation. However, street size and context, as well as service type and transit vehicle size, are strong factors in considering how best to serve a street.

Transitways demand detailed planning and consideration of context, with robust strategies for accommodating local goods movement and loading, especially where curbside access is a high priority but center-running designs are not possible.

Center Transitway

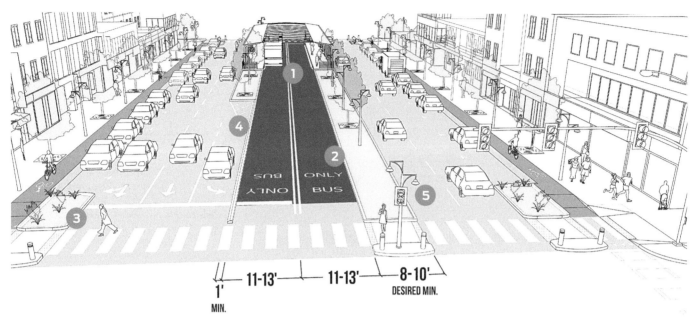

Center transitways accommodate very high transit frequency

Center transitways are separated from other vehicle traffic by medians or other vertical separation elements, and prioritize transit movements at intersections. Center transitways provide a high level of capacity and reliability for bus or rail service, and typically require the most space of any transit treatment, with a configuration similar to that of an off-street transitway. They can be configured as shown to support right-side median stops, or with center-median stops.

APPLICATION

Center transitways are used with high-quality, frequent bus or rail service on very large streets.

Where right-side boarding is required, such as for BRT services that also operate in curbside lanes, center transitways with right-side medians are a flexible option.

When left-side boarding is available, center transitways can be designed either along a median or on the median, with center-median stations.

BENEFITS

Center transitways, especially those separated by medians or raised above the roadway surface, provide very strong protection from traffic-related delays, both from friction between lanes and from unauthorized use of transit lanes.

Central transitways allow the highest running speeds among on-street transit facilities, since pedestrians interact with vehicles only at stations and crosswalks, and bicycle use of the transitway is prohibited. Placing buses in separated space in the center of a roadway improves travel time and reliability by reducing conflicts with parked cars, bicycles, and right-turn movements.

Median space can be used for stations, green infrastructure, greenways/multi-use paths, or other public spaces, depending on width.

Placed in the median of a multi-lane roadway, center-running rail lines can provide the most robust transit service thanks to dedicated lanes, larger stations, and high-capacity vehicles.

CONSIDERATIONS

Transit speed and reliability on transitways is limited primarily by dwell time. Key rapid transit elements, such as off-board fare payment, all-door boarding, and level or near-level boarding, should be applied to maximize the benefit of a median transitway.

Transit vehicles with only right-side doors must either use right-side platforms at stations, or use a contraflow bus configuration with center-boarding islands.

Stations for center-median transitways may take up more right-of-way width than curbside-running lanes, since boarding platforms and median strips must be placed between the transitway and travel lanes.

Right-boarding BRT stations allow the use of typical rolling stock, which often run on streets without dedicated lanes at the beginning or ends of their routes.

Center platforms may reduce overall space occupied by stations, though side-boarding islands can have space benefits when stations are split across an intersection.

Installation should be coordinated with land use changes that maximize potential for transit-oriented development. Land use regulations should be tailored to promote transit use and create a more inviting pedestrian realm.

Left-boarding center-median stations reduce this space consumption significantly.

CRITICAL

The width of a median transit lane must be carefully determined based on the design vehicle's width and dynamic envelope.

1 Dedicated transit lanes require median boarding islands in the roadway at each stop. These stops must be fully accessible and lead to safe, controlled crosswalks or other crossings.

2 BUS ONLY/LRT ONLY pavement markings (MUTCD 3D-01) emphasize the lane and deter drivers from using it.

3 Since pedestrians must cross to the center of the street to access stations, safe crossings are critical. See the *Urban Street Design Guide* for more guidance on crosswalks and crossings.

4 To avoid conflicts with center-running transit vehicles, left turns must be either prohibited or accommodated using left-turn lanes and dedicated signal phases

5 Transit signal heads should be used at intersections to give transit vehicles priority and avoid driver confusion with general traffic signals.

Ensure that pedestrian refuge islands adjacent to transitways are wide enough to allow large groups of people to wait, particularly near stations. Discourage pedestrians from waiting in unsafe locations in the roadway, especially near railways. Where spacing between parallel tracks provides no clear zone between passing LRVs, clearly indicate the danger area and discourage pedestrians from waiting in this area.

Intersections with pedestrian, bicycle or motor vehicle cross-traffic must be signalized.

RECOMMENDED

Intersection design should reflect the presence of the transitway, with markings through the intersection to show the transit vehicle travel path.

Red color markings or pavement should be used to emphasize dedicated median transit lanes and deter drivers from entering them. Color application may be limited to the intersection approach to save application and maintenance costs.

Should be implemented alongside complementary rapid transit elements, such as off-board fare payment, transit signal priority, and level boarding.

OPTIONAL

Construct transitways with concrete or other highly durable material, rather than asphalt, to minimize maintenance costs.

Median configurations can permit transit vehicles to bypass one another at stops, such as with a center-median transitway that has both local and express routes, an important consideration to avoid delays. Even if the initial service provided on the transitway serves all stops, building passing opportunities into the stations allows for greater service flexibility in the future.

Median-to-median crossing, Washington Ave., **MINNEAPOLIS, MN**

University Blvd., **SALT LAKE CITY, UT**

Side Transitway

Transit may be configured to operate in completely separated running ways at the sides of urban boulevards. Side transitways may operate either uni-directional or bi-directional service on one side of the street.

Side transitways maintain the enhanced capacity and flow of fully separated transitways while enabling pedestrians to board directly from the sidewalk. They may also create enhanced boarding areas and buffer active users from vehicle traffic.

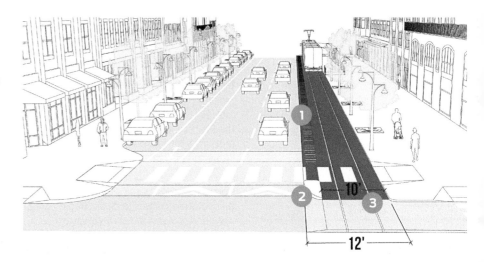

APPLICATION

Used with high-quality, frequent bus or rail service, especially on one-way streets.

May be applicable in contexts with few crossings or driveways (such as waterfronts or natural boundaries).

Bike facilities, including raised cycle tracks, can be simultaneously implemented and aligned with transit operations.

Where right-side boarding is required, such as for BRT services that also operate in curbside lanes.

BENEFITS

Placing the transitway in dedicated, separated space improves travel times by reducing conflicts with parked cars, bicycles, and some turning movements.

Side-running transitways can serve transit with potentially very high capacity and frequency, while improving the pedestrian and passenger experience of the street.

Compared to central median transitways, side transitways can reduce conflicts associated with pedestrian crossings and turning traffic, especially in edgefront conditions (see page 34).

CONSIDERATIONS

Turns across the transitway must be managed, and sometimes prohibited. Prohibiting right turns requires more guidance than left-turn prohibitions.

CRITICAL

1 Transitway must be physically separated from travel lanes either by grade differences or vertical elements.

All intersections with pedestrian, bicycle, or motor vehicle traffic must be signalized. To avoid conflicts with transit vehicles, left- and right-turning traffic across the transitway must be either prohibited or accommodated using turn lanes with dedicated signal phases.

When headways are long enough to prevent turning vehicles from blocking the transitway, either a lateral offset between turning vehicles and the transitway, or a dedicated turn lane that crosses the transitway, can be used.

2 Place signs and design elements (like curbs with tight corner radii) to direct turning traffic from cross streets away from the transitway, and into the proper general traffic lanes.

If parking is located next to a transitway, 4 feet of clear width must be available adjacent to the parking lane to accommodate loading.[1]

RECOMMENDED

Intersection design should reflect the presence of the transitway to highlight its path and deter conflicting movements. Crossings may be raised to the transitway grade at intersections and driveways, where applicable.

3 Pavement should be colored to emphasize dedicated lanes and deter drivers from entering them. BUS ONLY (MUTCD 3D-01) or LRT ONLY pavement markings may also be appropriate. Color application may be limited to the intersection approach.

Transitways should be implemented alongside complementary treatments such as all-door boarding, transit signal priority, and level boarding.

Provisions should be made to alert other street users when transit vehicle traffic approaches from unexpected directions.

Queen's Quay, **TORONTO, ON**

Market Street, **SAN FRANCISCO, CA**

Lane Elements

The physical and operational characteristics of transit vehicles create special demands for designing transit lanes. The use of color, selection of pavement and marking material, and means of separation contribute to the success of transitways.

Transitways and methods of separation can also contribute to the streetscape and help achieve pedestrian safety and stormwater management goals.

Pavement Material

PORTLAND, OR

ALEXANDRIA, VA

DENVER, CO

ASPHALT[1]

Asphalt is the most common street material, and the least expensive to implement.

Asphalt street surfaces are prone to deforming under the weight of a bus, especially during acceleration and braking. Thick courses of asphalt can address this issue, but concrete bus pads are usually needed at stops and stations.

Asphalt is not recommended for streetcar rail beds.[2]

CONCRETE

Concrete street surfaces are recommended for streets with heavy bus traffic, as concrete is stronger than asphalt and less liable to shifting under the heavy weight of buses.

Concrete is more expensive but lasts longer than asphalt. Especially in warm weather cities, concrete may have a lower life cycle cost than asphalt. High early strength concrete can allow service to return within several hours of paving.[3]

Where a bus route or lane is asphalt, concrete bus pads are recommended for locations where buses brake, including transit stops, signs, and traffic signals (see *Bus Pads*, page 103).

Embed rails in concrete to avoid track shifting and service interruptions due to resurfacing and other maintenance.

PAVERS

Distinctive paving enhances the transit streetscape, announcing the presence of a special urban realm, and extending the feel of public space from the sidewalk into the street. In large shared areas and plazas, pavers of different colors, textures, and orientation can be used to indicate where to expect transit vehicles.

Pavers are applicable to running ways, and streets where enhancing the public realm is desired. They are especially useful in shared plazas and transitways.

Large unit pavers made of concrete, brick, or stone (typically granite) are durable, and can be used for bus running ways or rail beds.[4]

Bricks and pavers are broadly applicable with streetcars, though may buckle under the stress of buses and heavy vehicles, especially where vehicles accelerate (stops and intersections).

Large block pavers distribute force from large vehicles turning and accelerating. Additionally, diagonal or interlocking paver configurations better distribute loads than square configurations.

Ensure pavers have adequate friction and skid resistance for people walking and biking.[5]

Green Transitway

Green transitways transform the character of a transit street, providing large planted areas along and between tracks or bus guideways. They represent one of the best examples of the coordinated pursuit of mode shift, water sustainability, and quality of life goals.

Green transitways create an attractive human and natural environment, complementing transit investments in a cost-effective way.[6]

St. Charles Ave., **NEW ORLEANS, LA**

APPLICATION

Planted transitways can be used for fully separated bus or rail transitways, both center- and side-running. They can be integrated into comprehensive stormwater management strategies.

BENEFITS

A large permeable surface provides substantially improved stormwater infiltration and retention.

Soil provides noise dampening benefits.

Green transitways can support rain gardens and other higher biomass or high absorption areas.

The addition of large areas of green on a street provides a major local amenity, enhancing the public space along the street.

CRITICAL

Provide a continuous green space between tracks and adjacent road beds. Discontinue green space at intersections and pedestrian crossings, and provide accessible paths for pedestrians through the transitway.

For rail, tracks can be completely set within a surface covered with grass or other low-maintenance, low-lying, non-trailing plants such as sedum. Anchor rails or concrete bus guideway on solid material under the surface. Tracks should be enclosed in a noise absorber, filled with a porous base layer, covered with an anti-root membrane, and covered with a porous paving grid that is then planted.[7]

For buses, grass can be planted between and adjacent to concrete running paths or guideways for bus wheels.

RECOMMENDED

Choose plant types based on durability, geographic and location-specific climate conditions, and water absorption capacity.

OPTIONAL

Green transitways can be designed as swales that drain stormwater from the street, with the swale surface at a lower grade than the adjacent roadway. In this case, deeper water penetration should be permitted through. In most climates, rails must be elevated to avoid flooding.

SW Lincoln St., **PORTLAND, OR**

Pavement Markings & Color

Red or terra cotta colored pavement highlights the prominence of the transit system, while at the same time visually enforcing dedicated transit space. Implementation of "red carpet" treatments in different contexts have reduced vehicle incursions by 30–50%, supporting on-time performance and reliability.[8]

Coloring application depends upon factors such as climate, use and stress, and age and condition of pavement.[9]

NEW YORK, NY

SAN FRANCISCO, CA

NEW YORK, NY

RED PAINT

Epoxy-based paint is a widely available semi-durable marking material.

As with other paints, glass beads and sand can be added for retroreflectivity and skid resistance. These components should be prioritized near crosswalks and on shared bus-bike lanes.

When possible, apply after resurfacing; paint adheres best to new asphalt, especially for epoxy paint. On existing pavement, aggressive pre-treatment (power-washing and shot-blasting) can increase adherence and performance.

RED THERMOPLASTIC

Red thermoplastic provides a consistent colored surface, and in amenable conditions has a low life-cycle cost. It applies well to almost-new and slightly worn asphalt. However, it may need frequent replacement under high volumes of heavy vehicle traffic, common on bus lanes. Cold-weather climates and some varieties of concrete can also limit the lifespan of thermoplastic.[10]

Thermoplastic can be applied to any surface but is most effective when applied to asphalt, and may have limitations bonding to concrete or in cold climates.

Anti-skid treatments can be applied to thermoplastic.

METHYL METHACRYLATE (MMA)

Methyl methacrylate (MMA) is an advanced polymer with better wearing than traditional thermoplastic, and may have a lower life-cycle cost, especially under heavy vehicle loads and when snowplowing is frequent.

CHICAGO, IL

SEATTLE, WA

SEATTLE, WA

EMBEDDED COLOR

Asphalt or concrete can be mixed with a red pigment, eliminating the need to reapply a red colored surface treatment.

Tinted asphalt uses special aggregate and binder. Tinted asphalt materials and implementation costs are somewhat higher than for untinted asphalt, but prevents multiple reapplications of color.

Repairs, such as patching and pothole filling, as well as utility trenching, complicate the use of embedded color, as repair materials must match or be colored to match the pavement.

Colored microsurface pavements have shorter life cycles, especially in harsh or snowy climates; color should be mixed through the entire top concrete layer.

High Friction Surface Treatments (HFST) can be embedded with colored glass to provide a distinctive and durable surface even when repaving is not possible. HFST can enhance both bus and bike traction on curves or downhill sections.

INTERMITTENT COLOR

Where red lanes are not employed for the length of a transit lane segment, a solid red stripe can highlight key sections of a transit lane such as stops or sections with turn prohibitions, which help to self-enforce lane restrictions.

To save the expense of applying red color to entire road segments, a red thermoplastic or painted backing can be applied around the "BUS ONLY" lane markings.

The backed message may not have the passive enforcement value of a completely red lane, but can increase the visibility of the restriction.

CONTRAST

Color variations subtly suggest street space and modal zones while increasing the use of space by people on foot in shared environments (see *Shared Transit Street*, page 44). High contrast enables people with low vision to distinguish between two spaces, including two spaces at the same grade.

Lighter colored pavers and concrete that have higher solar reflectance (albedo) can help maintain a cooler, more comfortable street environment.[11]

Unit pavers of a variety of sizes and colors can be used in on-street railbeds to designate the streetcar path. Use different colors, orientation, or texture of pavers to designate the edge of the travel path and discourage other vehicles from entering or blocking.

On routes where the bus is not limited to a fixed path, select large paving blocks, as smaller pavers are subject to shifting under the weight of a bus. Where a bus is provided a fixed path, concrete or large pavers can be used for the path of the bus wheels, with smaller paving blocks adjacent to the running way and between the two running courses, forming a visual guideway.

Separation Elements

Vertical elements increase separation and prevent incursions on transitways. The level of separation provided depends upon available width, traffic conditions, and local laws or traffic conventions. If compliance is high, softer (or less aggressive) treatments may be adequate to maintain the integrity of dedicated transit space.

Additionally, speed, loading, and parking activities may guide application of separation strategies.

Ensure placement and height of vertical elements do not impede travel paths or sight lines.

EUGENE, OR

HARD CURBS

Vertical curbs typically 4–6 inches in height can be installed for limited or block-length sections to physically prevent intrusion into the transitway.

Vertical reflective elements can improve the visibility of a hard curb.

Require curb ramps at crossings.

A mountable curb

MOUNTABLE CURBS

Curbs less than 6 inches tall can be rounded or sloped to warn other users of dedicated transit space while still providing flexible entry on limited occasions.

Curb slope should not exceed 2:3.[12]

To be mountable by bicycles, curb slope should not exceed 1:4. A non-mountable beveled curb with a 1:1 slope creates bike-friendly but not mountable separation.

Bicyclists will only be able to cross safely at a perpendicular angle.

Can be used on corners or roundabouts where a small curb radius is desired for design vehicles, while allowing large control vehicles like buses to mount the curb, creating a larger effective curb radius.

Roundabout with mountable curb,
EUGENE, OR

SALT LAKE CITY, UT

HOUSTON, TX

HOUSTON, TX

RUMBLE STRIPS

Rumble strips are a soft treatment to give a tactile cue to drivers when they encroach upon the transit lane.

Where transitways would be dangerous to enter, rumble strips are a low-cost treatment to reduce vehicle incursions.

These are typically reserved for high-speed streets, as they are neither safe nor comfortable for bicyclists or wheelchair users to cross, and are not as effective at restricting incursions as other treatments.

Rumble strips must not extend into pedestrian areas like crosswalks.

BOLLARDS

Vertical elements like bollards, concrete domes, or plastic "armadillos" provide visual and physical lane delineation.

Bollards should be 30–42 inches in height to achieve full visibility.[13]

Many types of bollards are available in a range of costs and designs, and can be integrated into the streetscape.

Assess design speeds, urban design guidance, and contextual characteristics to determine bollard design and style. Fixed bollards must be adequately anchored to absorb forces from vehicle impacts.

Bollards must be readily visible and include either retroreflective surface or lighting elements.

Bollards may be applied for full block segments or at specific locations where warning is desired.

LOW VERTICAL ELEMENTS

Low concrete domes can be applied to existing streets and provide both a visual and tactile cue to drivers to prevent incursion.

Plastic "armadillo"-shaped elements are an easy-to-install alternative.

Markings should be used to clearly delineate the presence of raised domes.

Plastic "armadillos", UNITED KINGDOM

Separation Elements *(continued)*

ALEXANDRIA, VA

PLANTING STRIPS

Planting strips enhance the streetscape while providing vertical and horizontal separation. Plantings require additional space and maintenance. Xeriscaping may provide an attractive low-maintenance alternative.

Plants must not block sightlines or impede the running way. Maintain some clearance between plantings and travel lanes or transitways where possible, or use plants that grow vertically without trailing. Shrubs require regular trimming and may not be desirable where clear sightlines are required. However, trees and shrubs are often suitable on fully separated transitways.

Trees that drop leaves, particularly all at once in the fall, can create slippery conditions for both bus and rail vehicles.

Avoid plantings that might grow to encroach on intersections to ensure pedestrian access and safe interactions with vehicles.

Bioswales and connected planters assist with stormwater management (refer to the *Urban Street Design Guide*).

Movable planters offer the flexibility of being easily reconfigured or removed. Self-watering planters capture more stormwater and require less care.

SAN FRANCISCO, CA

FULL-LANE TREATMENTS

Short vertical elements can be installed across a rail transitway or lane to deter general motor vehicles from entering.

Elements must not intrude into pedestrian spaces such as crosswalks.

BALTIMORE, MD

Signs & Signals

All of the signs and signals documented here are in use in the United States.

Most of the sign and signal options discussed in this document are available in existing U.S. MUTCD guidance, and specific configurations and uses may be available through the FHWA MUTCD experimentation process. Sign, signals and markings standards vary by state and may have changed since the time of publication, and should be checked during the design process.

NEW YORK CITY, NY

REGULATORY SIGNS

Regulatory signs include those used to communicate required or prohibited movements (see page 156).

Include turn restrictions on overhead signs or signal mast arms, particularly for movements that are not adjacent to the curb or a median on which a sign can be placed.

DENVER, CO

FLASHING BEACONS

Flashing beacons can be used to enhance overhead and other regulatory signage, indicating to drivers and other users when the transit lane is in force.

Flashing indications on signs may be used to alert street users during times of day when part-time transit lanes are in effect.

NEW YORK CITY, NY

OVERHEAD SIGNS

Overhead signs above transit lanes and transitways alert drivers and other street users by placing critical information about lane use in a prominent location.

If used on transit lanes, overhead signage should include information about permitted vehicles, time-of-day restrictions, and permitted turns.

Regulatory signage, such as turn restriction signage, can be placed overhead, directly above the movement it is regulating.

ALEXANDRIA, VA

DYNAMIC SIGNS

Dynamic signs can be used to alert other street users of approaching transit vehicles, and to regulate turns and other movements that are prohibited when transit vehicles are approaching.

Include dynamic elements on overhead signage.

Dynamic signs can be lit during times of day when part-time transit lanes are in effect.

ALEXANDRIA, VA

TRANSIT SIGNAL HEADS

Transit signal heads clarify that a movement or phase is exclusive to transit.

Traditionally used on rail lines, transit-specific signal heads may be used with buses as well.

Transit signals may be used when transit lanes or transit vehicles in mixed-traffic lanes have exclusive phases, including on transit lanes, transitways, or when a signal is used to give the transit vehicle a queue jump in mixed-traffic lanes.

Market Street, SAN FRANCISCO, CA

Lane Design Controls

At the outset of any redesign project, the project team sets forth key criteria governing the street design. These "design control" parameters critically shape decision making.

Enhancing transit function requires a proactive design approach—the complete assemblage of the street drives how users perceive their environment, and determines street capacity. While transit vehicles present geometric challenges, "over-designing" transit facilities limits the ability to balance multiple modes and provide a safe and vibrant street. Transit design controls, like all street design controls, should always be driven by the targeted outcome and the unique issues and opportunities to increase the character and efficiency of the street.

Design Vehicles

TRANSIT DESIGN VEHICLE	COMMON STREET TYPE

Standard 40' Bus

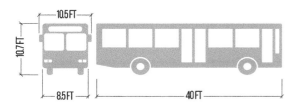

Neighborhood Transit Street
» Speeds are low to moderate.

Corridor Street
» Increased stop distance and lane width results in higher travel speeds.

Downtown Street
» Speeds are low to moderate with frequent stops.
» Congestion, parking, and standing vehicles are more significant than design speed in determining operating speeds.

Articulated 60' Bus

Corridor Street
» Clear rights-of-way accommodates larger capacity vehicles.
» Increased stop distance and lane width results in higher travel speeds. Assign additional width to lane buffers.

Downtown Street
» High-capacity or trunkline routes, especially in dedicated lanes.

Modern & Historic Streetcars

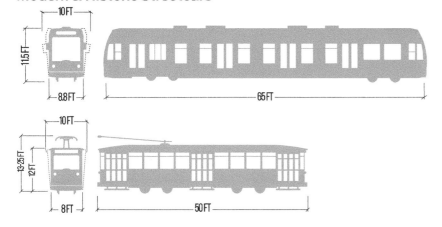

Neighborhood Transit Street
» Low to moderate speeds with frequent stops, typically 20 mph or less.
» Smaller length and width than LRVs allows operation in more constrained streets.

Corridor Street
» When operated on transitways or dedicated lanes, modern streetcars can be functionally similar to LRT, operating at up to 30–35 mph in some cases.
» Provide comfortable stations, especially for center-running streetcars.

Downtown Street
» May operate in mixed traffic or shared street conditions.
» Prevent blockage by stationary vehicles, including overhanging parked vehicles.

Modern Light Rail Vehicle

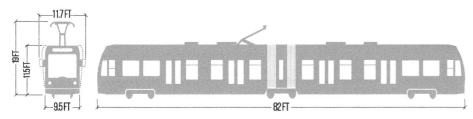

Corridor Street
» Longer stop spacing, and often in separated transitway, allows for increased speed, potentially 30–35 mph.

Downtown LRT Street
» Modern light rail may transition from exclusive guideway to street-grade or mixed traffic conditions as it enters downtown.

Vehicle Widths & Buffers

Street users and vehicles occupy different amounts of space depending on their size and speed. Lane design should accommodate transit vehicles at a speed that is safe within the overall street context, supporting consistent and reliable operations.

Buffers shown here are not lane widths, but represent the operating envelope and minimum distance to adjacent objects when in motion, and can overlap with adjacent lanes.

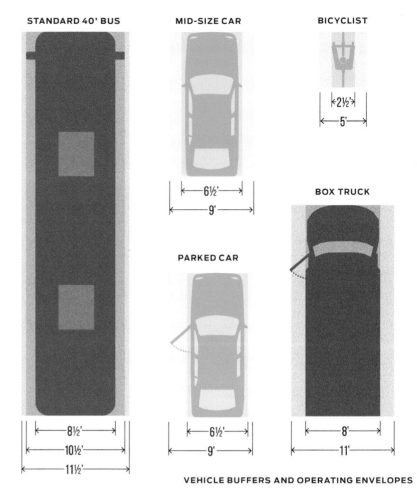

VEHICLE BUFFERS AND OPERATING ENVELOPES

DISCUSSION

The width of vehicle lanes affects street safety and travel speeds. Narrower lanes generally result in slower travel speeds while increasing street safety for all users. For private motor vehicles in particular, narrower lane width, down to 10 feet or narrower in special cases, is correlated with all-user safety benefits.

Lane widths are determined in the context of both the design vehicle, or the regular user, and the control vehicle, or the infrequent but largest user. The design vehicle uses one lane, while the control vehicle may intermittently require the use of multiple lanes (refer to the *Urban Street Design Guide* for additional information). On many transit streets, the transit vehicle is both the design and control vehicle—both the regular and largest user.

Vehicles have both clearly defined vehicle spaces (the size of the vehicle itself) as well as a buffer space (or operating space) which defines the space needed to operate comfortably at a moderate speed. Wider vehicles can be accommodated in narrower lanes on an infrequent basis—even where street space is constrained, vehicles may on occasion use a part of an adjacent lane where the whole street section provides enough space to do so safely. Overlapping buffer zones can be safely accommodated at slower speeds.

Buses are among the largest vehicles operating on city streets, with mirror widths often exceeding available lane space. Where buses operate in a narrow mixed-traffic lane, intrusion into adjacent lanes may sometimes occur, such as when two buses pass each other. Ensure that adjacent lanes in a street section can occasionally accommodate such movements when needed.

Encouraging safe transit movement while accommodating efficient operations requires a predictable, even, and low-speed environment. Narrower transit lanes that are co-implemented with signal and intersection treatments, in-lane stops, appropriate stop spacing, and adjacent buffer zones, allow transit to progress comfortably at consistent speeds.

While transit vehicles in constrained spaces are sometimes subject to mirror strikes, wider mixed-traffic lanes can increase the number and severity of total crashes in which transit vehicles are involved.

Where buses use a travel lane adjacent to a bicycle lane, both bus and bike operational comfort are enhanced by providing a buffer space between them where width is available.

Vulnerable users like bicyclists should always be given sufficient space to operate safely at a comfortable distance from fast-moving traffic or from larger vehicles like buses and trucks, outside of the door zone.

Design for rail vehicles must factor dynamic vehicle envelopes, critically around turns and elevation changes. Vehicles on a fixed guideway cannot move around obstructions.

On streets with existing vehicle speeds above 35 mph, it may be necessary to introduce narrower lanes along with other design measures to lower vehicle speeds to a safe level for transit and pedestrians, or to fit a dedicated transit facility.

Lane width considerations for specific facilities are included in Chapter 2: *Transit Streets* (see page 17).

Lane width considerations for specific facilities are included in Chapter 2: *Transit Streets* (see page 17).

RECOMMENDATIONS

Bus lanes may be 10–11 feet wide when offset, and 11–12 feet when configured curbside or in transitway adjacent to an opposing lane of bus traffic.

Where space is available, use buffers rather than widened lanes to reduce side-swipe risks without increasing design speed. In mixed-travel lanes, assign added width to buffer zones to visually narrow lanes.

Shared bus-bike lanes may be 10–11 feet wide along segments where neither is expected to overtake the other, such as where bus volumes are moderate or where bus speeds are low. Passing at stops may be accommodated with a 13-foot shared lane (see page 122).

Where wide trucks commonly park or load in a parallel parking lane, potentially obstructing transit service in the adjacent travel lane, consider a parking buffer or wider travel lane.

In-street rail vehicles, including streetcar/tram/trolley and multi-unit LRVs, can operate in travel lanes 10–11 feet wide, depending on vehicle model. Mirror clearance may be a more significant factor for streetcars than for buses. Guideway and vehicle operating space must remain clear of obstacles, such as wide vehicles parked in an adjacent lane.

ADJACENT LANE WIDTHS & USER ENVELOPES

Combine these pairs of adjacent uses to configure a street, accounting on a case-by-case basis for existing space constraints and operational characteristics.

The assembly of adjacent lanes should account for friction and user comfort; the buffer envelopes of users may overlap infrequently or at low speeds. Minimum widths may not provide a comfortable operating space over long distances.

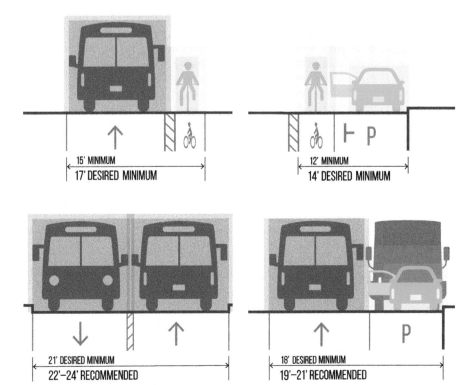

Design Speed

An active approach to design speed, sometimes called the safe system method, uses speed as an output affected by geometric design rather than an input alone.[1]

By setting a target speed for transit and general motorized traffic, designers can proactively create a safe walking and riding environment.

DISCUSSION

Human context is the primary determinant of safe vehicle speeds on any street. When designed for an appropriate speed, a street can both accommodate prevailing transit speeds, create a safe operating environment for transit, and provide a safe, comfortable street for people walking and bicycling to transit.

Speed limits are not the primary factor in urban travel time, especially when buses and streetcars operate in mixed traffic. Reducing speed limits may not have a measurable impact on transit performance, and may be beneficial where transit speeds are much lower than the pre-existing speed limit.

Desired vehicle speed can be achieved through proactive street design that encourages safe speeds, keeping to a minimum the total number of general through-traffic lanes, choosing a small corner radius, and providing a full urban streetscape, including trees and street furnishings (refer to the *Urban Street Design Guide* for more guidance).

Stopping distance is substantially longer for rail vehicles than buses. While most urban conditions require frequent stopping and low speeds for on-street routes, transitways may have higher speeds and may require longer stopping sight distance.

Immediately before a stop, shorter transition distances are acceptable for transit vehicles since deceleration has already begun.

CRITICAL

Design streets using target speed, a safe speed at which drivers should drive, rather than existing operating speed or statutory limit.

Align the design speed with target speed by implementing traffic calming measures, including narrower lane widths, roadside landscaping, speed cushions, and curb extensions. Traffic calming measures can be designed to slow general traffic while having little negative impact on transit vehicle operation.

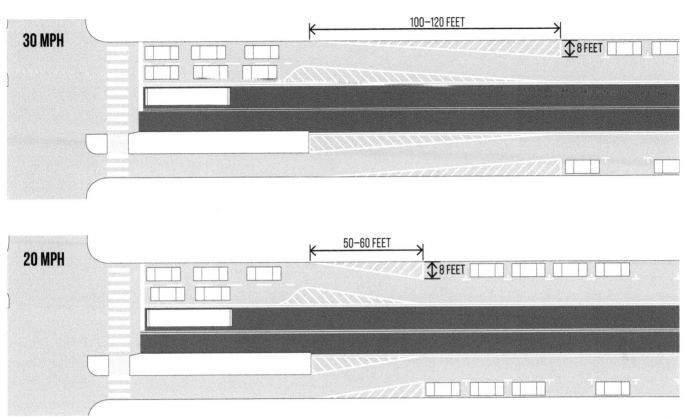

As speed increases, more space is required for safe design facilities. An 8-foot lateral transition requires more than twice as much distance at 30 mph (top) versus 20 mph (bottom) based on the standard calculation for transition length, $L=WS^2/60$.

RECOMMENDED

Reducing speed dispersion confers a transit benefit by making traffic flow more predictable. In mixed-traffic operations, it is desirable for the 95th percentile of observed target speeds to fall within 5 mph of top transit speeds.

In selecting the design speed basis for such values as signal progression speed, lane width, and transition taper length, it may be appropriate to choose a speed lower than the speed limit, unless the limit can be lowered locally to the desired design speed. Using the full speed limit to calculate taper lengths, for example, can result in lane transitions occupying most of a city block, even though a less gradual transition self-enforces a safe design speed.

Where space is not highly constrained, it is desirable to provide longer (more gradual) horizontal and vertical transitions for transit vehicles, providing improved passenger comfort. Use standard lane widths to encourage safe operating speeds.

In-lane stops in mixed-travel lanes—which often utilize boarding bulbs and islands and stabilize operating speeds by reducing the need for transit vehicles to shift lanes—should be implemented where feasible (see *Stop Placement & Intersection Configuration*, page 60).

Reducing design speed using lower signal progression speeds can confer benefits to transit performance while improving safety for vulnerable users, especially in downtown contexts with closely spaced signals, or where dwell times are low but stops are frequent (see page 150).

OPTIONAL

Shared transit streets may be assigned target speeds as low as 5–10 mph. At these speeds, rail vehicles or buses can operate safely in a traveled way shared by people walking.

Speed enforcement cameras have proven highly effective at reducing speeds and improving speed limit compliance by private motor vehicle drivers.[2]

6. Intersections

Intersections are pivotal conflict points for both safety and operations. Great streets are optimized for multiple modes and balance the converging demands of all users. Effective intersection design convenes elements of the street design toolbox including lane configuration, stop or signal control, transit stop location, pedestrian safety and access, management of turning movements, and bikeway location and design. In urban contexts, especially as density increases, design packages should combine and negotiate these elements to reduce risk to active users and create efficiency for transit operations.

Intersection Principles

MINIMIZE PERSON DELAY, MAXIMIZE SAFETY

Design and operate intersections to reduce the total amount of time that people—inside and outside of vehicles—spend waiting. Since walking is part of the transit trip, minimizing transit delay also involves a special emphasis on pedestrians. Compact intersections with urban-scale turn radii and pedestrian islands work with these goals, providing safe crossings at all legs of the intersection, while facilitating short signal cycles.

PRIORITIZE FOR RELIABILITY

Signal priority can be used both to keep transit runs on time and to reduce scheduled travel time. A combination of transit-friendly base signal timing and conditional priority can promote all transit runs and also manage headways, keeping transit predictable and comfortable for passengers and dispatchers alike. Where "transit first" or mode shift policy directives exist, preferential intersection treatments should be implemented aggressively to promote transit goals, consistent with pedestrian needs.

COMBINE SIGNALS AND DEDICATED LANES

Signal priority and dedicated lanes are most effective when implemented together. Providing a transit approach lane or a dedicated lane, alongside transit signal priority and in-lane stops, can eliminate delays from general traffic queuing. With dedicated lanes in place, a concurrent transit, through-vehicle, bike, and pedestrian phase can move before vehicle turn phases, making intersections both more convenient and safer. Make these improvements through close coordination between street departments and transit agencies.

SEPARATE PROBLEMATIC MOVEMENTS

Geometrically skewed movements, left turns across multiple lanes, and high-volume right turns can create both injury risks and delays on a transit street. Transit, through-moving vehicles, and people walking and biking can all benefit when problematic vehicle movements are provided with separate signal phases. Keep these and all phases short to prevent long transit and pedestrian wait times.

DEDICATE, THEN FILTER

Use the full palette of intersection design and traffic management techniques to filter vehicle traffic onto and off of transit streets, preventing congestion and improving the street environment. Where dedicated lanes are not possible, periodically diverting private through-traffic or selectively prohibiting turns keeps transit moving. On blocks with stations where space is at a premium, motor vehicle through-traffic or parking can be prohibited altogether, freeing space for other priorities.

PRIORITIZE IN CONTEXT

Different treatments work for different intersections. Analyze intersections in the context of block length, transit volumes and headways, pedestrian and bicycle volumes and crash history, motor vehicle traffic movements, crossing transit lines, and opportunities presented by the broader street network. Across all contexts, intersection design strategies should prioritize key movements and target the main sources of transit and pedestrian delay.

Signals & Operations

Traffic signals must not be considered in isolation, but rather as a system of multiple intersections. Because delay at traffic signals often accounts for one-quarter to one-third of a transit route's total trip time, it is important to consider settings and technology that optimize the performance of the system—ideally, to keep transit vehicles moving between stops. In many cities, traffic signals and progression were traditionally designed primarily for auto traffic with little regard for other street users, especially transit.

Signal strategies should focus on the goal of moving people rather than favoring a single mode. Specific actions can increase transit convenience, reliability, and predictability while improving general traffic operations for all users. With or without transit signal priority, signal timing plans should be optimized to reduce person delay rather than vehicle delay, favoring pedestrian mobility. The signal network helps achieve goals of both the local agency's policies as well as broader regional transit plans.

Transit Signal Progression

Transit signal progressions, a form of pre-timed or "passive" transit signal priority, are signal progressions (green waves) set to realistic travel speeds for on-street transit, often in the 12–20 mph range.

Signal progression speeds determine the pace of an urban street. However, signal progressions are frequently set without regard for stop-related delay, including dwell time and time lost to acceleration and deceleration at each stop. Progressions set at or near the speed limit can cause transit vehicles to fall behind the signal progression after making a stop, and long signal cycles impose additional delay on transit.

Using a short signal cycle with offsets that account for dwell time, especially at high-volume stops, allow buses and streetcars to remain within the 'green wave' of a signal progression. Short signal cycles combine well with low-speed progressions by further reducing the penalty for falling behind the signal progression.

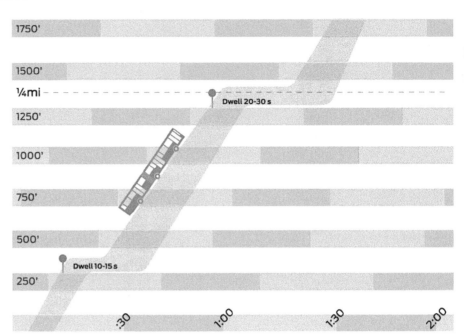

On one-way and high-frequency corridors, signal progressions timed at 12–15 mph can significantly improve average transit speed. Signal cycles integrate expected dwell times.

APPLICATION & CONTEXT

On signalized streets with a high volume of transit vehicles, typically more than 10 per hour or with combined headways less than 4 to 6 minutes, in mixed-traffic or dedicated lanes.

Where active transit signal priority is less feasible or has limited benefits, including streets with short distances between signals, streets with high pedestrian activity levels, and streets with short signal cycles.

Transit signal progressions are highly effective on one-way streets. On two-way streets, it may be necessary to prioritize the peak direction transit service if progressions are not possible in both directions.

BENEFITS

Reducing signal progression speeds to meet average transit running times allows buses and streetcars to keep up with the signal progression.

Especially on streets with transit lanes, or where most traffic clears within the vehicle platoon, transit vehicles can catch up to the signal progression after a stop.

The combination of a low-speed signal progression and short signal cycles can improve transit performance.

Timing signal progressions to lower speeds provides additional efficiency benefits to bicyclists, and promotes a safer urban street environment for all users by discouraging high speeds.

The combination of reduced variation and reduced average travel time by using transit signal progressions can result, over the course of a long, frequent transit route, in enough time savings to result in an additional run with the same number of vehicles.

To maximize the effect of passive signal priority, transit travel time variability should be reduced through stop consolidation and dedicated transit lanes.

CONSIDERATIONS

Signal progression speeds should be considered in the overall context of the street. Block length, crossing distance, and traffic volume are relevant to the selection of transit-friendly signal progression speeds.[1]

Private motor vehicle travel times may be increased when signal progression speeds are reduced, but since signal delay is a large portion of car travel time, short signal cycles may offset this increase for most trips.

On downtown streets with intersecting progressions or on transit corridor streets with high transit volumes, active transit signal priority can be impractical. Instead, signal timing can build typical dwell time at stops into the signal progression, or the progression can be set to a lower speed.

Include cross-street progressions in signal timing planning, especially for streets with high transit or total volume.

On streets with a mix of transit services, extra attention will be needed to set offsets to minimize delays. In some cases, signal timing changes will require prioritizing a rapid service over a local area.

RECOMMENDED

Set signals to a realistic transit travel speed between stops, including deceleration, dwell, and acceleration time, as well as right-turn delay if applicable. While specific speeds vary, blocks without a stop can often be set to 20–25 mph, while the block before a stop will be set to 12–15 mph due to deceleration, and the signal after the stop should account for both the full door-open-to-door-closed dwell time, and the low average speed achieved during acceleration.

Streets with transit in a dedicated lane may benefit from speeds of 15–20 mph if the bus can catch up to the progression after a stop.

A transit signal progression should allow a very high percentage of transit vehicles to arrive on the green signal phase at each signal along the street. For the target routes (not necessarily all routes on the street), first evaluate the arrival pattern of transit vehicles to each signal downstream of a stop. Set a target percentage of arriving vehicles, and adjust the signal offset such that a large percentage (such as 80% to 90%) arrive at the signal at least five seconds after the start of the green phase and ten seconds before the end of the green phase. Then adjust downstream signals accordingly, accounting for the new offset. The resulting progression should be somewhat faster than the existing transit travel time, since signal delay will be substantially reduced for the slowest runs. Reflect this new travel time in updated schedules.

In mixed traffic or in destination sections with frequent stops, transit operations typically benefit from signal progression speeds of 12–15 mph, which can coincide with comfortable signal pacing for active transportation modes.[2]

Alternating near-side and far-side stops makes the best use of transit-friendly progressions, placing the bus at the front of the traffic platoon after a near-side stop, and the back of the platoon after a far-side stop.

Signal progression speeds must be set lower than the speed limit, preventing transit operators and motorists from being incentivized to speed to catch the progression if they fall slightly behind. Transit-only streets with high pedestrian volumes may require lower speeds.

Where bikes and buses share a lane, prevailing bike speeds should be used to set transit progression speeds to prevent leapfrogging. Bike speeds are typically 12 mph for flat terrain, lower for uphill and higher for downhill sections, up to 20 mph.

Where peak-period traffic is much higher than midday or evening traffic, peak progression speeds should be very low, consistent with peak traffic and potentially with longer signal cycles. Slightly higher speeds, up to 20 mph on some streets, with shorter cycles, may be used at off-peak times.

CASE STUDY: GEARY BRT SIGNAL PROGRESSION

In 2014, San Francisco Municipal Transportation Agency (SFMTA) piloted a transit-friendly signal progression along Geary Street, a mile-long one-way corridor with frequent bus service.

Due to the presence of a dedicated bus lane, which minimizes variations in bus travel time. SFMTA implemented a signal progression, with dwell time offsets, averaging 18 mph. Using spreadsheet models, planners were able to assess travel time and dwell time distributions, with the goal of not only reducing travel time and delay along the corridor, but also minimizing variability in travel times, which creates increased operational difficulty and frustration for riders. SFMTA utilized automatic passenger counter (APC)

and automatic vehicle location (AVL) technology to collect data for the model.

The models found a high amount of variability in dwell times, further complicating implementation of an optimal signal progression. Planners opted for a progression that would favor "most" buses rather than "all" so as not to punish faster buses, or create sub-optimal coordination with other users (especially pedestrians).

Finally, the project set a goal of having buses arrive roughly 5 seconds after a signal turned green, with the rationale that a solid green allowed bus drivers to progress through the intersection at a smooth speed without hesitation.

After timing and tuning the signals, the project yielded notable improvements to both transit corridor travel times and variability. Over a single mile, the PM peak travel time fell by an average of 20 seconds, a 3.4% time savings. During the same PM peak, schedule deviation also fell 5.6%, reducing travel time variability and increasing transit predictability.

Active Transit Signal Priority

Transit Signal Priority (TSP) tools modify traffic signal timing or phasing when transit vehicles are present either conditionally for late runs or unconditionally for all arriving transit. TSP can be a powerful tool to improve both reliability and travel time, especially on corridor streets with long signal cycles and distances between signals. In urban contexts, TSP benefits are significantly amplified when implemented alongside other strategies like dedicated transit lanes. The most common tools are detailed on the facing page.

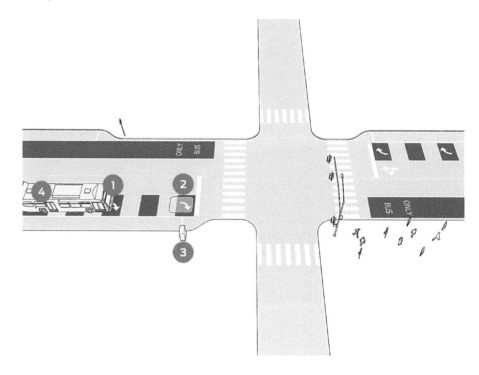

APPLICATION & CONTEXT

Where signals are a major source of delay for transit, particularly when signal delay is a significant portion of transit delay even at times or locations when traffic congestion is not a primary issue. For TSP to work, transit vehicles must be able to reach a signal, either with a dedicated lane or transitway, or by making use of an otherwise clear lane.

Corridors with relatively long signal cycles, or relatively long distances between signals, are good candidates for active TSP.

Specific intersections with long signal cycles or that favor the cross street and operate off of the progression of the rest of the corridor provide strong benefits.

Where transit routes turn, active TSP can extend turn phase time or reservice a turn phase to provide a clear turn lane and additional phase time for slow maneuvers.

Conditional TSP strategies are easiest to implement with moderate to long headways, allowing the signal cycle to gradually return to its non-priority timing. On higher-frequency corridors, decide whether to provide signal priority at every signal cycle, or only to late vehicles.[3]

For BRT and LRT, which often use larger vehicles to increase headways and reduce costs on high-capacity routes.

Unconditional signal priority or preemption should be considered at actuated signals.

BENEFITS

Active TSP can reduce transit delay significantly. In some cases, bus travel times have been reduced around 10%,[4] and delay was reduced up to 50% at target intersections.[5]

TSP is effective at intersections with routinely long queues, or on commonly delayed transit routes. TSP is most effective at intersections with a far-side stop or no stop, allowing the bus to clear the intersection without waiting at a signal.

CONSIDERATIONS

Signal priority usefulness depends on both geometric and operational factors like transit facility type, general traffic volume and capacity, signal spacing, and cycle length.

Active TSP may increase waiting times on cross streets, an especially important factor when transit lines intersect.

At high transit volumes, consider pre-timed strategies such as transit signal progressions. On streets with short distances between signals, a low-speed fixed signal timing strategy may confer more benefits to transit and multi-modal traffic than active TSP.

Active TSP requires a high degree of coordination between the agencies responsible for signals and transit vehicles and operations, with regard to on-board technology as well as signal technology and communications systems, transit schedules, and system goals. Coordination needs may require long-term agreements and planning of vehicle and signal equipment purchases based on goals, since not all equipment can perform all functions.

TSP Technology

1 Active signal priority uses a combination of on-board and wayside technology that determines what type of signal priority can be implemented. Conditional priority usually requires on-board automatic vehicle location (AVL), GPS, optical or laser communication, or other link between the transit vehicle and the signal system.

2 Active transit signal priority can be provided on transitways using in-ground loop detectors to identify arriving transit vehicles, since only authorized vehicles are present.

3 Intersection signal controllers and centralized traffic signal management systems are usually the longest-lifecycle elements of the system, and should be chosen with flexibility in mind and in direct coordination with transit agencies and technical specialists.

In most cases, implementing active TSP will require upgrading technology in the signal controller cabinet, on board transit vehicles, or both. However, a simple detection system that detects vehicle presence only, such as an in-ground loop detector, can be used to provide unconditional priority to transit vehicles operating on a transitway without the need for special equipment, as long as the intersection already has detection capability for other vehicles.

4 Using mobile Wi-Fi or other higher-bandwidth communication, transit vehicles can communicate their estimated time of arrival at an intersection, passenger load, schedule adherence, route number or type, and other attributes to the traffic signal controller or signal system. Various technologies can be used to detect when a transit vehicle has cleared an intersection and no longer requires priority. Advanced signal systems can use this information to prioritize signal priority requests, select the most appropriate TSP strategy for the situation, and end a priority phase as soon as it is no longer needed.

RECOMMENDED

Evaluate and plan TSP based on the goals of minimizing person delay and improving transit reliability. When active TSP is implemented at an intersection, priority should be provided to as many passenger arrivals as possible, based on clearance intervals and crosswalk capacity for crossing pedestrians.

For transit corridors with short headways (under 6 minutes) it may be beneficial to operate conditional TSP, providing priority only to late vehicles. On corridors with longer headways or with high reliability, TSP should generally be applied to all transit runs, with time savings incorporated into the service schedule.[6]

Where transit vehicle volume is high enough that not all arrivals can be provided with priority, late runs, more full vehicles, or rapid services should be prioritized.

Far-side stops maximize TSP efficacy, since arrival at the signal can be anticipated more easily than dwell time. However, near-side stops may be preferable at transfer points.

In mixed-traffic operations, active TSP is often more effective at off-peak periods. It is most effective at moderately high traffic volume, with volume-to-capacity (v/c) ratios of 0.5 to 0.7, and remains effective up to a v/c ratio of about 0.9.[7]

Signal preemption should be applied with great care, as it requires transit vehicle arrival to be anticipated far enough in advance to provide a full pedestrian clearance interval.

OPTIONAL

Adaptive TSP incorporates continuous detection along transit corridors, not just at intersection approaches, and may be integrated with automatic passenger counters (APCs), communication among transit vehicles and signal controllers, and real-time traffic data to determine TSP interventions with better precision and reduce general traffic impacts.[8]

Active Transit Signal Priority *(continued)*

GREEN EXTENSION provides extra time for a detected transit vehicle to clear an intersection. Green extension is most applicable when transit runs at the back of the vehicle queue, as is common at the first signal after a far-side stop. Green extension may be the easiest form of TSP to implement on urban streets since it does not require unexpectedly truncating a pedestrian phase.

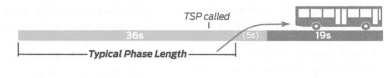

GREEN REALLOCATION shifts when in the signal cycle the green phase occurs—if the transit vehicle is on pace to arrive late, the green phase begins and ends late to accommodate transit. Phase reallocation provides similar benefits to phase extension, but with less impact to cross street traffic since the total green time per cycle does not change. This strategy requires AVL technology.

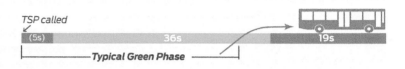

RED TRUNCATION provides a green phase earlier than otherwise programmed, clearing an intersection approach with a waiting transit vehicle sooner than otherwise. Red truncation requires the detection of the transit vehicle far enough away that the crossing pedestrian phase can clear. It is easiest to implement on long blocks or on transitways with predictable travel times.

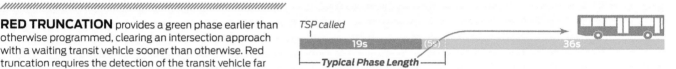

UPSTREAM GREEN TRUNCATION also known as a reverse queue jump, stops traffic behind a bus as boarding is completed, allowing the bus to re-enter the lane after a pull-out stop. Upstream green truncation can also be used to stop traffic at an intersection where transit makes a far-side in-lane stop, preventing queuing in the intersection. Green truncation is most effective on moderate frequency transit routes where delay upon reentry due to congestion is common. It can also benefit passengers alighting and crossing the street behind the bus.

PHASE INSERTIONS and **PHASE SEQUENCE CHANGES** describe the special bus-only phases or prioritization of turn phases used for shared turn/queue jump lanes, and are also helpful when buses make left turns.

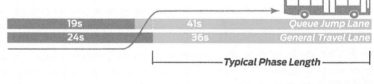

PHASE RESERVICING provides the same phase twice in a given signal cycle, such as a left-turn phase or a queue jump. Reservicing a phase can significantly reduce bus delay, particularly when the phase in question is relatively short.

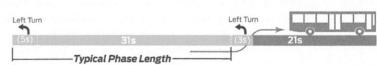

Signal Treatment	Lane Types	Stop Types
Green Extension	Transit Lane, Transitway, Mixed Travel	Far-Side; Pull-Out or In-Lane
Green Reallocation	Transit Lane, Transitway, Mixed Travel	Far-Side; Pull-Out or In-Lane
Red Truncation	Transit Lane, Transitway, Shared Right Turn/Queue Jump	Near-Side or Far-Side; Pull-Out or In-Lane
Upstream Green Truncation	Mixed Travel	Near-Side or Far-Side; Pull-Out
Phase Insertion/Phase Sequence Change	Transit Lane, Transitway	Any
Phase Reservice	Transit Lane, Transitway, Mixed Travel	Any

Active transit signal priority types and complementary geometric configurations

Short Signal Cycles

In mixed traffic, average transit speeds are slower than car traffic. Transit vehicles make regular stops, and tend to fall behind signal progressions.

On neighborhood streets and other small streets with high pedestrian activity levels, signals with short cycle lengths and progression speeds are favorable to lower-speed travel and let transit get back to the progression quickly. When transit has unpredictable dwell times, or where there is no coordinated signal progression, shortening signal cycle length can greatly reduce the time spent by transit vehicles waiting at red signals.

Dearborn St., **CHICAGO, IL**

APPLICATION & CONTEXT

On streets without a coordinated signal progression, including streets that take a "minor" role in the signal system, shorter cycles reduce side-street delay.

On signalized streets with frequent transit service, in mixed-traffic or dedicated lanes.

Where active transit signal priority is less feasible or has limited benefits, including streets with short distances between signals, and downtown streets with high pedestrian activity.

BENEFITS

Shorter signal cycles reduce net delay to transit vehicles, especially at near-side stop locations.[9]

Short signal cycles reduce overall pedestrian wait times and cross street delay, improving rider access to transit. With sufficient pedestrian crossing time, shorter cycles can improve pedestrian safety by reducing wait times and crossings against the signal.

CONSIDERATIONS

Shorter cycles may reduce the available time pedestrians have to cross the street. But pedestrian travel speeds vary widely, with mobility-impaired pedestrians traveling as slowly as 2 feet per second (f/s). Large pedestrian platoons, such as passengers alighting from a center platform, can also require more crossing time. Shorten crossing distances instead of lengthening signal cycles where possible. Pedestrians walking at 3 f/s can cross streets of up to 75 feet in 25 seconds, allowing evenly split 60-second cycles.

CRITICAL

In an urban context, the minimum signal cycle length is determined by pedestrian clearance times and crossing distance (street width). Pedestrians moving relatively slowly, in the range of 2.5 to 3 f/s, should be provided enough time to cross when starting at the beginning of a WALK signal, even if clearance intervals are calculated for 3.5 f/s. A minimum WALK time of 7 seconds is recommended, with a 4 second minimum required. (MUTCD 4E.06).

RECOMMENDED

Except where crossing distances exceed 70–80 feet, or where it is necessary to accommodate a third signal phase to separate turning vehicles from pedestrians, it is usually possible to set signal cycle lengths at 60 seconds.

On streets with neither a signal progression nor active transit signal priority, each signal cycle should include enough time to allow a bus to move from one stop to the next.

Turn Restrictions

Left turns consume an especially large amount of space and signal time, while queued right turns are especially problematic for transit operations in the right lane.

Prohibiting turns where they present issues, and shifting turn volume to the intersections where they can be best accommodated – with signal phases and turn lanes – can improve transit performance, general traffic performance, and walking and bicycling safety at the same time.[10]

More turn management strategies can be found in the next section, *Intersection Design for Transit* (page 158).

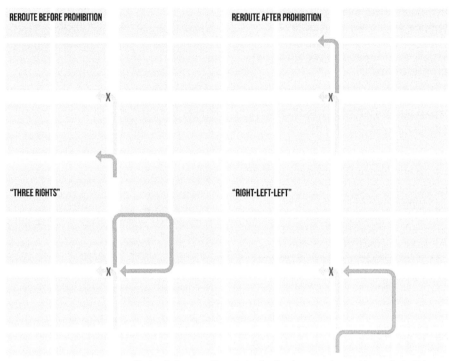

REROUTE BEFORE PROHIBITION

REROUTE AFTER PROHIBITION

"THREE RIGHTS"

"RIGHT-LEFT-LEFT"

Potential operational strategies to reroute problematic left turns

APPLICATION & CONTEXT

Turn restrictions may be applied on streets with or without dedicated transit lanes.

Left-turn restrictions are broadly applicable to multi-lane two-way streets, and may be beneficial on two-way streets with one lane per direction with very high transit volumes.

Left-turn prohibitions are an important component of high-capacity center-running transit services, such as center-running BRT and LRT. Streets with BRT and LRT should prohibit left turns from the transit lane, permitting them only from an adjacent lane with a dedicated turn phase.

Right-turn prohibitions are especially useful for intersections in downtown areas with high walking and bicycling levels, or for streets with right-side bike facilities, where permitting turns would result in long delays for transit vehicles running in the right lane.[11]

Turn management is required for side transitways.

Bicycle turns have minimal impact on transit and pedestrian traffic, and can be permitted even where other turns are prohibited.

BENEFITS

Left-turn restrictions may substantially reduce transit delays for all types of transit facilities except one-way street right-side facilities.

Left-turn restrictions may reduce the frequency of pedestrian injuries and the frequency of transit-involved motor vehicle crashes.[12]

Right-turn restrictions for curbside and offset transit lanes prevent transit delays from turning vehicles and may reduce the frequency of pedestrian injuries.

On two-way streets, left-turn restrictions can substantially increase the capacity of general-traffic lanes. In streets operating at or near capacity, this may enable the implementation of a transit lane while minimizing delays and queuing for general motor vehicle traffic.

CONSIDERATIONS

Where the turn to be prohibited has a moderate or high existing traffic volume, diversion is likely to occur. Alternate routes for the turn should be identified that would generate fewer conflicts between turning vehicles and pedestrians, transit service, and oncoming traffic.

Consider network connectivity when planning turn restrictions. Network analysis should at minimum identify alternate paths for vehicles to access the specific block that would no longer receive a turn, considering the availability of turn pockets, general intersection geometry, walking and biking volumes, and other aspects of turns. Some diversion paths may be less desirable than the original turn, while others can be safer and more efficient with relatively simple interventions.

Left-turn prohibitions may improve operations for right-side running transit operating in mixed-traffic lanes. However, right-turn volume increases must be accounted for when considering potential benefits for transit operations.

CRITICAL

Install NO RIGHT TURNS (MUTCD R3-1), NO LEFT TURNS (R3-2), NO TURNS (R3-3), or NO TURNS EXCEPT BICYCLES.

RECOMMENDED

Turn prohibition signs should be placed where they will be most easily seen by drivers who might be intending to turn. A NO RIGHT TURN sign should be installed adjacent to a signal face viewed by drivers in the right lane.

The NO LEFT TURN (or NO U-TURN or combination NO U-TURN/NO LEFT TURN: MUTCD R3-18) sign should be installed adjacent to a signal face viewed by road users in the left lane. A left-turn blank-out sign may be installed where left turns are prohibited while transit vehicles are present.

A NO TURNS sign should be placed adjacent to a signal face viewed by all road users on that approach, or two signs may be used (MUTCD §4D.34).

For bus lanes with turn restrictions, a solid lane line should be marked at the approach to the intersection along the bus lane.

If dedicated bicycle infrastructure is present on a street, bikes should be excepted from the turn restriction and provided with a short approach lane or other facility.

If turns can be made from a previous intersection, install wayfinding signage in advance of the prior intersection.

OPTIONAL

Wayfinding signage can be provided to direct vehicles to permitted turns or recommended diversion paths.

Vertical separation elements or other self-reinforcing geometric design elements may be installed to prevent or discourage prohibited turns.

Part-time turn prohibitions, usually applied during peak multi-modal traffic periods, are a useful tool for minimizing delays on streets without dedicated turn space. While peak-period left-turn prohibitions are a conventional strategy to increase general-traffic throughput—potentially resulting in higher traffic volumes over time—peak-period turn restrictions on left turns or right turns can substantially improve the performance and safety of either a peak-only transit lane or full-time transit lane.

RIGHT-TURN MANAGEMENT STRATEGIES (assumes one- or two-way street with right-side transit)

Transit Facility	Transit Service	Turn Conditions	Turn Strategies
Transit in Mixed Traffic	Frequent	Low amount of turn delay & high pedestrian/bike volume	Prohibit turns
	Frequent	Moderate amount of turn delay	Right-turn pocket, or prohibit turns
	Frequent bus, or any rail	High amount of turn delay	Right-turn lane at curbside, short offset transit lane for queue jump
	Low to moderate frequency bus	High amount of turn delay	Shared right-turn lane/queue jump
Curbside Transit Lane	Frequent bus, or any rail	Moderate amount of turn delay	Prohibit turns
	Frequent (5–15 min. headways)	High amount of turn delay	Shared right-turn lane with TSP (advanced or extended green)
Offset Transit Lane	Frequent (15 min. or less)	Moderate amount of turn delay	Right-turn pocket
		High amount of turn delay	Long right-turn lane to right of offset transit lane

LEFT-TURN MANAGEMENT STRATEGIES (assumes transit is most often operating in the center-most lane)

Transit Facility	Transit Service	Turn Conditions	Turn Strategies
Center Transitway	Any	Any condition	Prohibition preferred, or provide separate turn lane and phase
Center Transit Lane	Any	Any	Prohibition preferred, or provide separate turn lane and phase
Mixed Traffic (one lane, two-way)	Very Frequent	High amount of delay	Prohibit left turns, or provide separate turn lane and phase
	Frequent	High	Provide queue jump or left-turn lane

Third Street, **SAN FRANCISCO, CA**

Intersection Design for Transit

Making intersections efficient for transit operation and safe for people both inside and outside transit vehicles requires that a variety of design elements work well together: stop location and type, management of mixed-traffic turns, and bikeway location and design.

Geometry guides street users through intersections, working in tandem with signals to sort out conflicts and establish priority among users. The complexity, size, and intensity of use of intersections can create challenges for both transit reliability and pedestrian comfort and safety. Intersections can be organized by designating turn and through lanes, setting clear vehicle and walking paths through the intersection, and providing transit vehicles with a way to avoid general traffic queues and make use of signal priority treatments.

Shared Transit/Right-Turn Lane

On streets with a right-side dedicated transit lane that accommodates a moderate volume of right-turn movements, the transit lane can permit right turns approaching an intersection.

On streets with a right-turn lane but no transit lane, buses can be permitted to use the right-turn lane for through-movements.

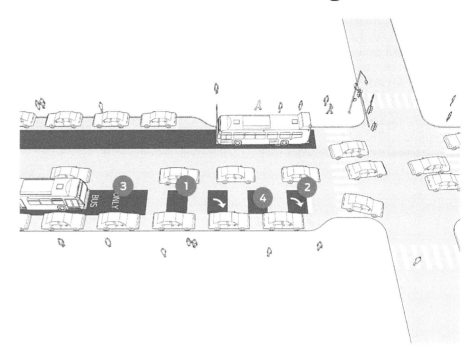

APPLICATION & CONTEXT

At locations where right-turning vehicles can typically clear through the intersection quickly.

Can accommodate moderate right-turn volumes at intersections where right turn on red is permitted and pedestrian volumes are low.

Can be applied to streets with or without dedicated transit lanes.

BENEFITS

Shared transit/right-turn lanes allow vehicles to make right turns across a transit lane.

CONSIDERATIONS

The operational benefits of permitting right turns from transit lanes accrue entirely to right-turning motor vehicles.

Where driver compliance is very low, permitting right turns from the transit lane may sometimes be safer than prohibiting turns.

If vehicle right-turn volumes are high enough for right-turn queues to occur with regularity, right turns should be accommodated separately from transit in a turn pocket (see page 160).

CRITICAL

1. The left-side line of the transit lane should be dashed for 50–100 feet in advance of the intersection.

2. Mark pavement with right-turn arrow. Install RIGHT LANE MUST TURN RIGHT and EXCEPT BUSES signs (MUTCD R3-7R & R3-1B).

3. Install BUS ONLY signs and markings on the receiving side of the intersection.

RECOMMENDED

4. Solid transit lane striping should drop to dashed striping 50–100 feet in advance of the intersection.

OPTIONAL

If provided as a shared right-turn/queue jump, a protected right-turn signal may be used, with a sign indicating RIGHT TURN SIGNAL (MUTCD R10-10) and EXCEPT BUSES. EXCEPT BICYCLES signs may also be provided.

Transit signals may be used to indicate when transit proceeds and when general traffic proceeds for both buses and rail vehicles.

On streets without bus lanes, a shared transit/right-turn lane can be provided to the right of general traffic through-lanes.

Right-Turn Pocket

Where right-turn volumes are high enough to interfere with transit operations but cannot be prohibited, providing a right-turn pocket to the right of the through transit lane reduces bus and streetcar delays.

Right-turn pockets should be considered only after other alternatives are exhausted, since they lengthen the time needed for safe pedestrian crossings, preclude the use of near-side curb extensions, and use valuable curbside space.

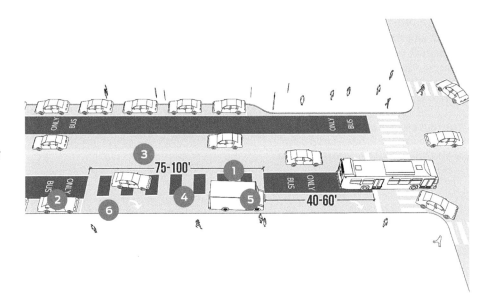

APPLICATION & CONTEXT

At intersections with high right-turn volumes on streets with a dedicated offset transit lane, or with substantial transit volume.

Applicable to buses and streetcars. At low speeds, applicable with multi-unit rail vehicles.

Apply only where impacts to the pedestrian realm can be avoided. Right-turn pockets should generally not be carved from existing sidewalks, as would be necessary for use with curbside transit lanes.

May be applied at intersections with far-side stops. May be applied at near-side boarding island stops, with right turns to the right of the boarding island.

Where right turns must be accommodated but would delay transit vehicles if present in the transit lane. At locations with high pedestrian crossing volumes and little offset distance, even low right-turn volumes can be problematic for transit.

Where a protected bike lane or raised cycle track exists to the right of the transit lane and/or curbside parking.

BENEFITS

Provides dedicated space for right turns while giving priority to through-moving transit.

Permits dedicated right-turn phases, potentially beneficial for pedestrian and bicyclist safety and operations at high-pedestrian intersections.

CONSIDERATIONS

Usually requires the removal of several parking spaces or other curbside uses.

Lengthens the pedestrian crossing, requiring longer pedestrian clearance phases and potentially delaying movement (including transit movement) on the cross street.

Usually precludes implementation of a near-side curb extension.

While a right-turn pocket may prevent vehicle queuing in the transit lane, ensure transit operations are not hindered by merging movements.

CRITICAL

1 A white skip line must be marked on both sides of the transit lane to indicate that vehicles may transition across it.

RECOMMENDED

2 The right-turn pocket should be provided to the right of an offset transit lane with a transition treatment to allow vehicles to cross the dedicated transit lane.

3 The transition zone should be 50–75 feet at low traffic speeds, and the dedicated transit lane should resume to create an approach area that accommodates at least one transit vehicle prior to the stop bar. With 40-foot buses, the transition zone should typically begin at least 100 feet from the crosswalk.

4 Red dashed bars, large red squares, or elephant's feet should be provided in the transition zone, consistent with the white skip lines, to emphasize that transit vehicles retain priority use of the lane.

5 The turn pocket should be 10–11 feet wide if routinely used by trucks at peak periods. 9 feet of width may be sufficient if passenger cars are the primary form of turning traffic at peak periods.

Pre-existing turning conditions should be observed carefully prior to design to ensure that transit vehicles can pass at peak transit-demand periods, often corresponding to peak queue periods.

6 Turn pockets should accommodate the longest routinely occurring queue, but should be no longer than necessary to clear blockages from the transit lane. All but the first 30 feet of the transition zone can be considered as part of the storage length, as peak traffic will transition extremely slowly.

OPTIONAL

Right-turn lanes can be used where general through-traffic is prohibited, requiring all private traffic to turn. Where transit transitions into a contraflow lane where all private vehicles are required to turn, it may be appropriate to transition right-turning traffic to a pocket and continue the transit lane through the intersection.

Transit lanes can be shifted to the left to create a longer right-turn lane. In this case, the transit lane functions like a transit approach lane. This configuration also permits the implementation of a boarding island between the transit lane and the turn lane.

For streets without transit lanes, a right-turn pocket can be paired with a short transit lane section at the intersection approach (page 164).

Dropped Transit Lane

On some narrow transit streets, mixed traffic is expected to use the transit lane both for right turns and to occasionally divert around vehicles waiting to turn left. If enforcement is robust and/or automated, dropping the transit lane approaching an intersection can clarify which movements are permitted.

The dropped transit lane will have a relatively low impact on transit operations, especially where the elimination of double-parking and curbside loading is more important for transit operations than eliminating intersection delay.

Other vehicles may enter the transit lane to circulate around left-turning vehicles, but must rejoin mixed-travel lanes after the intersection when dedicated transit lanes resume.

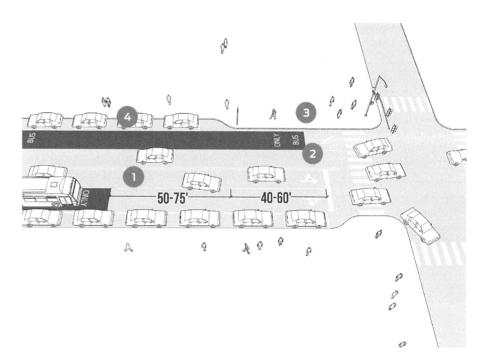

APPLICATION & CONTEXT

On transit lanes where automated enforcement is tied to the lane design, it may be important to formally permit through-movements in the transit lane at some intersections.

On two-way streets with one transit and one mixed-traffic lane per direction, where left turns are permitted but no left-turn pocket or lane is present. This condition is most relevant when left-turn volume is low, with one to two vehicles turning per signal cycle.

BENEFITS

Dropped transit lanes alleviate mixed-traffic delay and congestion at pinch points by permitting through-moving vehicles to merge right and bypass left-turning vehicles.

Buses and streetcars are generally able to maintain priority, as vehicles utilizing the dropped lane must merge and yield to through-traffic.

CONSIDERATIONS

Automated enforcement is important to successful implementation.

CRITICAL

1 Mark a skip line between the through mixed-traffic lane and the dropped transit lane to indicate to motorists that they may enter the transit lane, and install through/right arrows at the intersection approach.

Install RIGHT LANE BUS ONLY or other applicable sign where the transit lane resumes.

2 If private vehicles are permitted to continue across the intersection and merge left after the intersection, use lane reduction arrows (MUTCD Figure 3B-24 F) to direct vehicles back into mixed-travel lanes.

RECOMMENDED

End the transit-only lane 60–100 feet before the intersection, depending on left-turn volume.

3 If a stop is located at the intersection, provide a far-side in-lane or curbside stop.

4 For offset lanes, a parking lane line or parking T's should be provided wherever possible.

Install BUS ONLY word message markings at the end of the bus lane and where it resumes on the other side of the intersection.

Queue Jump Lanes

Queue jump lanes combine short dedicated transit facilities with either a leading bus interval or active signal priority to allow buses to easily enter traffic flow in a priority position. Applied thoughtfully, queue jump treatments can reduce delay considerably, resulting in run-time savings and increased reliability.[1]

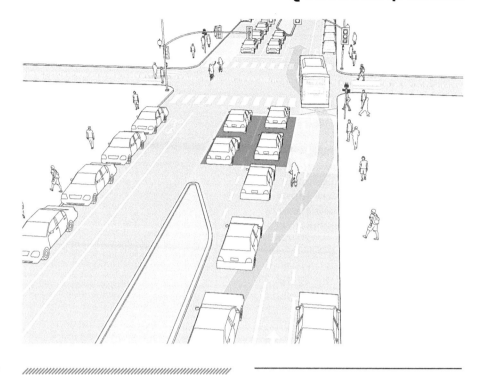

APPLICATION & CONTEXT

On signalized streets with low or moderately frequent bus routes, especially where transit operates in a right lane with high peak hour volumes but relatively low right turns.[2] In some locations, implementing restrictions may be necessary.

If applied as a longer transit approach lane (see page 164), buses may bypass longer queues.

Queue jumps can be applied at near-side, far-side, or non-stop configurations. At near-side pull-out stops, the bus completes loading before rolling forward onto a loop detector that gives priority.

At far-side or non-stop locations, the bus receives a priority signal treatment (see page 152), and proceeds either into a far-side stop or ahead of the traffic flow.

BENEFITS

A bus head start can significantly improve bus performance by routing vehicles through congested intersections ahead of traffic.[3]

CONSIDERATIONS

As congestion increases, bus head starts and bypasses become more effective.[4]

If vehicle right-turn volumes are high enough for right-turn queues to occur with regularity, right turns should be accommodated separately from transit in a turn pocket (see page 160).

In cities where yield-to-transit laws are enforced, the queue jump may operate effectively without a dedicated transit signal phase.

CRITICAL

Buses must have access to a lane and the ability to reach the front of the queue at the beginning of the signal cycle. Buses receive a head start with an advance green.

Separate signals must be used to indicate when transit proceeds and when general traffic proceeds. Transit signals can be either be a transit specific signal head (see page 139)[5] or a louvered or visibility-limited green indication, making it visible only to the right-most lane.

Where stops are located far-side, a signal phase progresses right-turning vehicles together with through-traveling buses. The queue jump lane must be long enough so buses can effectively bypass the expected length of congestion at the intersection at peak.[6]

Where stops are located near-side, right turns are prohibited from happening curbside. The bus pulls into the stop, completes boarding, and then pulls forward onto a loop detector to receive the advance green.

RECOMMENDED

Bus head starts may be made from a shared transit/turn lane or a short exclusive transit lane.

The length of a shared head start/right-turn pocket should be long enough to allow storage of right-turning vehicles and allow buses to reach the queue jump during each signal cycle.

If provided as a shared right-turn/queue jump, a protected right-turn signal may be used (MUTCD 4D-19), with a sign indicating RIGHT TURN SIGNAL (MUTCD R10-10) and EXCEPT BUSES.

Transit Approach Lane/Short Transit Lane

Short transit lanes on the approach to major intersections, sometimes paired with active signal priority, allow transit vehicles to bypass long queues that form at major cross streets.

Since these streets often have long signal cycles or break the progression of the transit street, they often present a significant source of delay across downtown, neighborhood, and corridor transit streets. Transit approach lanes let the transit vehicle stay in its lane, a major benefit to both bus and streetcar lines.

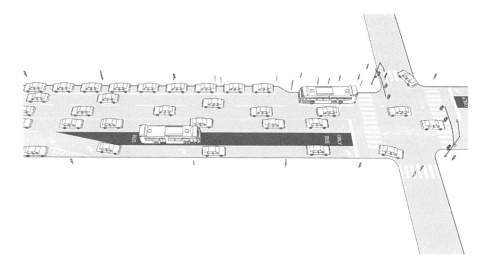

APPLICATION & CONTEXT

On streets that do not otherwise have dedicated transit lanes:

» At the approaches to signalized intersections where transit encounters long delays.

» At locations with a high volume of motor vehicle right turns.

» Signalized intersections with transit operating in a curbside or offset lane.

» Where a bicycle intersection approach is provided in a similar manner, with a dedicated lane and a right-turn pocket to the right.

» Where a right-turn/queue jump with signal priority is not practical, such as locations with long right-turn queues.

For streetcars in otherwise mixed traffic, the transit approach lane is often the best geometric configuration for transit priority without lateral shifts.

BENEFITS

Allow transit vehicles to bypass general vehicle queues and right-turn queues.

Transit vehicles proceed into the approach lane without changing lanes, an advantage over combined right-turn/queue lanes—this is especially important for retrofitting existing streetcar lines, and reduces delay for both bus and rail.

Allows separate signal phases or other accommodation of right-turning traffic.

CONSIDERATIONS

At locations with high and variable right-turn volumes, it may be difficult to plan a right-turn lane that prevents queues across the transit approach lane.

Motor vehicle queues will typically lengthen when a dedicated lane is provided to transit. On streets with short blocks, longer queues can block crossing multi-modal traffic. Motor vehicle queues can be managed by reducing the green signal time available upstream of a major intersection, requiring separate transit signals to achieve a benefit for transit.

Automated enforcement is often needed to create an effective transit lane on streets with a through or arterial function for motor vehicle traffic.

CRITICAL

The transit approach lane must be conspicuous and enforceable. Use clear signage and pavement marking to communicate to motorists the exclusivity of the transit approach lane.

86th St., **NEW YORK, NY**

RECOMMENDED

The dedicated approach lane should be long enough to allow the transit vehicle to fully bypass a routinely forming queue. Queue length calculations must account for the additional length of the queue after a general traffic lane is reassigned to a transit lane; in the example shown, this length is twice the pre-existing queue length.

Right turns either should be accommodated with a dedicated turn pocket/turn lane to the right of the transit approach lane, or should be restricted to prevent queuing in the transit lane.

OPTIONAL

Consider the use of flexible delineators or other vertical elements between the general through lane and the transit lane.

Transit stops may be located on either side of the intersection. Near-side stops, or mid-block stops for very long transit approach lanes, may be provided along the transit approach lane, using a boarding island if a right-turn lane is provided to the right of the transit approach lane.

Virtual Transit Lane

Virtual right-turn lanes permit right turns only when a transit vehicle is not present. When a transit vehicle approaches, right turns are prohibited. Transit signals are triggered to allow transit vehicles to pass through the intersection.

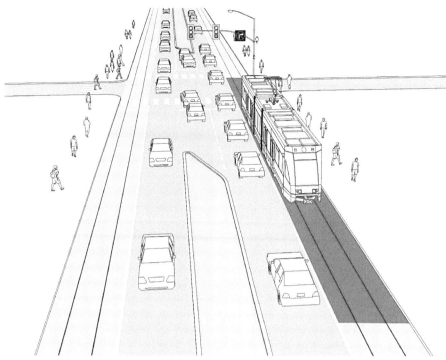

Turns are prohibited when a transit vehicles approaches the intersection

APPLICATION & CONTEXT

Streets with moderate transit service frequency, often with streetcar operating in a mixed-travel or shared turn lane.

At intersections where right-turning vehicles are subject to delays while yielding to pedestrians and bicyclists.

Prohibiting turns when transit is present may be beneficial with or without a dedicated transit lane, especially for streetcars.

BENEFITS

Transit priority is provided, with minimal impact on general network connectivity.

CONSIDERATIONS

Drivers planning to turn right may change lanes and wait in the second lane until right turns are permitted, increasing motor vehicle delay.

CRITICAL

Traffic signals must be transit responsive, using an AVL system, an operator control, or an advance loop detector.

The right-turn prohibition is communicated to drivers with a NO RIGHT TURN blank-out sign (MUTCD R3-1 or 1a) potentially accompanied by an LRV symbol blank-out sign.

Signage must communicate to vehicles that they are prohibited from entering the transit lane while the transit vehicle is present.

RECOMMENDED

A dedicated transit lane should be prominently marked and may be colored red on approach to the intersection before dropping into a shared right-turn/transit lane (see page 159). Dedicated lanes increase the transit vehicle's ability to reach the signal unimpeded.

OPTIONAL

A right-turn arrow may be used when transit vehicles are not present.

Bicycle Rail Crossings

With or without bike lanes, streetcar and light rail streets attract bicycle traffic. Making these streets safe for people using bikes is critical for preserving local destination access, and is often important for bike network connectivity.

If high-comfort bicycle facilities cannot be implemented on streetcar and light rail streets, parallel high-comfort bicycle routes should be provided in addition to basic destination-access bicycle accommodations on streetcar streets.

Yesler St., **SEATTLE, WA**

DISCUSSION

Bicycle tires can become stuck in rail flanges when in-street tracks are crossed at too low an angle, causing the bicycle rider to fall. Particular attention must be paid where streetcar tracks bend or turn, where light rail tracks cross a street, or where bicycle lanes or bicycle turning movements cross tracks.

Bicycling adjacent to tracks can also pose dangers, particularly pronounced when a bicyclist must be prepared to swerve to avoid unforeseen obstacles such as opening vehicle doors.

A variety of design techniques can prevent these injury-causing falls by directing bicyclists to cross tracks at higher angles, and by guiding people on bikes to ride a safe distance from rails while riding parallel to them.

APPLICATION

Bike-friendly track crossings are applicable wherever streetcar or light rail tracks turn across a bikeway (including any bike lane, bike boulevard, or cycle track), where a bikeway turns across tracks, and at any intersection where bike turns are accommodated, especially where two bike lanes intersect.

Bike-friendly trackway design is applicable to all mixed-traffic streetcar and light rail running ways.

CRITICAL

Where bicycle paths of travel cross a street-surface rail track, bicyclists must be directed to cross tracks at a high angle. While 90-degree crossings are preferred, 60 degrees is the minimum design angle for bikeways to cross in-street rails.

Bicyclists must be able to cross tracks fully upright and not leaning, with perpendicular or high-angle approaches established in advance of tracks to allow riders to right themselves.

RECOMMENDED

Rail Turns Across Bikeways

» A bike sneak is a short section of bicycle lane, protected bicycle lane, or raised cycle track that is bent out (bent toward the sidewalk) to direct bicyclists at a safe angle across turning tracks. Provide bicycle lane markings to direct bicyclists to the right, establishing sufficient space for a safe crossing of rails. Provide intersection markings, at or near a 90-degree angle to the curving track that return bicyclists to the bicycle lane on the opposite side of the intersection without entering the motor vehicle lane. The bike sneak can be marked, raised, channelized, or otherwise protected using a variety of means of separation, depending on the volume of bicyclists and the role of the street in the bicycle network.

» Crossing tracks at an angle less than 45 degrees should be discouraged, both on streets with and without a bicycle facility.

» Warning signage or markings should be used ahead of an intersection or other rail crossing where the natural travel path of a bicyclist, generally parallel to the lane line or curbline, would cross the rail at a low angle.

Bicycle Turns Across Rail

» Two-stage turn queue boxes direct bicyclists to cross rails at a safe angle when turning left across tracks, or turning right across tracks from a left-side bikeway. (Refer to the *Urban Bikeway Design Guide* for guidance on two-stage turn queue box design).

Bicycle-Friendly Trackways

» Bicycle lanes should include a buffer at least 3 feet wide to account for these instances, and prohibitions of dangerous misuse of the bike lane, such as double-parking, must be strictly enforced. Where possible, physically separating bicycle lanes from streetcar lanes is preferred. In addition to cycle tracks, placing rails on raised beds or transitway design treatments, such as rails in raised beds, or vertical separation, prevent bicycles from entering tracks. Vertical separation may be especially desirable in tight spaces. If curbs are greater than 2 inches, roll curbs or mountable curbs should be considered.

For more on bicycle networks, see *Bicycle Access & Networks* on page 186.

NW Lovejoy St., **PORTLAND, OR**

Peachtree Street, ATLANTA, GA

Transit Route Turns

Intersections on transit streets pose extra challenges: they must account for the size of transit vehicles and their large turning radii, as well as conflicts from other street users. But while buses and light rail vehicles may require more, or dedicated, street space, thoughtful intersection design can yield more efficient transit service facing fewer conflicts.

Turn Radii

Transit vehicles typically require an effective turning radius of approximately 20–30 feet, depending on lane width and presence of curbside parking lanes or buffer distance. Bikeways or parking lanes create additional space for large design vehicles to turn smoothly and safely (see page 158 for design alternatives).

At intersections, geometric decisions must balance efficient accommodation of transit turns with pedestrian safety. Curb radii should be designed as tightly as possibly to reduce pedestrian crossing distance without adversely affecting transit operations.

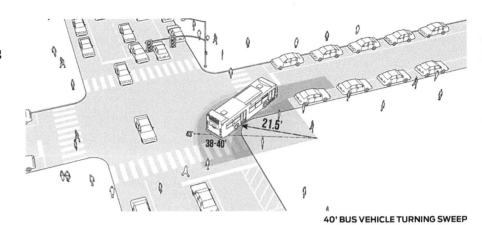

40' BUS VEHICLE TURNING SWEEP

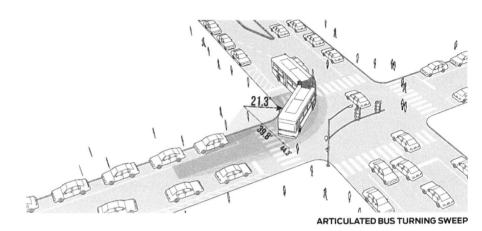

ARTICULATED BUS TURNING SWEEP

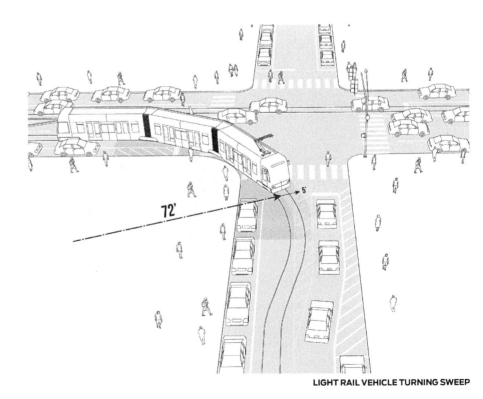

LIGHT RAIL VEHICLE TURNING SWEEP

40-FOOT BUS

A typical inner turning radius of a standard 40-foot bus is 21.5 feet, which is required to clear the curb. At its tightest turning angle, the rear overhang of the back bumper extends out to 43.3 feet.[1]

When considering curb extensions at intersections where a reduced pedestrian crossing distance is desired, the bus's effective turning radius may be accommodated by allowing the turning bus to use part of the on-coming travel lane to accommodate its wide sweep (see *Recessed Stop Line*, page 172).

To make turns at its tightest radius, the bus must slow significantly, which can cause run-time delays, especially if turns are frequent along a route.

Where parking lanes are adjacent to the curb, the effective radius available for turns increases, allowing a narrower lane width. Likewise, if the receiving street has multiple travel lanes, the bus can be accommodated using both lanes.

60-FOOT ARTICULATED BUS

Articulated buses, or extended coaches pivoting around a center bridge plate, are most commonly 60 feet long. They are generally the assumed operating vehicle in BRT or "open BRT" systems.

The turning geometry of a 60-foot articulated bus is quite similar to a 40-foot bus, the primary difference being the vehicle's ability to pivot around the center bridge plate.

Due to their extended length and capacity, articulated buses are not characteristically employed on smaller streets where fewer riders are likely to accumulate, so tight curb radii are a less significant consideration.

However, where articulated vehicles must turn around tight corners, special care must be taken for overhanging portions of the vehicle that pass over the corner of the curb, where pedestrians may be standing or walking.

MODERN STREETCAR/ LIGHT RAIL VEHICLE

Vehicle turning radius varies greatly, depending on streetcar/LRV age and design.

A standard three-section LRV centerline turn radius is 82 feet, though streetcars may have a smaller centerline radius between 45 and 60 feet.[2]

Light rail vehicles forced to turn necessarily use multiple travel lanes, and tracks must be designed to accommodate inherent turning constraints.

Extended vehicle length also requires additional time to complete turns, impacting traffic flow and potentially delaying street users.

Turn radii must be designed for the dynamic vehicle envelope, including mirrors and swaying, which, if blocked by parked or standing vehicles, can delay or result in damage to LRVs.

Light rail vehicles require additional acceleration and deceleration length approaching and exiting intersections.

A significant variable affecting rider comfort is superelevation, or the tilting of the vehicle as it turns, which may unbalance standing riders. Cross slopes must account for turning radii and speeds.

Recessed Stop Line

Buses may face challenging turning geometries when routed through small intersections, especially when transit service is operated in the curbside lane. Pulling the stop bar back from the intersection allows large transit vehicles to use two lanes around tight curb radii.

On-street parking and bikeways may provide space for a larger effective radius for transit vehicles to turn.

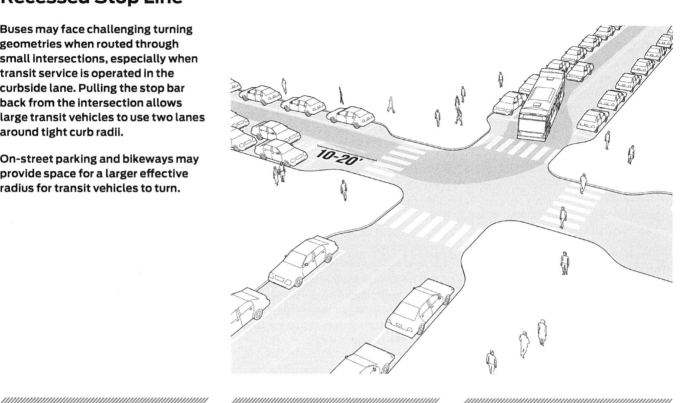

APPLICATION & CONTEXT

Where buses face challenging turning geometries in small intersections, especially when transit vehicles turn from curbside lane to curbside lane.

BENEFITS

Allows buses to make wide turns in tighter intersections, and enables tighter intersection geometry to reduce the typical turning speed of general traffic.

Where the effective turning radius of the transit vehicle is greater than the radius provided for the transit vehicle to turn from one travel lane into one receiving lane, recessing the stop line allows the transit vehicle to briefly use the opposing lane to complete the turn.

CONSIDERATIONS

Pedestrian safety and comfort is the most important turn radius consideration. Buses should only be used as a design vehicle for locations where buses turn frequently. If buses turn infrequently (such as during substitution, rerouting, or on low-frequency coverage routes), it is acceptable to allow buses to use the whole intersection for turns (see *Turn Radii,* page 170). On higher-frequency routes, use turn radii designed for buses, with other measures to reduce car turning speeds.

CRITICAL

Recess the stop line on the receiving street to allow the turning bus to use the full width of the receiving street, accounting for the inner and rear swept paths of the bus(see page 170).

RECOMMENDED

For stop bars more than 20 feet from the intersection, install STOP HERE ON RED (MUTCD R10-6), and STOP pavement marking.[3]

Plan transit routes to minimize difficult turns that might degrade the pedestrian environment and slow travel times (see *Contraflow Transit Street*, page 54).

OPTIONAL

Mountable curbs or "concrete pillows" may help to provide a smaller curb radius for slower target speeds, while allowing turns by large transit vehicles. Mountable curbs must be delineated with color or paving treatments that both prohibit cars from entering and alert pedestrians to look for buses.

Concrete pillow, **PORTLAND, OR**

Transit-Only Turns

Bus- or streetcar-only turn restrictions provide the safety and operational benefits of general motor vehicle turn prohibitions while permitting a critical bus movement.

APPLICATION & CONTEXT

May be applied at any intersection at which buses turn but general traffic left or right turns can be prohibited.

BENEFITS & CONSIDERATIONS

Transit vehicles require larger turn radii than most vehicles, a challenge to pedestrians. However, transit turns are less frequent.

CRITICAL

Install NO TURNS; EXCEPT BUSES signs at intersections (MUTCD R3-3 and R3-1A).

RECOMMENDED

Provide a through-only arrow signal head (MUTCD 4D-2C).

Install advance signage before intersection.

If a bus lane is present, a solid white lane line should be marked at the approach to the intersection along the bus lane.

Bikes should be excepted from the turn restriction and when possible provided with dedicated infrastructure.

OPTIONAL

Wayfinding signage directing motor vehicle drivers to permitted turns can be provided.

Dedicated Turn Channel

Unlike slip lanes, a dedicated turn channel is designed specifically for transit vehicles, and can be designated exclusively for their use, preventing excessive vehicle speeds.

APPLICATION & CONTEXT

Where frequent transit routes make regular right turns (or left turns from one-way streets), rail turns on small streets, and where width is available.

Entrances to on- or off-street terminals.

CONSIDERATIONS

The turn channel should be designed to accommodate smooth, low-speed turns by the transit vehicles that use it regularly. Especially for bus channels, overly wide channels encourage unsafe speeds and may invite unauthorized users.

RECOMMENDED

If used by general traffic, the turn channel should have the tightest turn angle that is able to accommodate transit vehicles—tighter angles slow traffic speeds, but improve sightlines and pedestrian crossing safety.[4]

Apply red color to designate the space as a transit-only area.

If the turn can be made only during a specific phase, install transit signals at the approach to the channel.

If designed for buses and permitting mixed traffic, the dedicated turn channel should rise to meet a crosswalk at a grade consistent with bus operations at the speed for which the curve has been designed.

For long transit vehicles, the turn can begin in a channel and be completed in the second lane of the receiving street, reducing the corner radius needed for the channel.

Install signage prohibiting general motor vehicle traffic, such as BUSES ONLY or STREETCARS ONLY signage, at the entrance to the channel.

SW Moody Ave., **PORTLAND, OR**

7. Transit System Strategies

Good street design for transit requires a balance between two goals: serving dense, mixed-use places, while providing reasonable travel times and reliable operations. Busy streets—where walking and bicycling are practical and pleasant—signal vibrancy, and also tend to be important destinations for people arriving by any mode. But these popular and busy streets also often result in slow and unreliable transit.

Transit speed and travel time not only affect customer satisfaction and ridership, they also underlie operating costs. The slower and more variable transit travel times are, the more transit agencies must spend to deliver the same frequency of service. Where transit runs in mixed traffic, it is common for transit travel times to decline slowly as the city develops. Transit agencies must then pay more to maintain the same frequency of service along slower routes rather than spending those resources offering more service.

Designing streets for transit, walking, bicycling, and driving is possible, but the right answer is different in different places, and it always requires both creativity and compromise.

Network & System Principles

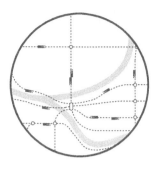

SYSTEMWIDE APPROACHES GO FARTHER

The street network is the transit network. Systemic street design and transit system enhancements—from fare collection and wayfinding to signal coordination and traffic network management—need to be selected and operated with transit in mind. Integrating ridership-supportive treatments into the daily practice of street engineering, development review, and transit operations continuously builds transit into the urban fabric.

FREQUENT, PREDICTABLE, CONVENIENT

Reliability rivals total trip time and cost in transit riders' priorities, and is essential to capturing ridership. Transit service is most valuable for riders when it is always coming soon throughout the day, allowing riders to easily take both routine and spontaneous trips.

RIDERSHIP REINFORCES PERMANENCE

Transit routes with high ridership are permanent fixtures in the street. Cities should work with transit providers to identify, plan for, and invest in well-utilized transit corridors. The value of transit design improvements is highest when focused on the frequent, high-ridership network that passengers feel is legible, reliable, and predictable.

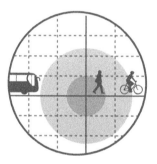

EQUITY GOES BEYOND COVERAGE

Transit is vital to economic opportunity, and must go beyond just providing an easy trip to downtown. Cities are increasingly multi-centered, with employment, activity clusters, and social connections distributed in new ways not always anticipated by the existing transit network. High-frequency, all-times networks that use transfers to reach more of the city in less time serve the multi-directional movements that people need for a complete urban life—and that make regional economies competitive and dynamic.

COMPLETE TRIPS NEED COMPLETE NETWORKS

Transit, walking, and bicycling are mutually supportive, and thrive on connected grid street networks. While not every street can provide the highest level of comfort to every mode, a complete active transportation network is indispensable in achieving the full potential of transit, expanding the reach of transit stops and multiplying the desirability of living or working near transit. When people use transit for one trip, bikes for another, and their feet for a third, all on the same corridor, the street has succeeded.

EASY TO RIDE, EASY TO RUN

Simple, mostly straight routes that follow street patterns are both rider-friendly and efficient to operate. Whether making a spontaneous trip to a new place or using a route regularly, passengers can take full advantage of the transit system when riding is easy to understand. Name stops and routes based on recognizable destinations and streets, keep routes direct, integrate fare payment procedures, and make planning and connecting in multi-leg trips as simple as possible.

SW Moody Avenue, PORTLAND, OR

Network
Strategies

Transit routes can be changed. Existing routes in many cities are the result of decades of incremental changes, rather than a reflection of current or underlying demand patterns. Cities change, and transit networks can both shape and respond to shifts in city form.

Transit Networks

At the largest scale, transit network design is a powerful tool that affects every aspect of a transit system and the daily lives of its passengers.

In large cities, transit networks are almost always multi-modal, with a wide variety of service types and even multiple network patterns. In an effective transit system, these modes connect and complement, rather than duplicate, one another.

In the following schematic diagrams, heavier lines represent more frequent or higher-volume service.

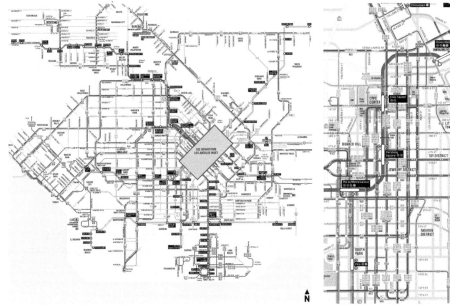

LA Metro's regional & downtown frequent transit networks, **LOS ANGELES, CA**

MULTI-HUB NETWORK

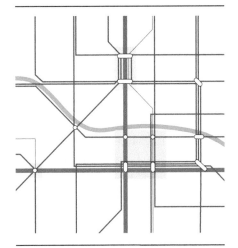

Cities with extensive off-street rail networks often plan surface transit as a feeder to rail. Bus routes originate and terminate at rail stations.

Operations in these systems strongly favor the trunklines, resulting in frequent or high-volume bi-directional service along these routes but much less frequent service to other locations.

Trunklines connect key hubs, making travel between dense centers quick and simple.

When buses are used for trunkline routes, robust rapid transit street design includes transitways and station-area planning.

Local routes on neighborhood streets benefit from comfortable stops, system information and branding, and other integration with the broader system.

APPLICATION

Cities with both buses and a dedicated-right-of-way rail system have historically structured the former primarily as a feeder service to the latter. Bus Rapid Transit can be used to upgrade new parts of the network into trunklines. At somewhat lower speeds and distances, streetcars and buses can also form a multi-hub network, with dedicated lanes or transitways in downtown.

Cities with multiple large economic or activity clusters require connectivity beyond downtown. Lower-density neighborhoods and activity centers often access core rail service via feeder surface transit.

BENEFITS & CONSIDERATIONS

Prominent stations can be major attractors for ridership and transit-oriented development activity. Keeping transfer points compact and walking-oriented is key to their development potential.

With targeted investments, surface bus networks may provide substantially faster travel for specific routes, even in systems with separate off-street transit. Bus networks are often simpler and less expensive to plan and build.

Service frequency, and subsequent investments, can be imbalanced toward rail, especially when the rail network is well established.

GUIDANCE

Because transfers are key to an effective network, the transfer process should be as simple and seamless as possible. Design transit hubs to be simple to navigate, and implement transfer-supportive fare payment methods.

Design rapid network to run primarily on either large streets with dedicated transit lanes or on other streets where reliable service can be provided.

GRID NETWORK

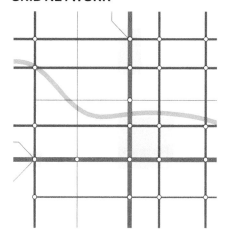

More trips can be made more quickly on a network of high-frequency routes with predictable, rapid-style service and comfortable stops, making transfers an acceptable part of commutes.

APPLICATION

Cities with distributed destinations including polycentric or corridor-based employment centers.

Cities with conventional 20th-century arterial grids.

BENEFITS & CONSIDERATIONS

Improves service for a very high percentage of existing passengers.

High potential to attract new passengers, especially those whose destinations are outside of downtown.

Some passengers may have longer trips to downtown or longer walks to rapid stops.

Straightened routes operating as part of a grid provides the ability to run higher frequency at a lower cost by reducing the total number of routes.

GUIDANCE

Design system as a grid so that most destinations can be reached from most origins with only one transfer, running through-services rather than terminating at key destinations.

Design rapid network to run primarily on either large streets with dedicated transit lanes or on other streets where reliable service can be provided.

Riders are willing to walk slightly farther to access higher-quality service, so stops and routes can be spaced farther apart; however, service must be frequent and reliable to ensure quality is not degraded.

Because transfers are key to an effective network, the transfer process should be as simple and seamless as possible. More destinations can be connected if riders can transfer conveniently along the grid with minimal added trip time.

RADIAL NETWORK

Many transit networks are oriented around a traditional set of destinations and have evolved only gradually over the past decades—often changing little since the introduction of the bus itself.

One-seat networks connecting to downtowns have long been a goal for transit systems competing with private automobiles. But in most cities, destinations are distributed, not just concentrated in downtown.

APPLICATION

In cities with a strong downtown core.

In cities where topography or irregular street patterns result in strong activity corridors feeding into a central hub.

BENEFITS & CONSIDERATIONS

Provides a one-seat ride for passengers traveling to the network hub.

Where population density or funding do not allow high-frequency routes, radial networks can still provide basic service across a city. Especially where travel times are reliable, as in smaller cities, a radial or hub network can be set up with "pulse" schedules where all routes arrive at a central hub at the same time.

Often requires that passengers travel downtown to transfer to another line. Destinations that are neither along the closest bus line nor downtown may be difficult to reach. However, select cross-town routes can provide important connections between branches.

As branches converge on downtown destination streets, capacity and congestion become major challenges to on-time performance.

Routes run less frequently due to decreased fare box recovery, so riders may need to proactively plan trips.

Trunk segments near downtown with multiple transit routes may be well served with frequent service, but diverging routes may be difficult to understand.

GUIDANCE

Investment in dedicated transit infrastructure along key trunkline segments shared by multiple routes will yield the greatest benefits.

Routes sharing a common trunk segment may have a common identifier, acting as a unified line that is easier to understand for passenger trip-planning closer to downtown.

Route Simplification

Direct, simple routes are easy to use, and save time compared with circuitous routes. Transit routes that have evolved in a piecemeal fashion over decades can be simplified to create more frequent and direct service.

Dedicated space and signal strategies pair well with projects that straighten a transit line along a main street, helping these changes add up to meaningful time savings.

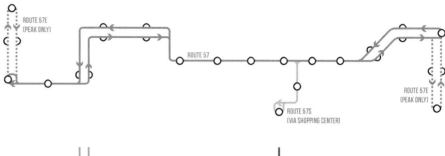

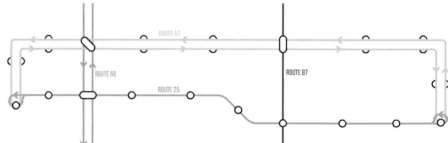

Simple, direct routes are easier for passengers to understand and often faster-running

APPLICATION

Routes that turn frequently or do not operate in alignment with the existing street grid.

Areas experiencing significant growth or changes in transportation demand including routes that are transitioning from a coverage role to a structural (local or rapid) role in the network.

Systems that have undergone many small, spot-level changes over a long period.

BENEFITS

Reducing the number of turns, especially through complex intersections, eliminates a large source of transit delay.[1]

Transit signal progressions, some forms of active signal priority, and dedicated space treatments are easier to achieve on a single main street.

Reducing route "branching" can allow routes to operate at high frequencies.

CONSIDERATIONS

When transitioning to a grid network that relies on transfers, service needs to be frequent and reliable to facilitate predictable trip times.

Moving or eliminating stops or routes requires local public discussion and an understanding of stakeholder needs. Route realignments in areas with inaccessible or disconnected pedestrian infrastructure are much more challenging to plan in a way that supports existing riders. These changes may be unsuccessful in saving costs, as paratransit trips may increase.

Though access distances can be increased, transit service changes should be designed to avoid entirely cutting off passengers from fixed-route service, with special concern for places where a large percentage or number of passengers are fully reliant on transit.

RECOMMENDATIONS

Long routes should be designed to mitigate the cumulative impacts of delay.

Long routes are a high priority for directness, and should be designed to mitigate the cumulative impacts of delay from turns and other causes.

Turns that serve specific destinations should be close to the beginning or end of a route so that only those passengers using that destination are directly impacted by the increased travel time.

To serve multiple large origins and destinations on separate streets, routes should be chosen to provide reasonable walking distances to both locations without diverting. Choosing to run transit on streets in the center, rather than the edge of districts with multiple destinations, can create a stronger route with more all-day and both-directions ridership.

Routing multiple lines to converge onto a single corridor can increase core frequency and justify higher-quality transit treatments.

Structure routes to serve destinations in a straight line.

Routes that divert from a main street to reach a particular stop reflect a preference for shorter walking distances for passengers who use that stop at the expense of travel time for those already on board. Diverging from the street into parking lots or large developments and campuses can be a major time expense; instead, stop on the street, and work with large landowners to develop frontages or improve internal walking circulation.

From Stops to Stations

Stop spacing is a powerful service-planning tool with relevance to both travel time and coverage goals. Consolidating existing stops is not simple, but converting a route from numerous low-ridership stops to better spaced, higher-capacity stations achieves the benefits of stop consolidation and accessible boarding at the same time.

Switching from stops to high-quality stations can serve to balance walking time and on-vehicle time, with benefits for both travel time and reliability. Prominent, attractive stations with elements like platforms and shelters are easier to construct when investments are concentrated in a smaller number of stops. Stops can become recognizable stations that anchor the transit service in a place.

Stations can be mobility hubs, attracting riders from a larger area with bike share, bike parking, and car share service integration.

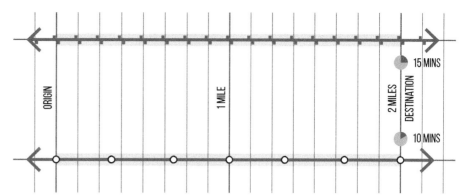

Converting two miles of route from 16 stops to 6 stations can boost speeds and reliability

APPLICATION & CONTEXT

Local services with eight or more stops per mile are prime beneficiaries of stop consolidation.

Scheduled reconstruction projects are opportunities to include stop consolidation and upgrades, vehicle procurements, and improvements to the pedestrian realm.

New vehicles, especially when procured to meet accessibility standards or to provide rapid service, provide an opportunity to install platforms and consolidate stops.

BENEFITS

Longer station spacing reduces dwell time associated with making more frequent stops; fewer stops allow faster and more consistent travel times, improving service quality for passengers and service cost for agencies. Savings can be used to reduce route cost or increase service frequency.[2]

More prominent stations reinforce the existence, permanence, and legibility of the route and its identity as part of a broader transit system.

Larger stops can accommodate more passengers with better amenities. Higher pedestrian volumes accessing transit stations reinforce safer pedestrian conditions, especially when sidewalks and crossings are upgraded.

More robust station-stop design can allow for faster boarding with level or near-level boarding and off-board fare payment.

Noise and air pollution are reduced when vehicles stop and start fewer times.

Stations allow space used for stops to be restored to other curbside uses, such as vehicle and bike parking, green infrastructure, or parklets.

RECOMMENDATIONS

Set stop spacing based on goals for the route. For general applications, convert to a pattern of stops 800 feet apart for local service, and ¼–½ mile for rapid lines.[3] Distancing stops evenly along the route enables simpler signal progression planning.

When local and rapid services both operate along the same street, more frequent local stops are more acceptable, and rapid stops can be spaced as much as one mile apart. Where local runs alone for long corridors and rapid service is unlikely to be added, consider 1,200–1,400 foot spacing.

Stop spacing for local services of more than 5 per mile can be useful when most passengers are going short distances. These conditions are often met on short routes, in retail and entertainment areas, where substitutes for walking are a primary reason for the service, or where design and street conditions render the delay caused by stops less relevant.

Adjust stop spacing to the street grid and the surrounding transit network, especially reducing the distance to transfers.

Transition from making stops on demand to stopping at every station. Predictable stops and dwell times simplify service and trip planning.

Pair stop consolidation with station investments, including near-level boarding platforms, high-quality shelters and seating, green infrastructure, bike parking, bike share, and real-time passenger information systems (see Ch. 3: Stations & Stops, page 57; and Ch. 4: Stop Elements, page 91).

Prioritize near-level or level boarding and comfortable waiting areas that do not block pedestrian through movement. Universal design enables more comfortable use for all passengers, including those with disabilities, and speeds boarding and alighting while easing the demand on operators.

All-door boarding (which can be supplemented with off-board fare collection) reduces dwell time.

Fares & Boarding

Fare collection and boarding can be time consuming, accounting for half to a third of vehicle revenue time. Strategies that streamline fare collection and allow for multi-door boarding can dramatically speed up passenger boarding time, reducing dwell time and total run-time.

Modern on-board PoP fare payment using an RFID payment card, **SAN FRANCISCO, CA**

Fare control officer checking proof-of-payment tickets, **SAN FRANCISCO, CA**

FARE PAYMENT METHODS

Cash Payment

» Cash fares are paid to the driver upon boarding. Cash payment is time-consuming and should be discouraged.
» In systems using proof-of-payment (PoP) fare control, riders paying cash receive a PoP ticket from the driver showing fare was paid.

Ticket Vending

» Passengers purchase a ticket at a vending machine, which acts as a proof-of-payment.
» Tickets may be bought at on-board or off-board vending machines.

Radio Frequency ID (RFID) Card

» Fares are paid using cashless RFID cards, which must be tapped at a reader to be validated.
» On-board RFID readers are placed either at multiple doors as with PoP systems, or at the front door alone for systems with driver fare control.
» Off-board RFID readers are placed at the stop. Riders scan their RFID cards before boarding the bus, reducing boarding times.

Mobile App

» Tickets are purchased via smart phone using a mobile application.
» Tickets may be instantly valid, or may require on-board validation by scanning a QR code.
» Passengers must present the electronic ticket to driver upon boarding, or to fare control officers upon request.

FARE CONTROL METHODS

Proof-of-Payment (PoP)

» Passengers receive a proof-of-payment (PoP) which must be presented to fare control officers upon request. PoPs may be physical or electronic "tickets."
» Many modern systems allow fares to be paid using cashless RFID cards or mobile apps.
» Cash payments may be made to the driver, who will provide a ticket or receipt as proof-of-payment. Alternately, tickets may be purchased from an on-board vending machine.
» PoP tickets are typically valid for a specified amount of time after purchase or validation, such as 60 or 90 minutes.
» PoP fare payment is required in systems that permit multi-door boarding.
» PoP fare control requires consistent enforcement to be effective.
» Fare inspectors make random checks to ensure riders have a valid ticket. Passengers without a ticket are assessed a fine.

Driver Fare Control

» Most traditional bus and streetcar services use driver-controlled fare payment.
» All passengers must board at the front door, where the driver ensures fares are paid.
» Cash fares are paid into a farebox by the driver at the front door.
» RFID cards must be tapped at a reader near the front door upon boarding.
» Tickets, including physical tickets, mobile tickets, and passes must be presented to the driver for visual inspection.
» Driver fare control can slow operations as drivers must collect fare payment in addition to operating the vehicle.

Turnstile Control

» At enclosed stations, turnstiles may be used to control passenger entry.
» Fares may be paid using machine-readable tickets, RFID cards, or other fare media like tokens.
» Access may be manually controlled by a station attendant, who can collect cash or tickets.
» Gated systems are difficult to implement at on-street stations. High platforms and active enforcement are usually needed.

Off-board RFID card reader and real-time arrival display, **SEATTLE, WA**

Select Bus Service off-board PoP ticket vending machine, **NEW YORK CITY, NY**

A multi-day mobile ticket is validated on-board by scanning a QR code, **AUSTIN, TX**

PoP PAYMENT STYLES

On-Board PoP Payment

» RFID farecards must be tapped upon boarding.
» Systems using PoP fare control can place RFID readers at multiple doors, allowing for passengers to board at any door.
» In systems using driver fare control, an RFID card reader is placed near the front door.
» On-board ticket vending machines can be installed where physical PoP tickets are required and installing machines at every stop is not feasible.
» Some mobile apps require that mobile tickets be validated by scanning a QR code upon boarding.

Off-Board PoP Payment

» Off-board RFID readers or ticket vending machines are placed at the stop. Riders scan their RFID cards before boarding the bus, reducing boarding times.
» Off-board fare collection can significantly reduce passenger boarding times, with dwell per passenger falling from about 4 seconds to 2–2.5 seconds.
» Providing off-board ticketing machines may be expensive.
» See *Fare Vending* (page 99) for more information about off-board fare vending.

VEHICLE BOARDING TYPES

Multi-Door (or All-Door) Boarding

» Passengers may board at multiple doors.
» Used with PoP fare systems.
» Reduces per-passenger dwell time significantly, especially at high-use transit stops.
» Faster boarding times move buses faster in congested areas, and move pedestrians faster on crowded sidewalks.
» Passengers must board with a valid ticket, tap their RFID card or validate their ticket upon boarding, or purchase a ticket from the driver or an on-board vending machine.
» Gather information before and after implementation; invest in automatic passenger counters, or employ short-term counting staff, to assess boarding times, volumes, and improvements.

Front Door Boarding

» All passengers board through the front door.
» Traditional transit operations commonly use driver fare control, requiring drivers to both operate the vehicle and collect fares, and resulting in slowed operations.

Case Study: MUNI ALL-DOOR BOARDING, SAN FRANCISCO

In San Francisco, SFMTA implemented all-door boarding on a systemwide basis in 2012, extending to buses a practice already in place for light rail. Passengers tap prepaid cards at card readers located at all doors, or board with timed paper transfer tickets. Cash customers pay at the front door, saving the expense of on-street fare collection machines. Since a proof-of-payment system was already in place for non-cash passengers, San Francisco shows the specific benefit of all-door boarding. At busy stops, a 38% reduction in entry/exit time was found for buses: 1.5 seconds per customer, in a system with 100 boardings per bus in the peak hour. Transit travel speeds increased 2% on average after implementation. Coupled with improved enforcement, fare evasion dropped from 9.5% to 7.9%, reducing estimated fare loss nearly $2 million.[4]

Pedestrian Access & Networks

A transit trip is door-to-door, not stop-to-stop. Fully connected and comfortably designed pedestrian networks are an indispensable precursor to great transit systems and to the urban activity levels that transit is designed to support. Since a wide range of potential riders will walk farther on comfortable, active, pedestrian-friendly urban streets than in vehicle-dominated conditions, transit reaches its greatest potential in walkable urban places.

The directness and clarity of the pedestrian network in the transit walkshed has immediate relevance to the safety of transit passengers, and must be prioritized in ridership-oriented transit street design and planning. Good sidewalks save money, since disconnected walking networks can prevent efficient transit routing patterns or add to demand for expensive paratransit trips.

Bus stop at 2nd Ave. and Marion St., **SEATTLE, WA**

NETWORK

The transit walkshed—the distance people will walk to a transit stop—is not a fixed distance. Though the quarter-to-half-mile transit walkshed is often cited, riders will walk farther in a comfortable walking environment or if doing so reduces trip time, eliminates transfers, or reaches more reliable and rapid service.

Access to transit is improved with direct pedestrian paths of travel that provide the shortest distance to transit stops for the largest number of potential riders. Short block lengths and a high density of intersections will maximize the area reachable on foot in a reasonable length of time.

Design intersections with short crossing distances using curb extensions, boarding bulbs and boarding islands, refuge islands, and pedestrian plazas where applicable. Short signal cycles favor pedestrians and transit, enabling frequent and convenient crossings. Interim treatments, described in depth in the *Urban Street Design Guide*, should be used to regularize and shorten crossings when capital improvements are not immediately available.

Safe pedestrian crossings should be provided at all transit stops, including mid-block stops, unless the distance to the next crossing is short, typically 100 feet or less. Where block length is longer than the distance between stops, as on some transit corridors, boulevards, and conventional arterial streets, controlled mid-block crossings must be provided at mid-block stops to provide basic passenger safety. Locally used signal warrants should not be used to prevent the provision of these crossings. Pedestrian crossings on transit streets should be signalized or stop-controlled unless shared street design, raised crossings, or other design elements result in very low speeds, generally 10 mph or lower.

Avoid forced crossings. Incomplete intersections that require pedestrians to cross multiple legs to continue in a straight line are a source of pedestrian delay, and can raise pedestrian crash rates.

The movement of transit passengers is as important in the design of transit stations as the movement of transit vehicles. Within and around a transit stop, pedestrians should be able to travel in direct paths whenever possible, and safety measures should be designed so that the station remains a welcoming environment.

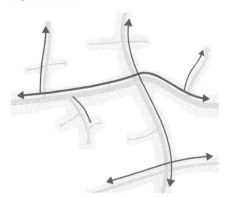
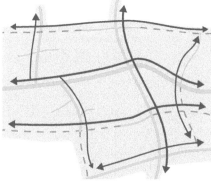

Well-connected street networks with frequent intersections cut travel times and distances, and allow people to access more places in the same amount of time.

COMPLETENESS

Continuous sidewalks connected by legal and safe pedestrian crossings must be provided on both sides of urban streets with transit service. Where few pedestrians are present, pedestrians and bicyclists may be accommodated on shared-use paths on one or both sides of a street. Gaps in the pedestrian network and other substandard conditions force pedestrians to walk unsafely and severely limit the attractiveness of transit as a mode by indicating that pedestrians should not be present on a street.

Transit-served streets without existing pedestrian facilities should be prioritized for sidewalk construction to provide a connected pedestrian network and avoid forcing transit riders and other pedestrians to walk in motor vehicle traffic. Where sidewalks cannot be constructed on a reasonable schedule, fill gaps in sidewalk coverage by providing interim sidewalks at the grade of the street, using vertical separation elements, edge markings, and pavement color and/or texture. Where interim sidewalks meet a crosswalk, provide detectable warning strips.

Where sidewalks cannot be provided, as in extremely constrained rights-of-way, streets should be regulated as shared spaces. Target speeds of 10 mph or less should be used in most such cases, using all geometric measures necessary to reduce traffic speeds.

On transit streets, alleys and driveways should cross the sidewalk at sidewalk-grade. Place detectable warning strips at the sides of major driveways across the sidewalk.

Stop- and signal-controlled intersections may also feature raised crossings along the transit street sidewalk.

DESIGN

The walking zone, or width of sidewalk that is dedicated to walking (uninterrupted by vegetation, utilities, or furniture), must be at minimum 4 feet wide to accommodate a wheelchair, and should be at least 6 feet wide on all urban streets. On most transit streets, a 10–12 feet pedestrian clear path is desirable and can be achieved using 20-feet wide sidewalks from building line to curb. Downtown locations may benefit from wider sidewalks.

Transit shelters and other stop elements must not interfere with pedestrian through paths (see page 93).

LEGIBILITY

The transit stop is the gateway to the neighborhood, and can include maps and directional signage to key destinations. Cities and transit operators should collaborate with civic groups, BIDs, and local stakeholders to coordinate pedestrian wayfinding and corridor branding. Provide wayfinding beyond the stop location, allowing transit riders to find destinations on other streets and guiding pedestrians to the transit stop.

HUMAN ENVIRONMENT

Sidewalks are a human environment. Transit relies on pedestrian networks that are hospitable in normally occurring conditions, allowing people to walk to their destinations and to assume that walking conditions will be safe and comfortable. Sidewalks that provide people with a place to walk at a distance from large vehicles, with shade in hot weather, opportunities for shelter from rain, and places to sit, can support longer walks to transit and attract a larger number of transit riders.

Human-scale lighting should be provided on sidewalks. Desired light levels should be established and met to ensure that sidewalks are usable and safe at night throughout the walkshed of transit stops and along all streets that can be used for through pedestrian travel.

Street trees and planting strips enhance the pedestrian experience and promote satisfaction with transit service (see page 104). Place vegetation between vehicle and pedestrian travel paths.

Building facades with active ground floors enhance both real and perceived street safety, and should be required in redevelopment on most transit streets. Active ground floors include both retail and residential uses that open onto the street.

Use transit stops to expand the range of pedestrian travel, with seating and shelters.

Active ground floors activate the sidewalk, **SEATTLE, WA**

Bicycle Access & Networks

Bicycle and transit riders are often the same people on different trips. Riders switch modes depending on the length, destination, and purpose of their trip, who they are traveling with, and where else they might go. Bike and transit systems can be planned as complementary modes that add more value together than apart.

Bicycle networks extend the reach of transit, providing an easy way for many transit riders to make first- and last-mile connections. Integrating bike share and personally owned bicycles with transit is a key step in creating an urban mobility system that covers the entire city or urban area.

Orange Line BRT bus with bike rack, **LOS ANGELES, CA**

COMPLEMENTARY NETWORKS

Not all transit streets will attract high bicycle volumes or provide a high-comfort bike facility. In some cases, such as high-volume transit streets without a general traffic lane, it may be impossible to safely accommodate bicycles even for local access. In these cases, high-comfort bicycle routes should be provided on nearby parallel streets, generally no more than 300–400 feet away, with special attention paid to bike parking and wayfinding.

Providing for safe bicycle operations at low speeds is an acceptable design strategy on streets where it is not physically possible to provide dedicated, high-comfort bike facilities.

Where bikeways run parallel to a transit street without dedicated bike facilities, provide wayfinding to major destinations that minimizes bike travel on the transit street. Provide on-street bike parking at intersections of the transit street to conveniently accommodate bicyclists accessing destinations on the transit street.

BICYCLE ACCESS TO TRANSIT

Nearby or parallel high-quality transit and bicycle facilities are mutually supportive, enhancing one another's effectiveness. Where it is not possible to install high-comfort bikeways on a transit street, provide a high-comfort bicycle route on a nearby parallel street.

Bikeways should be provided on transit streets in a manner consistent with local bicycle planning priorities and policies. On one-way streets and large two-way streets, numerous opportunities exist to provide a high level of comfort to both modes (see Ch. 2: *Transit Streets*, page 17).

On streets with bus and general traffic lanes but no dedicated bikeway, consider using bus-bike lanes (see page 122). These design strategies acknowledge that bicycle travel demand is present on every street, and that bus facilities are particularly attractive to bicyclists.

Bicycle wayfinding signage should be used to guide bicyclists to transit stops, especially for rapid services and other transit lines with significance for long trips.

Secure bike parking and bike share provide a large number of passengers with bike-to-transit access, and allow the use of bikes at both ends of a transit trip without carrying the bike on transit. Bicycle parking should be provided near transit stops and stations (see page 105).

Bike share stations can be co-located with transit stops to form mobility hubs. Unless directly adjacent to a transit stop or platform exit, the location of a bike share station should be noted on wayfinding signage at the stop or station (see page 105).

BIKES ON TRANSIT

Transit vehicles can carry bicycles inside or outside the vehicle. Articulated low-floor buses, streetcars, and light rail vehicles can all accommodate interior bicycle access, ideally through a center door with large interior clear areas. Racks can be designed to hold bikes in either an upright or a hanging position; not all passengers and not all bikes can use racks that require lifting. Peak-period transit ridership can complicate interior bicycle access due to space constraints.

Front-end exterior racks with capacity for two to three bicycles, or upright or hanging rear racks, are a common bus feature. Exterior rack loading time adds to stop dwell time, sometimes significantly. Loading a bicycle onto an exterior rack takes 20–30 seconds.[5]

Accessing an exterior bike rack may present challenges for passengers, depending on curb height. For near-level or level boarding, platforms should be 5 feet longer to permit front-end bike racks. Where exterior bike racks are used with high platforms, identify how passengers can step to or from street level with a bicycle.

Where bike volumes are high, it is difficult to accommodate them on transit vehicles. In these cases, bike parking at origin stations and bike share at destination stations is the best alternative.

Bike on hanging bike hook inside a LRV, **PORTLAND, OR**

Bike cage with specialized turnstiles for increased security, **BOULDER, CO**

System Wayfinding & Brand

Clear branding and route legibility are critical features of an easy-to-use transit system. A strong, unified brand makes a transit system look like just that: a system to get everywhere you need to go. Predictable, incremental wayfinding and brand identification guides riders through the entire trip.

A shelter branded for rapid service, with system map. **SAN FRANCISCO, CA**

APPLICATION

Use wayfinding signage to guide riders to the transit stop, especially where stops for opposing travel directions of the same route are not located immediately nearby each other, as on one-way street pairs.

At popular transit destinations such as shopping areas, civic centers, inter-city rail stations, airports, and entertainment venues, clear signage helps riders easily find stops.

BENEFITS

At busy transfer nodes, wayfinding guides riders promptly to connecting routes.

Information and wayfinding features located away from transit stops help riders choose between travel options in advance, and then find the right stop depending on the travel option chosen.

Strong branding reinforces user confidence by displaying a recognizable and unified identity. The transit station often serves as a recognizable landmark with strong neighborhood identity.

Information alerting riders about nearby, transit-accessible destinations at stops allows passengers to make more informed decisions about travel options.

Distinction between types of service, such as local and rapid, can be highlighted through distinctive branding of stops.

CONSIDERATIONS

Simple network structures and rider procedures are inherently easier to understand and may require less instruction.

RECOMMENDED

Wayfinding elements should be clearly placed at regular intervals, especially at confusing areas and at decision points, where potential riders choose a transit route and travel path to access transit.

Name stops, stations, and destinations to reinforce brand and recognizability. At locations with multiple lines or stops, name all the stops for a geographic element and provide platform letters or numbers to distinguish boarding areas.

Place wayfinding in visible and predictable locations, such as overhead or at eye-level.

Wayfinding should show both the number/name of a route and its direction/destinations.

Distinctions among frequency are more useful to passengers than distinctions among modes. On maps, provide distinct thicker lines or bolder colors for frequent services. Match color, icons, and names across the system.

All wayfinding signage and materials should be consistent with regional or agency brand; using consistent logos, colors, and fonts reinforces visibility and identity.

Include tactile or audible cues, providing directional guidance at decision points and signs confirming the route taken, especially in confusing or difficult-to-navigate areas.

For station-area destinations, indicate direction and travel times in easily understood units, such as blocks or approximate walking time.

Halsted Street, **CHICAGO, IL**

Performance Measures

Making the case for transit streets involves choosing measurements that accurately reflect both the benefits and costs of a project, including those relevant to decision makers and to local stakeholders. This element of the street design process may differ greatly from metrics internal to either a transit operating agency or a streets department.

Beyond measures of movement, the safety, comfort, public space value, and spatial efficiency of a street are all important for understanding whether a transit street supports goals related to the people, neighborhood and city it is designed for.

Measure the Whole Street

When the highest-capacity mode on a street can keep moving, transit riders aren't the only beneficiaries. Evaluating a transit street project involves comprehensively measuring how well the street works as a transportation corridor, but also how it works as a public place and as an investment.

Transit operating agencies and street transportation departments have internal metrics used for understanding capacity and quality of service for each mode, with metrics being particularly well developed for transit service. This section discusses street measurements at the corridor and network level.

There are many additional goals that may be relevant to a project, including local and citywide environmental or mode shift goals. Cities should apply performance measures that relate to their specific policy goals, and provide feedback to project and program management based on these goals.

MOBILITY AND ACCESS

Measure how well a transit street moves people, goods, and services, considering capacity, volume, travel time, and reliability. Set multiple time periods for evaluation, such as full weekdays, weekends, and typical peak periods. Peak periods generally span several hours. Evaluating for peak 15-minute periods may lead to results prejudicial to all-day operation.

Counting People

Total person movement and total person capacity are primary performance measures for transit streets that encompass the current and long-term potential of a street to serve the city.

Count transit riders, people in private motor vehicles, people walking, and people riding bicycles. Use automated counts when available for walking, bicycling, and motor vehicle traffic, combined with short manual samples of vehicle occupancy to assess total person movement. Automatic passenger counters (APCs) precisely track ridership numbers and characteristics. Measuring ridership and boardings through specific segments and corridors enables highly localized analysis of transit performance.

Use average person capacity per lane to understand the effects of a design and the number of people moved per lane, at peak times and all day, as a performance measure for motorized modes. This measure is significantly more accurate than using vehicle capacity, vehicle delay, or vehicle traffic volume alone.

Market St., **SAN FRANCISCO, CA**

Transit Travel Time

Planned trip time combines average travel time and variation to generate a single number, such as the 50th or 85th percentile travel time, reflecting a typical traveler's experience of the mobility system. Comparing these numbers across modes for a trip along the street, or for a set of trips around the network, helps evaluate the real time saved by transit street design changes. Pedestrian travel time which is affected by the completeness of the pedestrian network and by signal timing and the distance between crossings, should be added to provide a more accurate view of total travel time.

At the network level, the planned travel time can be used to evaluate the effects of a transit street project on the performance of the system as a whole. When applied to the entire city or region in relation to demographic and employment location data, planners can evaluate the number of jobs, businesses, or other neighborhoods accessible by transit within a target travel time. The equity of the transportation system can be evaluated using this method, by comparing the level of access provided to each neighborhood.

Across modes, delay compared with free-flow movement is important for understanding the potential value of various transit priority treatments, but is less meaningful when considering personal mobility. Use delay and queuing to inform intersection-specific design treatments, such as the size of pedestrian refuge areas or upstream traffic signal management. Changes to vehicle queue length at key intersections may be relevant to the perception of a project's impacts, and should be understood in the context of overall street operations and impacts on cross streets.

Access to the City

A primary metric for evaluating the effectiveness of a transportation system is the number of destinations—rather than the physical territory or distance—reachable by residents in set amounts of time. Applying this measure to the transit-walking system creates a master effectiveness metric that can be applied to evaluate potential large transit investments or changes in transit network structure.[1]

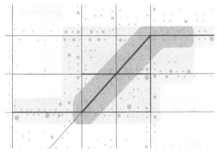

Mapping destination access

Private Motor Vehicles

In measuring results for general motor vehicle traffic, travel time and variation in travel time are often more relevant to drivers than common measures like vehicle delay and vehicular Level of Service. As for transit riders, change in the 85th percentile travel time is a useful measure for understanding results for typical users. Crowd-sourced and fleet-sourced traffic speed datasets can provide a network-level view of these changes over time. These include fleet GPS data, toll pass reader data, and data from companies that provide mobile map software or cellular phone service.

Motor vehicle traffic is often perceived to be negatively impacted by transit, but motor vehicle drivers may directly benefit from specific street design treatments, and receive indirect benefits from transit projects at the network level. Motor vehicle travel times may decrease if transit vehicle movements are simplified, or if designated transit lanes clear double-parking and vehicles queuing to turn from a former mixed-traffic lane.[2]

Measuring vehicle traffic volume (throughput) before and after project implementation can provide information about mode shifts and spatial or temporal diversion, when network-level traffic data is available. As development occurs along a transit corridor, quantifying the total number of people using the street demonstrates the total value of the places along the street, and is a relevant measure for understanding the new destinations available to motorists in a given travel time.

Consider network-level evaluation for transit street elements that are expected to lengthen a street's travel time for private vehicles, but may add significant transit capacity and eventually reduce vehicle trip demand. As mode shift occurs on the corridor, traffic volumes may decrease or remain constant.

At the city or region level, vehicle miles traveled and transit passenger miles traveled are key performance measures whose direction indicates whether a city is becoming more or less dependent on private vehicle travel. Commute mode split is an important and commonly used measure, and should be supplemented by measures of mode split for other trip types.

Curbside Management

Loading, parking, and curbside management are important regulatory facets of transit street project planning and evaluation. Transit street design treatments sometimes increase or decrease parking supply. Changes in on-street parking supply can be quantified by calculating the percentage change to the number of residential or commercial (metered) spaces available within a short walk of the transit corridor.

In cities, goods movement efficiencies are relevant for both travel time and loading. The number of illegally parked or double-parked trucks, or the time spent by a truck looking for a loading space, can be used to measure the effectiveness of curbside management for goods movement along a transit street.[3]

Measure the Whole Street *(continued)*

SAFETY

Comprehensive safety across modes can be measured along a street and compared with other streets. A comprehensive approach to injury prevention includes a focus on both fatal and life-altering injuries, and the potential for such injuries.

Multi-modal safety should be measured in terms of risk per distance of street (i.e. injuries per mile) or risk per user (i.e. injuries per million daily users). If total injuries are used as the numerator, separate motorized and active numbers should be calculated to avoid hiding the less frequent, but more severe, active-mode crashes. Alternatively, a measure of all-modes KSI (people killed or severely injured) per street mile or per million daily users provides a single measure of the risk that people bear when traveling on the street.

Since severe crashes are relatively rare events, it may be necessary to evaluate the safety of a street before statistically significant or reliable data is available on KSI crashes.

For faster analysis, changes in the top or 99th percentile vehicle speeds, or the percentage of vehicles operating above the target speed, may be used to understand the effectiveness of safety measures and changes in the risk of serious injury to transit occupants and pedestrians, soon after a project is implemented.

Conflict counts, which measure the number of evasive actions taken to avoid an imminent crash at a specific location, can be used in conjunction with other engineering assessment tools to understand the safety performance of a particular street redesign.

At the city or regional level, the number of transportation injuries, severe injuries, and deaths; and injury rates per capita are primary safety performance metrics. The safety performance of transit vehicles and systems can be measured in injuries or crashes per revenue mile or injuries per passenger mile traveled. However, since limiting or reducing the total miles of vehicle travel in a region is a major motivation for transit investments, evaluations of multi-modal safety should avoid denominating by distance traveled.[4]

Safety can be evaluated at an operational level more quickly than crash data analysis permits, allowing potentially life-saving changes. 95th percentile vehicle travel speed and the percent of vehicles exceeding the speed limit or exceeding the street's target speed can be used to evaluate the effectiveness or consistency of traffic operational measures on the street. Measures of conflicts per day between motor vehicles and pedestrians or bicyclists can be used to quickly assess whether specific safety issues have been addressed by a design treatment.

PUBLIC SPACE & SOCIAL LIFE

The amount of space available for stationary activities, including social, civic, and market activities, is an important component of a transit street's potential benefits. Measure the acreage or width of sidewalk space and other public space made available as a result of a transit project.

The quality of public space is a leading indicator for both transit and business potential. Public space canvassing, which counts the number of people engaged in stationary activity in a place, is a measure of public space quality and availability. For projects with a public space component, this measure provides hard data to support quality-of-life conclusions. Supplement these observational counts with survey data on public space quality and project satisfaction for a more comprehensive understanding of the experiential quality of a public space.

Sidewalk comfort and safety can be quantified using measures relevant to human comfort, including the availability of shade, adequate street lighting, and active ground floor uses. Develop measures specific to the project, climate, and social life of the street.

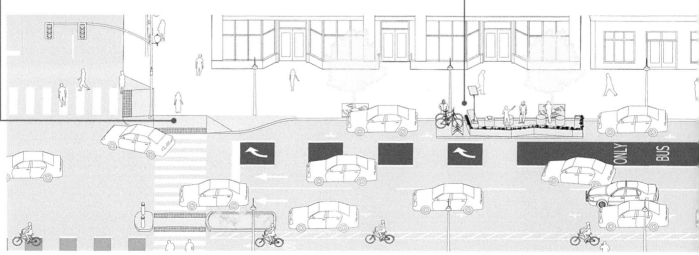

HEALTH, SUSTAINABILITY, & ENVIRONMENT

When transit performs at a high level, it competes with automobile travel rather than with walking. Changes in vehicle mode travel have very important impacts on public health and environmental sustainability that relate to the policy landscape of transit. Many cities have adopted sustainability goals that include greenhouse gas emissions reductions, and many have regulatory obligations related to local air quality.

Physical activity related to added or improved transit can be measured in daily time spent being active or distance walked or biked. Increases in physical activity may be correlated with changes to the built environment that increase transit ridership, such as increased density or walkability.

Increasing transit mode share on a street can dramatically improve the street's air quality, with benefits for public health and sustainability. Air quality can be measured and compared across modes as emissions per occupant mile, with greenhouse emissions and particulate emissions singled out as areas of special concern.[5]

Surface permeability ratio, pavement reflectivity, and surface air temperature are affected by the amount of paved area, and the type and color of material used.

ECONOMIC PRODUCTIVITY

Transit street productivity can be measured in terms of business, residential, and institutional benefits. Capital investment is an important measure for large transit-oriented development projects, but may miss the value added to existing buildings when transit access improves.

Business Sales

Local business sales can be measured using sales tax receipts and related data. This is a good short- or medium-term measure that is more accurate and faster than using real estate sales, and may be more readily available than commercial lease data. In New York City, a study performed using this measure found that corridors and major intersections with bus improvements experienced retail sales growth of 50% to 71%, against a baseline of 18–22% for their borough (county) as a whole.[6] Storefront occupancy is another medium-term measure for retail streets, with easy data collection and methodology.[7]

Development and Redevelopment

Development density and new local development, in square footage or dollar investment, are long-term measures of economic and land use benefits of transit projects, especially for projects involving rezoning or redevelopment. The Healthline BRT in Cleveland, Metroway BRT in Alexandria and Arlington, VA, Phoenix light rail, Portland streetcar, and Charlotte LYNX light rail are all examples of projects with large local development results associated with a transit project and other coordinated investments.[8]

Cost Savings from Transit Productivity

Transit service quality and efficiency are related, with time savings directly related to cost savings. Faster travel time means maintaining the same frequency of service with fewer transit vehicles in circulation on the route, freeing resources for other routes. Increased frequency and shorter wait times, or operating cost savings, can be quantified by transit providers to inform the public discussion, especially related to infrastructure investments.

City governments also benefit from transit street investments, most directly from additional property, sales, or other taxes per acre. Evaluating these returns on public investment in comparison with a business-as-usual development scenario shows specific value to the public.

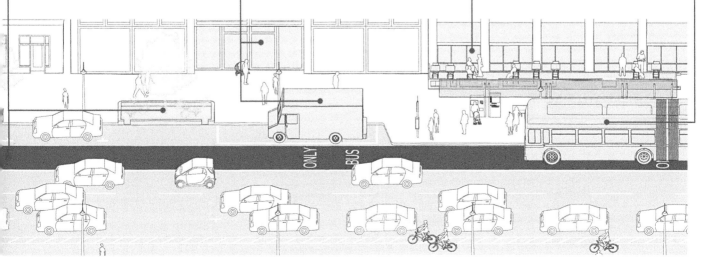

8. Resources

AASHTO	American Association of State Highway Transportation Officials
ADAAG	Americans with Disabilities Act Accessibility Guidelines
APBP	Association of Pedestrian and Bicycle Professionals
APTA	American Public Transportation Assocation
ADA	Americans with Disabilities Act (1990)
ADA Std.	ADA Standards for Accessible Design
BRT	Bus rapid transit
CFR	Code of Federal Regulations
FHWA	Federal Highway Administration
FTA	Federal Transit Administration
ITE	Institute of Transportation Engineers
LRT	Light rail transit
LRV	Light rail vehicle
MUTCD	Manual on Uniform Traffic Control Devices
NACTO	National Association of City Transportation Officials
PoP	Proof-of-Payment
PROWAG	Public Right-of-Way Accessibility Guidelines
RFID	Radio Frequency Identification
ROW	Right of way
TCQSM	Transit Capacity and Quality of Service Manual (a publication of the Transportation Research Board)
TRB	Transportation Research Board

Bus

A single-unit or articulated pneumatic-tire on-street transit vehicle, regardless of running way or service pattern.

Bus Rapid Transit (BRT)

BRT refers to a high-quality, high-capacity line with frequent service, widely spaced stops, multi-door level or near-level boarding, and either dedicated space or signal treatments to remove most traffic-related sources of delay.

Bus Rapid Transit, Closed

Closed BRT lines, like those in Curitiba, Bogota, and Mexico City, feature specialized bus vehicles using dedicated infrastructure. These systems often use center-running transitways and high-floor left-boarding buses, achieving level boarding at all doors and very short dwell times per passenger. These services are sometimes independent of the rest of the transit system.

Bus Rapid Transit, Open

Open BRT lines can operate both on dedicated transitways and on streets in mixed traffic. Transitways designed for open BRT often use right-door boarding, so that other bus services can share the facility. Near-level boarding is more common than level boarding. Some BRT systems have buses with both left and right doors, allowing BRT vehicles to operate both in a specialized transitway and on the right. Like streetcars and light rail, these systems can operate in mixed traffic or in pedestrian-priority settings.

Control Vehicle

A large but infrequent user of a particular street, such as a truck or bus on neighborhood streets. On smaller streets, control vehicles are expected to slowly and cautiously negotiate with other street users. The control vehicle dictates how street design might accommodate a larger vehicle's needs, for example by using the whole intersection or multiple lanes to complete a turn.

Critical, Recommended, & Optional

Within guidance sections, the words **Critical**, **Recommended**, and **Optional** have a technical meaning defined in the *About the Guide* section. **Critical** is paired with the verbs "must" and "shall." **Recommended** uses the term "should," and **Optional** uses the terms "may" and "can." "May" and "can" may appear in "critical" only when if-then statements are used when discussing a particular treatment.

Design Vehicle

A frequent user of a given street which dictates the minimum required turning radius.

Light Rail and Light Rail Vehicle (LRV)

A multi-unit rail transit vehicle designed to operate on either separate rights-of-way or on-street transitways, regardless of service pattern.

Protected Bike Lane, or Parking-Protected Bike Lane

The protected bike lane is a physically separated bicycle facility which is constructed within the road bed, and runs at the same grade as motor vehicle traffic. It can be separated from general travel lanes with a combination of pavement markings and vertical barriers such as on-street parking, flexible bollards, planters, or hard curbs.

Raised Cycle Track

Bikeways in the right-of-way that are provided above the street grade, whether at sidewalk level or between sidewalk and street level, are referred to as raised cycle tracks. Refer to the *Urban Bikeway Design Guide* for detailed guidance.

Rapid Service

Buses and streetcars with widely spaced stops, all-door boarding, or other systemic improvements but no dedicated space are referred to as Rapid service in this guide.

Retroreflective

Materials that are retroreflective have been designed so that when light is shined on them, they reflect light back in the direction of the light source. Retroreflective materials are applied to increase the conspicuity of road design elements, including bollards, signs, and markings.

Streetcar

A single-unit or articulated single-unit rail transit vehicle designed to operate on streets, in either mixed traffic, dedicated lanes, or a separated on-street transitway, regardless of service pattern.

Transit Signal Priority (TSP)

Transit Signal Priority, also referred to as "Active Transit Signal Priority" or "TSP," refers to signalization strategies where the existing signal cycle pattern is changed only when transit vehicles are present and based on actuation.

Notes

1. Introduction

1   Leinberger, Christopher B., and Patrick Lynch. Foot Traffic Ahead. Report. June 2014. Accessed 2016. http://www.smartgrowthamerica.org/documents/foot-traffic-ahead.pdf.

National Association of Realtors. 2015 Community Preference Survey. Report. June 2015. Accessed January 2016. http://www.realtor.org/reports/nar-2015-community-preference-survey.

MAKING THE CASE FOR TRANSIT

2   Per billion passenger miles traveled, bus and urban rail have by far the lower fatality rates of any travel mode, 0.11 and 0.24 respectively. 7.28 persons were killed per vehicle passenger mile, per the same 2000–2009 dataset.

Litman, Todd. A New Transit Safety Narrative. Journal of Public Transportation 17(4), National Center for Transit Research, Tampa, FL: 2015.

3   Oak Ridge National Laboratory. Transportation Energy Data Book, edition 34, "Chapter 8: Household Vehicles and Characteristics." US Department of Energy, Washington, DC: 2015.

4   A reasonable planning-level capacity for a dedicated transit lane is 80 buses per hour; assuming 100 riders per vehicle (a comfortable articulated bus capacity), 8,000 riders per hour can be moved through a single transit lane. At two-minute headways (or 30 buses per hour), a standard 40-foot bus, assuming 60 passengers, moves 1,800 passengers per hour.

High-capacity LRVs, running four cars per train with a capacity of 125 riders, have a capacity of 15,000 passengers per hour.

Ryus, Paul (PI), Alan Danaher, Mark Walker, Foster Nichols, William Carter, Elizabeth Ellis, and Anthony Bruzzone. "Ch 6, Bus Transit Capacity." Transit Capacity and Quality of Service Manual, Third Edition. TCRP Report 165, Transportation Research Board, Washington, DC: 2013.

RTD FasTracks. Streetcar and Light Rail Streetcar and Light Rail Characteristics. Regional Transportation District, Denver, CO: 2012.

5   60 people per meter per minute, allowing 1.5 sq. meters per pedestrian and a 75 meter per minute walking speed.

Ryus, Paul (PI), Alan Danaher, Mark Walker, Foster Nichols, William Carter, Elizabeth Ellis, and Anthony Bruzzone. "Ch 6, Bus Transit Capacity." Transit Capacity and Quality of Service Manual, Third Edition. TCRP Report 165, Transportation Research Board, Washington, DC: 2013.

Zhou et al. measured 2,500 bikes per meter per hour on cycle tracks in downtown Hangzhou.

Dan Zhou, Cheng Xu, Dian-Hai Wang, and Sheng Jin. Estimating Capacity of Bicycle Path on Urban Roads in Hangzhou, China. Submitted to the 94th Annual Meeting of the Transportation Research Board, Washington, DC: 2014.

6   James G. Strathman, Thomas J. Kimpel, and Steve Callas. Headway Deviation Effects on Bus Passenger Loads: Analysis of Tri-Met's Archived AVL-APC Data. Transportation Northwest Regional Center 10, University of Washington, Seattle, WA: 2003.

7   The TCQSM defines dwell time as the time spent serving passenger movements and the time spent opening and closing the bus doors. Everything else that causes a bus to sit at the curb is delay.

Ryus, Paul (PI), Alan Danaher, Mark Walker, Foster Nichols, William Carter, Elizabeth Ellis, and Anthony Bruzzone. "Ch 6, Bus Transit Capacity." Transit Capacity and Quality of Service Manual, Third Edition. TCRP Report 165, Transportation Research Board, Washington, DC: 2013.

8   A study of development investment around transit stations found significant returns from bus rapid transit especially, due to its relatively lower cost to implement. Cleveland's HealthLine BRT and Portland's MAX Blue Line LRT leveraged the most overall TOD investment of corridors studied—$5.8 billion and $6.6 billion, respectively, though the Cleveland BRT leveraged approximately 31 times more TOD investment per dollar spent on transit than Portland's MAX Blue Line LRT due to project cost.

Hook, Walter, Stephanie Lotshaw, and Annie Weinstock. More Development for Your Transit Dollar: An Analysis of 21 north American Transit Corridors. Insitution for Transportation & Development Policy, New York, NY: 2013.

9   Table of "Deterrent Effect of Various Kinds of Travel Time," Exhibit 4-5.

Ryus, Paul (PI), Alan Danaher, Mark Walker, Foster Nichols, William Carter, Elizabeth Ellis, and Anthony Bruzzone. "Ch 6, Bus Transit Capacity." Transit Capacity and Quality of Service Manual, Third Edition. TCRP Report 165, Transportation Research Board, Washington, DC: 2013.

2. Transit Streets

TRANSIT STREETS

1   Repurposing street space for transit can have a strong safety impact as well—research from around the world has demonstrated that rededicating lanes for exclusive transit use can reduce crashes 12–15%; other transit priority designs have reduced crashes more than 60%.

Duduta, Nicolae, Claudia Adriazola-Steil, Carsten Wass, Dario Hidalgo, Luis Antonio Lindau, and Vineet Sam John. *Traffic Safety on Bus Priority Systems: Recommendations for integrating safety into the planning, design, and operation of major bus routes.* The WRI Ross Center for Sustainable Cities, Washington, DC: 2015.

2   Bus lanes on a major street, coupled with all-door boarding and spot improvements at three intersections, improved corridor transit travel times on average 19-23%, with negligible impact to vehicle traffic.

Beaton, Eric B, Evan Bialostozky, Patrick Dougherty, Taylor Reiss Gouge, and Theodore V Orosz,. *Designing the Modern Multi-Modal Urban Arterial: A Case Study of the Webster Avenue Bus Rapid Transit Project.* Paper presented at the Transportation Research Board 93rd Annual Meeting, Washington, DC: 2014.

3   Factors like presence of bicycle and pedestrian facilities, mixed land uses, and transit stop amenities have all shown significant positive correlations with transit ridership. However, the most significant indicator to ridership is transit level of service—transit frequency, transit alternatives, and route density—at a given stop location.

Dill, Jennifer, Marc Schlossberg, Liang Ma, and Cody Meyer. *Predicting Transit Ridership At The Stop Level: The Role Of Service And Urban Form.* Submitted to the 92nd Annual Meeting of the Transportation Research Board, Washington, DC: 2013.

4   Multi-modal users may compose a larger share of transit riders in the Neighborhood context; quality pedestrian and bicycle infrastructure enhances access and capacity, as transit service is less intense than in Downtown contexts.

Coffell, Kathryn, et al. *Guidelines for Providing Access to Public Transportation Stations.* TCRP Report 153, Transportation Research Board, Washington, DC: 2012.

5   *Evaluation of Lane Reduction "Road Diet" Measures and Their Effects on Crashes and Injuries.* Highway Safety Information System, Federal Highway Administration, Washington, DC: 2010.

Stamatiadis, Nikiforos, and Adam Kirk, *Guidelines for Road Diet Conversions.* University of Kentucky, Lexington, KY: 2012.

6   Examples of higher standards for sidewalks include downtown Washington, DC (16 feet + 6-foot buffer), Chicago (varies, 10–12 feet depending upon context), San Francisco (9–17 feet depending upon context), and Boston (varies based on context, but minimum is 7 feet in downtown street types).

Design & Engineering Manual. District Department of Transportation, Washington, DC: 2009.

Boston Complete Streets Design Guide. Boston Transportation Department, Boston, MA: 2013.

STREET TRANSFORMATIONS

1   Speed cushions have less of an impact calming traffic speeds compared to speed humps, but research has found that bus drivers experience less stress and experience minimal (if any) delay crossing over.

Johnson, LaToya and AJ Nedzesky. *A Comparative Study of Speed Humps, Speed Slots and Speed Cushions.* ITE Annual Meeting, Washington, DC: 2004.

2   A pilot smart parking program in San Francisco found that dynamic pricing reduced average search times by 43%, and doubled the frequency with which blocks met their parking occupancy targets. Additionally, traffic speed improved on piloted corridors, and VMT decreased daily.

SFMTA. *SFPark Pilot Project Evaluation.* San Francisco Municipal Transportation Agency report: June 2014.

3   Harmful ultra-fine particles contained in vehicle exhaust have been shown to dissipate as distance from traffic increases—cycle tracks and sidewalks located opposite parking are exposed to 20-40% less micro-particles than traffic-adjacent facilities.

Kendrick, Christine, Adam Moore, Ashley Haire, Alexander Bigazzi, Miguel Figliozzi, Christopher Monsere, and Linda George. *The impact of bicycle lane characteristics on bicyclists' exposure to traffic-related particulate matter.* 90th Annual Meeting of the Transportation Research Board, Washington, DC: 2010.

4   Transit-Only Lane Enforcement using vehicle-mounted video cameras in San Francisco has been cited for reducing transit delays along Geary Boulevard 3–7%, and 15–20% on the 2-Clement and 3-Jackson bus routes.

San Francisco Municipal Transportation Agency. *Transit-Only Lane Enforcement.* MuniForward white paper, 2015.

5   In Melbourne, Australia, trams operate on the Bourke Street and Swanston Street corridors with average peak hour frequencies ranging from 50 to 75 trains per hour.

Robinson, Geoff. "Swanston Street North Proposed Tram Platforms." Presented to Future Melbourne Committee, Apr. 5, 2011.

6   On the Macrobús BRT corridor in Guadalajara, introduction of the central median has been credited with reducing injury crashes 35%. Each additional meter shortened from pedestrian crossings was found to decrease pedestrian crashes 6%.

Duduta, Nicolae, Claudia Adriazola-Steil, Carsten Wass, Dario Hidalgo, Luis Antonio Lindau, and Vineet Sam John. *Traffic Safety on Bus Priority Systems: Recommendations for integrating safety into the planning, design, and operation of major bus routes*. The WRI Ross Center for Sustainable Cities, Washington, DC: 2015.

7   Portland utilizes a quarter-cycle offset signal timing pattern, which offsets signal timings throughout a relatively consistent downtown street grid. Signal progression is determined by block lengths, resulting in a low-speed progression of 12–16 mph that benefits bicyclists and transit riders. Simultaneously, the timing creates a "reverse progression" for pedestrians walking 4 mph.

Koonce, Peter, Lee Rodegerdts, Kevin Lee, Shaun Quayle, Scott Beaird, Cade Braud, Jim Bonneson, Phil Tarnoff, and Tom Urbanik. *Traffic Signal Timing Manual*: Ch. 6, Coordination. Federal Highway Administration, US Department of Transportation, Washington, DC: 2008.

8   If a bus becomes disabled in the contraflow lane, it may be helpful to provide additional space for other buses to pass, as entering the opposing traffic direction is not desired.

Ryus, Paul, Kelly Laustsen, Kelly Blume, Tom Urbanik, and Scott Beaird. *Improving Transportation Network Efficiency Through Implementation of Transit-Supportive Roadway Strategies*. TCRP A-39, Transportation Research Board, Washington, DC: 2015.

3. Stations & Stops

STOP DESIGN FACTORS

1   Far-side placement confers benefits especially at complex intersections, heavy turn volumes, and where the bus turns.

Baldwin, Ben, Heather Boll, Alan Lehto, Jessica Tump, and Young Park. *Bus Stops Guidelines*. TriMet, Portland, OR: 2010.

2   Assuming buses require a 7-second critical gap to remerge, each 100 vehicles per hour in the adjacent travel lane adds roughly a second of delay—100 vph adds 1 second of delay, 500 vph adds 4 seconds, and 1,000vph adds roughly 12 seconds of delay on remerge. The TCQSM also assumes a pull-in maneuver requires 3.3 seconds, equating to more than 15 seconds of additional dwell time on a street with 1,000 vph where the bus is required to pull-out to stop.

Ryus, Paul (PI), Alan Danaher, Mark Walker, Foster Nichols, William Carter, Elizabeth Ellis, and Anthony Bruzzone. "Ch 6, Bus Transit Capacity." *Transit Capacity and Quality of Service Manual, Third Edition*. TCRP Report 165, Transportation Research Board, Washington, DC: 2013.

3   If a large number of vehicles turn behind the stopped transit vehicle at a far-side location, they will likely block the intersection, resulting in traffic congestion and delay.

"Ch 7, Station, Stop, and Terminal Capacity." *Transit Capacity and Quality of Service Manual, Third Edition*. TCRP Report 165, Transportation Research Board, Washington, DC: 2013.

4   Additionally, in constrained situations, buses may also be compelled to pull in so that the front and back of the bus overhang the sidewalk on entry and exit, creating a hazard for pedestrians.

Transport for London. *Accessible bus stop design guidance*. Bus Priority Team technical advice note BP1/06, Transport for London, UK: 2006.

5   Traffic modeling was used to demonstrate that moving a stop from near- to far-side alone changed travel times more than 4%; implementing with TSP and a queue bypass lane further amplified travel time reductions with the far-side configuration.

Bugg, Zachary, Jon Crisafi, Kevin Lee, Tom Urbanik, and Paul Ryus. *Effect of Transit Preferential Treatments on Vehicle Travel Time*. Kittelson & Associates, Inc. *ITE Mid-Colonial District Annual Meeting*: 2015.

6   Near-side stops may facilitate destination access, boarding during red signal phases, and legible transfers in certain contexts, but generally favor vehicle traffic.

KFH Group. *Guidelines for the Design and Placement of Transit Stops*. Washington Metropolitan Area Transit Authority, Washington, DC: 2009.

7   Cities determine preferred stop length based on available right-of-way, target speed, and agency experience. These charts reflect a range that exists across different US cities.

    Transit Stops & Stations: Stop Spacing, Location, and Infrastructure. San Francisco Municipal Transportation Agency, San Francisco, CA: 2015.

    KFH Group. *Guidelines for the Design and Placement of Transit Stops*. Washington Metropolitan Area Transit Authority, Washington, DC: 2009.

    Delaware Valley Regional Planning Commission. *SEPTA Bus Stop Design Guidelines*. Philadelphia, PA: 2012.

8   Bulb and boarding island widths are usually constrained by available right-of-way to 6–10 feet, depending upon configuration, so additional rider capacity is dispersed along the bulb length. All-door boarding has also demonstrated effectiveness in distributing riders along platforms.

    Fitzpatrick, Kay, Kevin M Hall, Stephen Farnsworth, and Melisa D Finley. *Evaluation of Bus Bulbs*. TCRP Report 65, Transportation Research Board, Washington, DC: 2001.

9   5–10 feet between each queuing vehicle.

    Boyle, Daniel K. *Better On-Street Bus Stops*. TCRP Synthesis 117. Transportation Research Board, Washington, DC: 2015.

10 Bridge plates rising less than 3 inches require 1:4 max slope, or 12 inches of length for 3 inches of rise. For 3–6 inches of rise, 1:6 max slope is required, and 1:8 max slope is regulated for 6–9 inches, increasing the length required up to 72 inches for a 9-inch rise. Shorter rises allow more compact ramp deployment.

    "Part 38—Accessibility Specifications for Transportation Vehicles." *ADA Accessibility Specifications*. Federal Transit Adminstration, Washington, DC: 2007.

11 In Seattle buses were retrofitted with larger tires to reach a 14-inch level-boarding platform shared with light rail.

    Kantor, David, Gregg Moscoe, and Cliff Henke. *Issues and Technologies in Level Boarding Strategies for BRT*. Journal of Public Transportation, 2006 BRT Special Edition. Tampa, FL: 2006.

12 Handrails must be provided on any ramp rising greater than 6 inches, and ramps may not rise greater than 30 inches. For ramps to doors more than 30 inches above curb level, a landing and turn is required for each 30 inches of rise.

    "Ch. 405.8: Transportation Facilities." *2010 ADA Standards for Accessible Design*. US Access Board, United States Department of Justice, Washington, DC: 2010.

13 An absolute minimum 3 feet of clear continuous width must be provided per ADA Accessibility Guidance, though proposed US guidance suggests a 4-feet minimum continuous width.

    "403 Accessible Routes." *2010 ADA Standards for Accessible Design*. US Access Board, United States Department of Justice, Washington, DC: 2010.

    "R302.4, Technical Requirements." *Proposed Accessibility Guidelines for Pedestrian Facilities in the Public Right-of-Way*. US Access Board, Washington, DC: 2011.

14 36-inches is the absolute minimum required by ADA Standards (ADAAG §403), though a 48-inch minimum is proposed by PROWAG guidance (§R304.2).

    "403 Accessible Routes." *2010 ADA Standards for Accessible Design*. US Access Board, United States Department of Justice, Washington, DC: 2010.

    "R304.2, Technical Requirements." *Proposed Accessibility Guidelines for Pedestrian Facilities in the Public Right-of-Way*. US Access Board, Washington, DC: 2011.

15 "Proposed guidelines require detectable warning surfaces to be installed on newly constructed and altered curb ramps and blended transitions at pedestrian street crossings."

    "Detectable Warning Surfaces on Curb Ramps and Blended Transitions." *Regulatory Assessment of Proposed Accessibility Guidelines for Pedestrian Facilities in the Public Right-of-Way*. US Access Board, Washington, DC: 2011.

16 Although most ADA guidance pertaining to transit platforms refers specifically to rail, which requires a 24-inch wide detectable warning strip along the length of platform edges, cities have applied the same standards and design criteria to BRT platforms, especially where boarding height is greater than 6 inches above the roadbed.

    Parsons Transportation Group. *Van Ness Avenue Bus Rapid Transit: BRT Design Criteria*. Report for San Francisco County Transportation Authority, San Francisco, CA: 2008.

17 Detectable warning strip may be placed at curb's edge at the door zone of any bus stop to indicate boarding position.

    APTA. *Bus Stop Design and Placement Security Considerations*. American Public Transportation Association, Washington, DC: 2010.

18 *Boston Complete Streets Design Guide*. Boston Transportation Department: 2013.

STOP CONFIGURATION

1   A study in London found that passengers were able to board up to 50% faster per passenger from bulbs than from curbside pull-out stops.

Transport for London. *Accessible bus stop design guidance*. Bus Priority Team technical advice note BP1/06, Transport for London, UK: 2006.

2   In one application on San Francisco's Mission Street, bulbs expanded available queueing space at the stop 64%, and resulted in a 132% increase in space available to each pedestrian. Additionally, vehicle and bus speeds both increased 7-46% from previous bus bay operation. When bus bays were still in use, buses often did not pull completely from the traffic stream and still created delays. While buses making in-lane stops do delay traffic while dwelling, they require less time to pull back in, resulting in mutual benefits to vehicle and transit traffic.

Fitzpatrick, Kay, Kevin M Hall, Stephen Farnsworth, and Melisa D Finley. *Evaluation of Bus Bulbs*. TCRP Report 65, Transportation Research Board, Washington, DC: 2001.

3   On Dexter Avenue in Seattle, an important corridor through a rapidly growing neighborhood, side-boarding islands have been crucial to maintaining bus travel times. Average transit trip time through 1.5 mile segment has increased 0.4 seconds in three years post-implementation, during which time traffic volume increased 19% from 11,800 to 14,100 ADT. Bicycle ridership also increased 39% over the same period.

Chang, Dongho. *Expanding Networks to Seattle's Job Centers*. Presentation, Seattle Department of Transportation: September 2015.

4   A slope between 1:10 and 1:25 is recommended by FHWA.

Goodman, Daniel, et al. *Separated Bike Lane Planning and Design Guide*. Federal Highway Administration, Washington, DC: 2015.

5   Rabito, Luciano, et al. *Separated Bike Lane Planning & Design Guide*. Massachusetts Department of Transportation, Boston, MA: 2015.

6   Sidewalk width standards vary by municipality, but 4' is the ADA minimum width requirement. 6' is a common standard sidewalk width requirement. Because 8' width is required for the boarding zone, sidewalks at stops should be at minimum 8' at stops, though at least 10' is preferred, and 14 feet is required where shelters are placed (4'-foot clear path along the curb, 4-foot shelter width, and 6-foot sidewalk width).

DDOT Sidewalk Installation Guidelines and Policy. District Department of Transportation, Washington, DC: 2015.

Street Design Manual, 2nd Edition. New York City Department of Transportation, New York, NY: 2013.

Streets and Sidewalks Maintenance Standards. Department of Public Works, City & County of San Francisco, CA: 2007.

7   Transit signal heads require a design exception for use with buses, and are evaluated on a case-by-case basis.

Barr, Joseph, Jordan Beveridge, Carl Clayton, Alan Danaher, Jack Gonsalves, Bob Koziol, and Sean Rathwell. *Designing Bus Rapid Transit Running Ways*. American Public Transportation Association, Washington, DC: 2010.

8   KFH Group. *Guidelines for the Design and Placement of Transit Stops*. Washington Metropolitan Area Transit Authority, Washington, DC: 2009.

9   Implementation of sidewalk and transit stop improvements along a transit corridor in Portland yielded a 12% reduction in paratransit trips taken by conditionally eligible riders, sugesting accessibility and stop improvements draw riders to fixed route service.

Thatcher, Russell, and Caroline Ferris. *Strategy Guide to Enable and Promote the Use of Fixed-Route Transit by People with Disabilities*. TCRP Report 163, Transportation Research Board, Washington, DC: 2013.

10 Multiple cities including San Francisco, Washington, and Portland have undertaken efforts to consolidate stops and increase spacing in order to provide more reliable service.

KFH Group. *Guidelines for the Design and Placement of Transit Stops*. Washington Metropolitan Area Transit Authority, Washington, DC: 2009.

Baldwin, Ben, Heather Boll, Alan Lehto, Jessica Tump, and Young Park. *Bus Stops Guidelines*. TriMet, Portland, OR: 2010.

11 At some mid-block locations, unsignalized crossings, and streets with high speeds, Z-crossings that help to direct pedestrian sightlines towards oncoming traffic may be appropriate, but are not appropriate in most urban contexts.

Station and Support Facility Design Guidelines User Guide: A Supplement to the Regional Transitway Guidelines. Metropolitan Council, Minneapolis, MN: 2012.

12 The mini-high platform serves one door of the rail vehicle, typically the front door, and constitutes any boarding height over 14 inches.

This is Light Rail Transit. Transportation Research Board, Washington, DC: 2000.

13 Portland's TriMet has instituted skip-stop configurations to great effect along its 5th Avenue transit mall, accommodating 175 buses per hour by staggering buses into four groups, placing two stops per block. The street is able to nearly triple its stop capacity by distributing riders among boarding groups.

Ryus, Paul (PI), Alan Danaher, Mark Walker, Foster Nichols, William Carter, Elizabeth Ellis, and Anthony Bruzzone. "Ch 6, Bus Transit Capacity." *Transit Capacity and Quality of Service Manual, Third Edition*. TCRP Report 165, Transportation Research Board, Washington, DC: 2013.

4. Station & Stop Elements

STOP ELEMENTS

1 A comparison of perceived and real wait time at transit stops with benches and shelters found that as wait time increases, stops with even basic shelters or seating can significantly reduce wait-time perception, especially when wait time approaches 10 minutes.

Fan, Yingling, Andrew Guthrie, and David Levinson. *Perception of Waiting Time at Transit Stops and Stations*. Working paper, University of Minnesota, Minneapolis, MN: 2015.

2 Transit agencies should evaluate existing structures, lighting conditions, and stop element design to provide 360° sightlines from within and approaching the bus stop.

APTA. *Bus Stop Design and Placement Security Considerations*. American Public Transportation Association, Washington, DC: 2010.

3 Where New York's Select Bus Service incorporated PoP fare collection, average per passenger boarding time was reduced to 1.5 seconds. In-lane stops, coupled with off-board fare collection and all-door boarding, reduced average dwell time an estimated 28% on the Bx41 bus in New York, and 38% on the Bx12.

Beaton, Eric B, Evan Bialostozky, Oliver Ernhofer, Theodore V Orosz, Taylor Reiss, and Donald Yuratovac. *Designing Bus Rapid Transit Facilities for Constrained Urban Arterials: a Case Study of the Webster Avenue BRT Running Way Design Selection Process*. Paper presented at the Transportation Research Board 92nd Annual Meeting, Washington, DC: 2013.

4 Trash receptacles may include aperatures or solar compaction capability, based on pedestrian traffic and safety considerations. Avoid placing receptacles blocking access paths, near critical structures, or in enclosed alcoves and alleyways. Collection, visibility, and maintenance are key considerations.

Pitard, Bill, Sean Ryan, and Randy Clarke. *Trash and Recycling Receptacles for Transit Facilities*. American Public Transportation Association, Washington, DC: 2013.

5 Rider surveys in Tampa found that 70% of riders feel more satisfied with transit service since they began using a real-time arrival mobile app. 60% of riders in Atlanta reported improved satisfaction, and 71% reported spending less time waiting for transit.

Brakewood, Candace. *Evaluating the Impacts of Real-Time Transit Information in Tampa and Atlanta*. Webcast, Center for Urban Transportation Research, University of South Florida, Tampa, FL: 2014.

6 Bus stop signs must adhere to ADA sign and display design requirements, including visual contrast, glare, appropriate character size and spacing, and iconography. However, schedules, timetables, and system maps are exempted.

"810.4 Bus Signs." *2010 ADA Standards for Accessible Design*. US Access Board, United States Department of Justice, Washington, DC: 2010.

7 Kassel curbs may encumber additional risk of overpulling onto the curb where the the bus makes a signficant "pull in" movement.

Transport for London. *Accessible bus stop design guidance*. Bus Priority Team technical advice note BP1/06, Transport for London, UK: 2006.

8 Typical Kassel curbs taper down and away from the centerline roughly 3–4%.

Brett Landscaping and Building Products, *Kassel Kerb Data Sheet*. http://www.brettpaving.co.uk/download/clientfiles/files/uploads/469.414 Kassel 07.pdf. Accessed Dec. 2015.

9 A comparison of actual and perceived wait times revealed that riders exposed to poor air quality and high traffic noise at the transit stop overestimate a 10-minute wait by more than 2 minutes. However, when mature trees are present at the stop, they underestimate the same wait by 3 minutes.

Lagune-Reutler, Marina, Andrew Guthrie, Yingling Fan, and David Levinson. *Transit Riders' Perceptions of Waiting Time and Stops' Surrounding Environments*. Working paper, University of Minnesota, Minneapolis, MN: 2015.

Watkins, Kari Edison, Brian Ferris, Alan Borning, G Scott Rutherford, and David Layton. *Where is my Bus? 13 Impact of Mobile Real-Time Information on the Perceived and Actual Wait Time of 14 Transit Riders*. Transportation Research Part A, Vol.45 No 8, 2011.

5. Transit Lanes & Transitways

TRANSIT LANES

1 Asha Weinstein Agrawal, Ph.D., Todd Goldman, Ph.D., and Nancy Hannaford. *Shared-Use Bus Priority Lanes on City Streets: Case Studies in Design and Management*. Report No. CA-MTI-12-2606, Mineta Transportation Institute, San Jose, CA: 2012.

2 Enforcement strategies vary based on state and local laws and statutes. Some cities classify bus lane violations as civil infractions (enforcable by civilian agents and/or by automated cameras), or have contractual agreements between police departments and DOTs to establish enforcement responsibilities.

   Asha Weinstein Agrawal, Ph.D., Todd Goldman, Ph.D., and Nancy Hannaford. *Shared-Use Bus Priority Lanes on City Streets: Case Studies in Design and Management*. Report No. CA-MTI-12-2606, Mineta Transportation Institute, San Jose, CA: 2012.

3 By equipping its entire transit fleet with enforcement cameras, San Francisco's Muni has seen delay reductions on routes with transit-only lanes ranging from 3 to 15% throughout the day. During afternoon peak, when delay is most significant, Muni has observed even better delay reductions, ranging from 7 to 20%.

   San Francisco Municipal Transportation Agency. *Transit-Only Lane Enforcement*. MuniForward white paper, 2015.

4 Research suggests that lane widths less than 12 feet on urban and suburban arterials do not increase crash frequencies.

   Potts, Ingrid, Douglas Harwood, and Karen R. Richard. *Relationship of Lane Width to Safety on Urban and Suburban Arterials*. Paper presented at the TRB 86th Annual Meeting, Washington, DC: January 2007.

   ....

   Relationship Between Lane Width and Speed. Parsons Transportation Group, Washington, DC: 2003.

5 Where it is infeasible to provide a separated bicycling facility (e.g. cycle track), bike routes should be provided on an immediately parallel street. Where bikes must cross rail tracks, provide a Two-Stage Queue Box (see NACTO's *Urban Bikeway Design Guide*) to cross bikes at a preferred angle. Alta Planning + Design. *Bicycle Interactions and Streetcars: Lessons Learned and Recommendations*. Prepared for Lloyd District Transportation Management Association, Portland, OR: 2008.

TRANSITWAYS

1 Passenger loading zones for accessible parking spaces may require 8 feet of clear width if a ramp is expected to be deployed.
   "Ch. R3, Technical Requirements." *Proposed Accessibility Guidelines for Pedestrian Facilities in the Public Right-of-Way*. US Access Board, Washington, DC: 2011.

LANE ELEMENTS

1 Regardless of material selection, all pavements that pedestrians access must be "firm, stable, and slip resistant."

   "R302.7, Technical Requirements." *Proposed Accessibility Guidelines for Pedestrian Facilities in the Public Right-of-Way*. US Access Board, Washington, DC: 2011.

2 Lawrence G Lovejoy, et al. *Track Design Handbook for Light Rail Transit, Second Edition*. TCRP 155, Transportation Research Board, Washington, DC: 2012.

3 Steven H Kosmatka, Beatrix Kerkhoff, and William C Panarese. "Ch. 17: High-Performance Concrete," *Design and Control of Concrete Mixtures, 14th Edition*. Portland Cement Association, Skokie, IL: 2003.

4 *London Bus Lane and Bus Stop Construction Guidance*. Local Government Technical Advisers Group. London, UK: 2013.

5 Pavers, like all pavements that pedestrians access must be level and maintained for accessibility.

   "R302.7, Technical Requirements." *Proposed Accessibility Guidelines for Pedestrian Facilities in the Public Right-of-Way*. US Access Board, Washington, DC: 2011.

6 "Low Impact Development (LID)." US Environmental Protection Agency, accessed August 15, 2015, http://water.epa.gov/polwaste/green/index.cfm.

   ....

   Garrison, Noah, and Karen Hobbs. *Rooftops to Rivers II: Green Strategies for Controlling Stormwater and Combined Sewer Overflows*. National Resources Defense Council, Washington, DC: 2011.

   ....

   "Managing Urban Runoff." US Environmental Protection Agency, Washington, DC: accessed August 15, 2015, http://water.epa.gov/polwaste/nps/urban.cfm.

   ....

   "Why Green Infrastructure." US Environmental Protection Agency, Washington, DC: accessed August 15, 2015, http://water.epa.gov/infrastructure/greeninfrastructure/gi_why.cfm.

7   Schreiter, Hendrikje. *Green Tram Tracks: The Advantages of Implementing Vegetation Systems in Tram Tracks*. Institute for Agricultural and Urban Projects at the Humboldt-University, Berlin: 2010.

8   Currently, color treatments require an experimentation request.

Official Ruling 3(09)-24(I) – Application of Colored Pavement: Aug 15, 2013.

Manual on Uniform Traffic Control Devices, 2009 Edition. Federal Highway Administration, Washington, DC: 2009.

9   Red color application on Church Street in San Francisco improved corridor travel times 14% for buses, and reduced travel time variability 27%, with negligible impact on vehicle travel times.

SFMTA. *Church Street Pilot Transit Lanes*. San Francisco Municipal Transportation Agency report, 2015.

10 In tests on high-volume bus routes, thermoplastic performed better than paint but resulted in similar life-cycle costs. Pre-treatment such as shot-blasting and cleaning improves the application of thermoplastic to older asphalt.

Carry, William, Eric Donnell, Zoltan Rado, Martin Hartman, and Steven Salici. *Red Bus Lane Treatment Evaluation*. Institute of Transportation Engineers, Washington, DC: 2012.

11 "EPA Cool Pavements Compendium." US Environmental Protection Agency, Washington, DC: accessed September 20, 2015. http://www.epa.gov/heatisld/resources/pdf/CoolPavesCompendium.pdf.

12 Along the US 1 transitway in Alexandria, VA, a 4-inch mountable curb was included at key locations to accommodate emergency vehicles.

"Route 1 Transitway, Docket Item #13." Planning Commission Hearing, May 1, 2012, City of Alexandria, VA.

13 *Better Streets Plan: Policies and Guidelines for the Pedestrian Realm*. City & County of San Francisco, CA: 2010.

LANE DESIGN CONTROLS

1   The Safe System Approach acknowledges that human error is inevitable, but by reducing speeds to under 30 km/hour, drivers have more time to react and cause less bodily harm during crashes.

NSW Centre for Road Safety. *"Safe System" — The Key to Managing Road Safety*. Roads and Traffic Authority, New South Wales Government, Australia: 2011.

2   A speed camera program in Montgomery County, VA, yielded a 10% reduction in mean speeds and a 59% reduction in the likelihood that a vehicle was traveling more than 10 mph above the speed limit at camera sites over seven years.

Wen Hu and Anne T. McCartt. *Effects of Automated Speed Enforcement in Montgomery County, Maryland, on Vehicle Speeds, Public Opinion, and Crashes*. Insurance Institute for Highway Safety, Arlington, VA: 2015.

6. Intersections

SIGNALS & OPERATIONS

1   In Portland's application of a 13 mph progression on its dense downtown grid generated a "reverse progression" for pedestrians traveling 4 mph.

Koonce, Peter. *Transforming Traffic Signals to Support Sustainability: Applications, Ideas, & Research*. Transportation Research and Education Center, Portland State University, Portland, OR: 2011.

2   Pangilinan, Christopher, and Kristen Carnarius. *Traffic Signal Timing for Optimal Transit Progression in Downtown San Francisco*. SFMTA, Presented to Institute of Transportation Engineers, Washington, DC: 2014.

3   In most applications, when a transit vehicle receives a priority phase (~10 sec), the dedicated time is restored by deducting time from up to four subsequent cycles. If headways are too short, the signal cycle can never be restored and may cause adverse delay.

Harriet R Smith, P Brendon Hemily, and Miomir Ivanovic. *Transit signal priority (TSP): A Planning and Implementation Handbook*. ITS America, Washington, DC: 2005.

4   TSP applications using AVL technology was demonstrated to reduce total bus trip times during peak hours between 4 and 15% in Minneapolis. Applications in Portland, Seattle, and Los Angeles noted 8–10% travel time decreases.

Jia Hu, Byungkyu (Brian) Park, and A. Emily Parkany. *Transit Signal Priority with Connected Vehicle Technology*. Transportation Research Record 2418, Journal of the Transportation Research Board, Washington, DC: 2014.

5   A number of studies of TSP implementation on streetcar routes in Toronto recorded widely varying travel time improvements, even up to 50% reductions in delays at some intersections. Factors such as stop siting, service frequency and ridership, and separation from traffic all impacted TSP effectiveness in reducing spot delay.

Danaher, Alan R. *Bus and Rail Transit Preferential Treatments in Mixed Traffic*. TCRP Synthesis 83, Transportation Research Board, Washington, DC: 2010.

6 Where headways are shorter than 4 minutes, the probability increases that transit vehicle behind another transit vehicle that receives a priority phase will be delayed as the signal cycle corrects itself. With high frequency, a fixed progression confers greater benefit to transit.

Chada, Shireen, and Robert Newland. *Effectiveness of Bus Signal Priority: Final Report*. National Center for Transit Research, Tampa, FL: 2002.

7 In isolation, TSP is most effective at v/c ratios between 0.5 and 0.7, which significantly benefits reducing transit delay up to 0.9. When using techniques like connected vehicle technology and green reallocation (which maintains phase length but shifts the green time based on transit arrival, instead of green extension, which simply adds green time) phases, TSP simulations showed a benefit of 85-88% delay reduction.

Jia Hu, Byungkyu (Brian) Park, and A Emily Parkany. *Transit Signal Priority with Connected Vehicle Technology*. Transportation Research Record 2418, Journal of the Transportation Research Board, Washington, DC: 2014.

8 Field test of adaptive TSP showed intersection delay at one congested location was reduced for all users: 43% for buses, 16% for general traffic, and 12% for cross-street traffic.

Li, Meng, Yafeng Yin, Wei-Bin Zhang, Kun Zhou, and Hideki Nakamura. "Modeling and implementation of adaptive transit signal priority on actuated control systems." *Computer-Aided Civil and Infrastructure Engineering*, 26, no. 4: 2011.

9 With shorter cycle lengths, the penalty to the transit vehicle for missing the green phase is smaller; additionally, shorter cycles generate shorter queues, reducing the likelihood that the transit vehicle will be blocked from reaching the stop by traffic.

Furth, Peter, and Joseph SanClemente, "Near-Side, Far-Side, Uphill, Downhill: Impact of Bus Stop Location on Bus Delay." *Transportation Research Record: Journal of the Transportation Research Board*, No. 1971, Transportation Research Board of the National Academies, Washington, DC: 2006.

10 Turning movements account for 32% of collisions involving buses and pedestrians. Two-thirds of those collisions involve left-turning buses hitting pedestrians.

Pecheux, Kelley Klaver, Jocelyn Bauer, Sheryl Miller, Jennifer Rephlo, Harry Saporta, Samantha Erickson, Sue Knapp, and Jason Quan. *Guidebook for Mitigating Fixed-Route Bus-and-Pedestrian Collisions*. TCRP Report 125, Transportation Research Board, Washington, DC: 2007.

11 In dense intersections for walking and biking, restricting turns, including right turns on red, has a safety benefit for vulnerable road users, but without physical design changes requires periodic enforcement. Additionally, if turns are restricted at a spot, a suitable alternative must be provided to maintain compliance.

Antonucci, Nicholas, Kelly Kennedy Hardy, Kevin L Slack, Ronald Pfefer, and Thomas R Neuman. *Guidance for Implementation of the AASHTO Strategic Highway Safety Plan, Vol. 12: A Guide for Reducing Collisions at Signalized Intersections*. NCHRP 500, Transportation Research Board, Washington, DC: 2004.

12 In New York, left-turn crashes involving severe pedestrian injuries outnumbered right-turn crashes 3 to 1. Additionally, pedestrians struck crossing at signals had the signal in 57% of cases.

Viola, Rob, Matthew Roe, and Hyeon-Shic Shin. *The New York City Pedestrian Safety Study & Action Plan*. New York City Department of Transportation, New York, NY: 2010.

INTERSECTION DESIGN FOR TRANSIT

1 Implementation of queue jumps with TSP at 13 locations on a rapid transit route in West Valley City, UT, saw a 13–22% reduction in travel times, and a 22% increase in bus speed.

Zlatkovic, M, A Stevanovic, and Z Reza. *Effects of Queue Jumpers and Transit Signal Priority on Bus Rapid Transit*. Transportation Research Board Compendium of Papers, Washington, DC: 2013.

2 Thresholds may vary by municipality, but common thresholds include routes "with average headway of 15 min or less; when traffic volumes exceed 500 vehicles per hour in the curb lane during a.m. or PM peak hours; when the intersection operates at a level of service D or lower; and when cost and land acquisition are feasible."

Kent, Fred III, Stephen Davies, Cynthia Abramson, Erika Hanson, and Meg Walker. *Transit-Friendly Streets: Design and Traffic Management Strategies to Support Livable Communities*. Transportation Research Board, TCRP 33, Washington, DC: 1998.

3 MicroSim modeling showed a 3-17% reduction in delay combining queue jump lane and near-side stop with active TSP compared to a far-side stop with TSP with no queue jump.

Zhou, Guangwei, and Albert Gan. *Design of Transit Signal Priority at Signalized Intersections with Queue Jumper Lanes*. Journal of Public Transportation, Vol 12, no. 4, Tampa, FL: 2009.

4   VISSIM modeling was used to demonstrate that transit gains the greatest benefit from a full queue bypass lane approaching a far-side stop. As v/c ratio approaches 1.0, queue bypasses (greater than the length of the average traffic queue) with TSP become increasingly effective at reducing transit and general traffic delay.

Bugg, Zachary, Jon Crisafi, Kevin Lee, Tom Urbanik, and Paul Ryus. *Effect of Transit Preferential Treatments on Vehicle Travel Time.* Kittelson & Associates, Inc. *ITE Mid-Colonial District Annual Meeting*: 2015.

5   Though effectiveness is dependent on wide-ranging characteristics, far-side stop locations have been shown to improve travel time savings more than near-side locations. MicroSim models have been used to indicate that locating a near-side stop 25-100 feet of the intersection increased average net delay up to 10 seconds, while far-side location in this configuration reduced net delay .5 seconds.

Bugg, Zachary, Jon Crisafi, Kevin Lee, Tom Urbanik, and Paul Ryus. *Effect of Transit Preferential Treatments on Vehicle Travel Time.* Kittelson & Associates, Inc. *ITE Mid-Colonial District Annual Meeting*: 2015.

Cesme, Burak, Selman Z. Altun, and Barrett Lane. *Queue Jump Lane, Transit Signal Priority, and Stop Location: Evaluation of Transit Preferential Treatments using Microsimulation.* Presented to the Transportation Research Board, Washington, DC: 2014.

6   As of 2015, use of a transit signal head for bus movements in general traffic requires a design exception, though has been applied in cities such as Austin, TX.

"Part 4. Highway Traffic Signals." *Manual on Uniform Traffic Control Devices, 2009 Edition.* Federal Highway Administration, Washington, DC: 2009.

TRANSIT ROUTE TURNS

1   AASHTO. *Guide for Geometric Design of Transit Facilities on Highways and Streets, 1st Edition.* American Association of State Highway and Transportation Officials, Washington, DC: 2014.

2   However, some cities with historic streetcar lines have much shorter centerline radii; Philadelphia's is as little as 35.4 feet. However, limited capacity affects the likelihood that such small streetcars will be installed in the future.

Graebner, JH, RE Jackson, and LG Lovejoy. *Trackway Infrastructure Guidelines for Light Rail Circulator Systems.* American Public Transportation Association, Washington, DC: 2007.

3   An advance stop bar can be applied with "STOP" stencil, as well as "Stop Here" sign (R1-5b).

"Chapter 3B.16 - Pavement and Curb Markings." *Manual on Uniform Traffic Control Devices, 2009 Edition.* Federal Highway Administration, Washington, DC: 2009.

4   "Provide a low-angle right turn (about 112 degrees). This angle slows down the speed of right-turning vehicles and improves driver visibility of pedestrians within and approaching the crosswalk."

Daisa, James M, and Brian S Bochner. *Design Walkable Urban Thoroughfares: A Context Sensitive Approach.* Institute of Transportation Engineers & Congress for New Urbanism, Washington, DC: 2010.

7. Transit System Strategies

NETWORK STRATEGIES

1   Conversion of one-way street to one-way with a contraflow transit lane on Sansome Street in San Francisco resulted in a 36-47% decrease in mean corridor travel time at peak for the 12, 15, and 42 bus lines during peak hours. Additionally, travel time variability fell by almost 80% for the corridor. Simplifying and converging three routes onto the Sansome Street corridor allowed significant travel time savings and service increases for passengers, and much more predictable service planning for Muni.

Mirabdal, Javad, and Bond Yee. *First Transit Contra Flow Lane in Downtown San Francisco.* City and County of San Francisco, prepared for the Institute of Transportation Engineers, Washington, DC: 1999.

2   Eliminating one stop, even if passenger boarding takes longer at other stops, can save 15 seconds or more, with additional savings if a pull-out stop and re-entry delay are avoided.

Ryus, Paul (PI), Alan Danaher, Mark Walker, Foster Nichols, William Carter, Elizabeth Ellis, and Anthony Bruzzone. "Ch 6, Bus Transit Capacity." *Transit Capacity and Quality of Service Manual, Third Edition.* TCRP Report 165, Transportation Research Board, Washington, DC: 2013.

3   In Portland, a 6-8% increase in stop spacing yielded a 5.7% reduction in travel time without affecting ridership. In San Francisco, buses gained 4.4–14.6% increases in speeds upon reducing average stop spacing from 5.9 to 2.5 stops per mile.

El-Geneidy, AM, JG Strathman, TJ Kimpel, and DT Crout. *Effects of Bus Stop Consolidation on Passenger Activity and Transit Operations*. Transportation Research Record 1971, Transportation Research Board, Washington, DC: 2006.

Diaz, RB and D Hinebaugh. *Characteristics of Bus Rapid Transit for Decision-Making*. Federal Transit Administration, Washington, DC: 2009.

4   *All-Door Boarding Evaluation Final Report*. San Francisco Municipal Transportation Agency, San Francisco, CA: 2014.

5   Riders typically require 20–30 seconds to load a bicycle onto a front rack, including deploying the rack and securing the bicycle.

Ryus, Paul (PI), Alan Danaher, Mark Walker, Foster Nichols, William Carter, Elizabeth Ellis, and Anthony Bruzzone. "Ch 6, Bus Transit Capacity." *Transit Capacity and Quality of Service Manual, Third Edition*. TCRP Report 165, Transportation Research Board, Washington, DC: 2013.

PERFORMANCE MEASURES

1   Transit can increase access to destinations by either extending the distance passengers can travel or helping to decrease distance between passengers and destinations. Investments in transit service and stations can influence urban development and improve destination density and accessibility, even for non-riders.

Walker, Jarrett. "Ch. 1 – What Transit Is and Does." *Human transit: How clearer thinking about public transit can enrich our communities and our lives*. Island Press, Washington, DC: 2011.

2   Even while reducing the number of travel lanes to dedicate transit lanes and protected bikeways on 1st and 2nd Avenues in Manhattan, both streets maintained traffic volumes while slightly increasing travel speeds along the corridors.

New York City Transit & New York City Department of Transportation. *+selectbusservice: M15 on First and Second Avenues Progress Report*. New York, NY: 2012.

3   "Reducing parking duration by 10–20% can have the same effect as creating hundreds of new parking spaces in a neighborhood, while improving traffic flow." Smart parking programs on Church Avenue and along commercial corridors in the Park Slope neighborhood in Brooklyn increased unique visitors by up to 18%, and resulted in a 21% increase in corridor travel speed and 19% increase to travel speed reliability.

New York City Department of Transportation, *Measuring the Street*. New York City, NY: 2012.

4   Transit passenger fatality rates were 0.02 per 100 million passenger miles traveled in 2010, while motor vehicle fatality rates were 1.08 per 100 million VMT in 2013, with average vehicle occupancy of 1.55 in 2011, resulting in a 0.69 fatality rate per 100 million occupant miles traveled.

FARS Encyclopedia 1994–2013. National Highway Traffic Safety Administration, US Department of Transportation, Washington, DC: accessed Dec. 2015.

5   Measuring transit-related emissions impacts involves calculating per-passenger transit vehicle emissions, as well as avoided car trips (mode shift), congestion relief, and impacts on land use that further support transit efficiency.

Recommended Practice for Quantifying Greenhouse Gas Emissions from Transit. Climate Change Standards Working Group, American Public Transportation Association, Washington, DC: 2009.

6   New York City Department of Transportation, *The Economic Benefits of Sustainable Streets*. New York City, NY: 2013.

7   Implementation of dedicated transit lanes and protected bike lanes on First and Second Avenues in New York City coincided with a 47% drop in commercial vacancies along the corridor, compared with a 2% increase borough-wide over the same period.

New York City Department of Transportation, *Measuring the Street*. New York City, NY: 2012.

8   Nelson, Arthur, and Joanna Ganning. *National Study of BRT Development Outcomes*. University of Utah, report developed for the National Institute for Transportation and Communities, Portland, OR: 2015.

Introduction

WHY TRANSIT MATTERS

Koonce, Peter, Paul Ryus, David Zagel, Young Park, and Jamie Parks. "An Evaluation of Comprehensive Transit Improvements—TriMet's Streamline Program." *Journal of Public Transportation 9.3*, Tampa, FL: 2006.

Ryus, Paul (PI), Alan Danaher, Mark Walker, Foster Nichols, William Carter, Elizabeth Ellis, and Anthony Bruzzone. *Transit Capacity and Quality of Service Manual, Third Edition*. TCRP Report 165, Transportation Research Board, Washington, DC: 2013.

+selectbusservice, M15 on First and Second Avenues: Progress Report. New York City Department of Transportation and New York City Transit, New York, NY: 2011.

Walker, Jarrett. *Human transit: How clearer thinking about public transit can enrich our communities and our lives*. Island Press, Washington, DC: 2011.

Transit Streets

TRANSFORMATIONS

Carry, William, Eric Donnell, Zoltan Rado, Martin Hartman, and Steven Scalici. *Red Bus Lane Treatment Evaluation*. Institute of Transportation Engineers, Washington, DC: 2012.

Integration of Transit into Urban Thoroughfare Design: Draft White Paper.

Chicago Department of Transportation. *Complete Streets Chicago: Design Guidelines*. City of Chicago, IL: 2013.

The BRT Standard, 2014 Edition. Institute for Transportation and Development Policy, New York, NY: 2014.

Kim, Sangyoup, Jaisung Choi, and Yongseok Kim. *Determining the Sidewalk Pavement Width by Using Pedestrian Discomfort Levels and Movement Characteristics*. KSCE Journal of Civil Engineering, 15(5): 883-889, New York, NY: 2011.

Vanasse Hangen Brustlin, Inc., Foursquare Integrated Transportation Planning, and National Bus Rapid Transit Institute. *Bus Priority Treatment Guidelines*. National Capital Region Transportation Planning, Washington, DC: 2011.

Project for Public Spaces, Inc. *Transit-Friendly Streets: Design and Traffic Management Strategies to Support Livable Communities*. TCRP Report 33, Transportation Research Board, Washington, DC: 1998.

Stations & Stops

STOP DESIGN FACTORS

Delaware Valley Regional Planning Commission. *SEPTA Bus Stop Design Guidelines*. Philadelphia, PA: 2012.

Design of On-street Transit Stops and Access from Surrounding Areas. American Public Transportation Association, Sustainability and Urban Design Program, Washington, DC: 2012.

Furth, Peter, and Joseph SanClemente, "Near-Side, Far-Side, Uphill, Downhill: Impact of Bus Stop Location on Bus Delay." *Transportation Research Record: Journal of the Transportation Research Board*, No. 1971, Transportation Research Board of the National Academies, Washington, DC: 2006.

Guidelines for the Location and Design of Bus Stops. TCRP Report 19. Transportation Research Board, Washington, DC: 1996.

Mishalani, Rabi G, Mark M McCord, and John Wirtz. *Passenger wait time perceptions at bus stops: Empirical results and impact on evaluating real-time bus arrival information*. Journal of Public Transportation 9.2(5), Tampa, FL: 2006.

United States Access Board. "Ch. 4 Accessible Routes." US Department of Justice, Washington, DC: accessed Nov. 2015 (https://www.access-board.gov/guidelines-and-standards/buildings-and-sites/about-the-ada-standards/ada-standards/chapter-4-accessible-routes).

United States Access Board. "Detectable Warnings Update, March 2014." *ADA Standards*. US Department of Justice, Washington, DC: accessed Nov. 2015 (https://www.access-board.gov/guidelines-and-standards/streets-sidewalks/public-rights-of-way/guidance-and-research/detectable-warnings-update).

United States Access Board. "Ch. 8 Special Rooms, Spaces, and Elements, Std. 810: Transportation Facilities." *ADA Standards*. US Department of Justice, Washington, DC: accessed Nov. 2015 (https://www.access-board.gov/guidelines-and-standards/buildings-and-sites/about-the-ada-standards/ada-standards/chapter-8-special-rooms,-spaces,-and-elements#810 Transportation Facilities).

United States Access Board. "Ch. 7 Communication Elements and Features, Std. 705: Detectable Warnings." *ADA Standards*. US Department of Justice, Washington, DC: accessed Nov. 2015 (https://www.access-board.gov/guidelines-and-standards/buildings-and-sites/about-the-ada-standards/ada-standards/chapter-7-communication-elements-and-features#705 Detectable Warnings).

STOP CONFIGURATIONS

Fitzpatrick, Kay, Kevin M Hall, Stephen Farnsworth, and Melisa D Finley. *Evaluation of Bus Bulbs*. TCRP Report 65, Transportation Research Board, Washington, DC: 2001.

Ryus, Paul (PI), Alan Danaher, Mark Walker, Foster Nichols, William Carter, Elizabeth Ellis, and Anthony Bruzzone. "Ch 6-7, Bus Transit Capacity and Rail Transit Capacity." *Transit Capacity and Quality of Service Manual, Third Edition*. TCRP Report 165, Transportation Research Board, Washington, DC: 2013.

Station & Stop Elements

STOP ELEMENTS

Baldwin, Ben, Heather Boll, Alan Lehto, Jessica Tump, and Young Park. *Bus Stops Guidelines*. TriMet, Portland, OR: 2010.

Broome, Nathan. *Bicycle Parking Guidelines, 2nd Edition*. Association of Pedestrian and Bicycle Professionals, Lexington, KY: 2010.

City of Cambridge Bicycle Parking Guide. Community Development Department, Environmental and Transportation Planning, City of Cambridge, MA: 2013.

Delaware Valley Regional Planning Commission. *SEPTA Bus Stop Design Guidelines*. Philadelphia, PA: 2012.

Schweiger, Carol L. *Real-Time Bus Arrival Information Systems*. TCRP Synthesis 48, Transportation Research Board, Washington, DC: 2003.

Station and Support Facility Design Guidelines User Guide: A Supplement to the Regional Transitway Guidelines. Metropolitan Council, Minneapolis, MN: 2012.

Texas Transportation Institute. *Location and Design of Bus Stops on Major Streets and Highways*. TCRP Report 19, Transportation Research Board, Washington, DC: 1996.

Transit Lanes & Transitways

TRANSIT LANES

APTA Bus Rapid Transit Working Group. *Designing Bus Rapid Transit Running Ways*. American Public Transportation Association, Washington, DC: 2010.

Beaton, Eric B, Evan Bialostozky, Oliver Ernhofer, Theodore V Orosz, Taylor Reiss, and Donald Yuratovac. *Designing Bus Rapid Transit Facilities for Constrained Urban Arterials: a Case Study of the Webster Avenue BRT Running Way Design Selection Process*. Paper presented at the Transportation Research Board 92nd Annual Meeting, Washington, DC: 2013.

Hillsman, Edward L, Sara J Hendricks, and JoAnne K Fiebe. *A Summary of Design, Policies, and Operational Characteristics for Shared Bicycle/Bus Lanes*. Florida Department of Transportation Research Center, Tallahassee, FL: 2012.

Levinson, Herbert, et al. *Bus Rapid Transit, Vol. 1: Case Studies in Bus Rapid Transit*. TCRP Report 90, Transportation Research Board, Washington, DC: 2003.

Levinson, Herbert, et al. *Bus Rapid Transit, Vol. 2: Implementation Guidelines*. TCRP Report 93, Transportation Research Board, Washington, DC: 2003.

Panero, Marta, Hyeon-Shic Shin, Allen Zedrin, and Samuel Zimmerman. *Peer-to-Peer Information Exchange on Bus Rapid Transit (BRT) and Bus Priority Best Practices*. Rudin Center for Transportation Policy and Management, New York, NY: 2012.

Vuchic, Vukan R. "Bus semirapid transit mode development and evaluation." *Journal of Public Transportation 5.2*, Tampa, FL: 2002.

TRANSITWAYS

Danaher, Alan R. *Bus and Rail Transit Preferential Treatments in Mixed Traffic*. TCRP Synthesis 83, Transportation Research Board, Washington, DC: 2010.

Eccles, Kimberly A, and Herbert S Levinson. *Design, Operation, and Safety of At-Grade Crossings of Exclusive Busways*. TCRP Report 117, Transportation Research Board, Washington, DC: 2007.

Pena, Angel A. *DC Streetcar Design Criteria*. District Department of Transportation, Washington, DC: 2012.

LANE ELEMENTS

NYC DOT Transportation & Planning Management. *Typical Pavement Markings*. New York City Department of Transportation, New York, NY: 2015.

TxDOT. "Section 4: Pavement Marking Material Descriptions," Pavement Marking Handbook. Texas Department of Transportation, Austin, TX: 2004. Accessed August 2015. http://onlinemanuals.txdot.gov/txdotmanuals/pmh/pavement_marking_material_descriptions.htm.

Cornwell, PR, JA Cracknell, and G Gardner. *Design Guidelines for Busway Transport*. Overseas Development Administration and Transport Research Library, Berkshire, UK: 1993.

LANE DESIGN CONTROLS

APTA Streetcar Subcommittee Work Group. *Modern Streetcar Vehicle Guideline*. American Public Transportation Association, Washington, DC: 2013.

AASHTO. *Guide for Geometric Design of Transit Facilities on Highways and Streets, 1st Edition*. American Association of State Highway and Transportation Officials, Washington, DC: 2014.

Guidelines for Accessible Building Blocks for Bicycle Facilities. San Francisco Municipal Transportation Agency, Mayor's Office, Department of Public Works, and Planning Department. City & County of San Francisco, CA: 2014.

Light Rail Design Criteria. Utah Transit Authority, Salt Lake City, UT: 2007.

Pena, Angel A. *DC Streetcar Design Criteria*. District Department of Transportation, Washington, DC: 2012.

Sando, T, and R Moses. *Integrating Transit Into Traditional Neighborhood Design Policie—The Influence of Lane Width on Bus Safety*. Florida Department of Transportation: Tallahassee, FL: 2009.

Streetcar Design Criteria. Utah Transit Authority, Salt Lake City, UT: 2007.

Intersections

SIGNALS & OPERATIONS

Boyle, Daniel K. *Commonsense Approaches for Improving Transit Bus Speeds*. TCRP Synthesis 110, Transportation Research Board, Washington, DC: 2013.

Chada, Shireen, and Robert Newland. *Effectiveness of Bus Signal Priority: Final Report*. National Center For Transit Research, Tampa, FL: 2002.

Koonce, Peter. *Prioritizing Transit in a Connected Vehicle World*. ITE Journal. Institute of Transportation Engineers, Washington, DC: December 2012.

Gardner, Kevin, Chris D'Souza, Nick Hounsell, Birendra Shrestha, and David Bretherton. *Review of Bus Priority at Traffic Signals around the World*. Prepared for UITP Working Group: Interaction of buses and signals at road crossings. International Assocation for Public Transport: 2009.

INTERSECTION DESIGN FOR TRANSIT

AASHTO. *Guide for Geometric Design of Transit Facilities on Highways and Streets, 1st Edition.* American Association of State Highway and Transportation Officials, Washington, DC: 2014.

Barr, Joseph, et al. "Select Bus Service on Bx12 in New York City: Bus Rapid Transit Partnership of New York City DOT and Metropolitan Transportation Authority New York City Transit." Transportation Research Record: Journal of the Transportation Research Board 2145, Washington, DC: 2010.

Beaton, Eric, et al. "Designing Bus Rapid Transit Facilities for Constrained Urban Arterials: Case Study of the Selection Process for the Webster Avenue Bus Rapid Transit Running Way Design in New York City." Transportation Research Record: Journal of the Transportation Research Board 2352, Washington, DC: 2013.

OmniTrans. Transit Design Guidelines: Final Report. OmniTrans, San Bernardino, CA: 2013.

INTERSECTION GEOMETRY

APTA Streetcar Subcommittee Work Group. *Modern Streetcar Vehicle Guideline.* American Public Transportation Association, Washington, DC: 2013.

Light Rail Design Criteria. Utah Transit Authority, Salt Lake City, UT: 2007.

Pena, Angel A. *DC Streetcar Design Criteria.* District Department of Transportation, Washington, DC: 2012.

Streetcar Design Criteria. Utah Transit Authority, Salt Lake City, UT: 2007.

Track Design Handbook for Light Rail Transit. TCRP 155, Transportation Research Board, Washington, DC: 2012.

Transit Design Guidelines: Final Report. OmniTrans, San Bernardino, CA: 2013.

TRANSIT ROUTE TURNS

Pecheux, Kelley Klaver. *Guidebook for Mitigating Fixed-Route Bus-and-Pedestrian Collisions.* TCRP Report 125. Transportation Research Board, Washington, DC: 2008.

Transit System Strategies

NETWORK STRATEGIES

Nielsen, Gustav, and Truls Lange. *Network Design for Public Transport Success—Theory and Examples.* Norwegian Ministry of Transport and Communications, Oslo, Norway: 2008.

Ryus, Paul, Kelly Laustsen, Kelly Blume, Tom Urbanik, and Scott Beaird. *Improving Transportation Network Efficiency Through Implementation of Transit-Supportive Roadway Strategies.* TCRP A-39, Transportation Research Board, Washington, DC: 2015.

Shrestha, Ranjay M, and Edmund J Zolnik. *Eliminating Bus Stops: Evaluating Changes in Operations, Emissions and Coverage.* Journal of Public Transportation 16.2, Tampa, FL: 2008.

PERFORMANCE MEASURES

FL DOT Public Transit Office. *Best Practices in Evaluating Transit Performance.* Florida Department of Transportation, Tallahasee, FL: 2014.

Hu, Wen, and Anne T McCartt. *Evaluation of automated speed enforcement in Montgomery County, Maryland.* Insurance Institute for Highway Safety, Arlington, VA: 2015.

Kittleson & Associates, Inc., et al. *A Guidebook for Developing a Transit Performance-Measurement System.* TCRP Report 88. Transportation Research Board, Washington, DC: 2003.

McCahill, Chris, and Mary Ebeling. *Tools for measuring accessibility in an equity framework.* Prepared for Congress for New Urbanism 23rd Annual Meeting. State Smart Transportation Initiative, Madison, WI: 2015.

Public Transportation: Benefits for the 21st Century. American Public Transportation Association, Washington, DC: 2007.

Public Transportation and the Nation's Economy: A Quantitative Analysis of Public Transportation's Economic Impact. Washington: Cambridge Systematics, Inc., October 1999.

Tomer, Adie. *Where the Jobs Are: Employer Access to Labor by Transit.* Metropolitan Policy Program, Brookings Institute, Washington, DC: 2012.

Credits

Project Steering Committee

ARLINGTON, VA

Larry Marcus, Arlington County

ATLANTA, GA

Norman Lopez, Jr., City of Atlanta
Becky Katz, City of Atlanta

AUSTIN, TX

Jim Dale, PE, City of Austin
Robert Spillar, PE, City of Austin

BALTIMORE, MD

Caitlin Doolin, City of Baltimore
William Johnson, City of Baltimore

BOSTON, MA

Vineet Gupta, City of Boston

BOULDER, CO

Bill Cowern, PE, City of Boulder
Joe Paulson, PE, PTOE, City of Boulder
Natalie Stiffler, AICP, City of Boulder

BURLINGTON, VT

Chapin Spencer, City of Burlington

CAMBRIDGE, MA

Tegin Bennett, City of Cambridge
Cara Seiderman, City of Cambridge

CHARLOTTE, NC

Judy Dellert-O'Keef, City of Charlotte
Krystel Green, City of Charlotte
Tom Sorrentino, City of Charlotte

CHICAGO, IL

Kevin O'Malley, City of Chicago
Keith Privett, City of Chicago
Nathan Roseberry, PE, T.Y. Lin
Malihe Samadi, City of Chicago
Dave Seglin, City of Chicago

DENVER, CO

Ryan Billings, City and County of Denver
Emily Snyder, City and County of Denver
Brian Welch, AICP, Regional Transportation District

EL PASO, TX

Fred Lopez, AICP, City of El Paso

FORT LAUDERDALE, FL

Karen Mendrala, City of Fort Lauderdale

HOBOKEN, NJ

Susan Poliwka, City of Hoboken

HOUSTON, TX

Christof Spieler, Houston Metro
Jeffrey Weatherford, City of Houston

INDIANAPOLIS, IN

Justin Stuehrenberg, IndyGo

LOS ANGELES, CA

Martha Butler, LA Metro
Zaki Mustafa, LADOT
Seleta Reynolds, LADOT

Project Steering Committee *(continued)*

LOUISVILLE, KY

Aida Copic, AICP, Transit Authority of River City
Rolf Eisenger, City of Louisville

MADISON, WI

David Dryer, City of Madison

MINNEAPOLIS, MN

Lucy Galbraith, AICP, Metro Transit
Jennifer Hager, City of Minneapolis
John Pierce, Metro Transit

MONTRÉAL, QC

Luc Couillard, Ville de Montréal

NEW YORK, NY

Eric Beaton, NYC DOT
Taylor Reiss Gouge, PE, NYC DOT
Chris Pangilinan, MTA
Aaron Sugiura, NYC DOT
Buckley Yung, MTA

OAKLAND, CA

Christine Calabrese, City of Oakland
Stephen Newhouse, AC Transit

PHILADELPHIA, PA

Logan Axelson, DVRPC
Jennifer Barr, AICP, SEPTA
Mike Carroll, City of Philadelphia
Patricia Ellis, City of Philadelphia
Tanya Flint, SEPTA
Erik Johanson, SEPTA
Betsy Mastaglio, DVRPC
Andrew Stober, City of Philadelphia
Ema Yamamoto, City of Philadelphia

PHOENIX, AZ

Jenny Grote, PE, PTOE, City of Phoenix
Mark Melnychenko, City of Phoenix
Eileen Yazzie, City of Phoenix

PITTSBURGH, PA

Andrew Dash, City of Pittsburgh
Patrick Roberts, City of Pittsburgh

PORTLAND, OR

Ben Baldwin, TriMet
Teresa Boyle, Portland Bureau of Transportation
Peter Koonce, Portland Bureau of Transportation
Ken Zatarain, TriMet

PUEBLA, PU

Ari Fernando Valerdi Moroni, IMPLAN City of Puebla

SAN DIEGO, CA

Linda Marabian, City of San Diego

SAN FRANCISCO, CA

Peter Albert, SFMTA
Jamie Parks, SFMTA
Britt Tanner, SFMTA
Dustin White, SFMTA

SALT LAKE CITY, UT

Becka Roolf, Salt Lake City
Julianne Sabula, Salt Lake City

SAN JOSÉ, CA

Zahi Khattab, City of San José
Lauren Ledbetter, Valley Transportation Authority

Contributors

David Bragdon, TransitCenter
Alan Danaher, PE, PTOE, AICP, Parsons Brinckerhoff
Andy Kosinski, PE, Fehr & Peers
Stephanie Lotshaw, TransitCenter
Megan Mittman, AICP, Fehr & Peers
Andres Ramirez, OmniTrans
Zach Smith, APTA
Matt Tingstrom, APTA
Shin-pei Tsay, TransitCenter
Rich Weaver, APTA

SEATTLE, WA

Bill Bryant, City of Seattle
Scott Kubly, City of Seattle
Paulo Nuñes-Ueno, City of Seattle

SOMERVILLE, MA

Jennifer Molina, City of Somerville

TORONTO, ON

Justin Bak, City of Toronto
David Kuperman, City of Toronto

VANCOUVER, BC

Dale Bracewell, City of Vancouver
Neal Peacocke, City of Vancouver

VENTURA, CA

Derek Towers, City of Ventura

WASHINGTON, DC

Jamie Carrington, AICP, WMATA
Jim Hamre, WMATA
Sam Zimbabwe, DDOT

Technical Review Team

Steve Durrant, Alta Planning + Design
Nick Falbo, Alta Planning + Design
Joe Gilpin, Alta Planning + Design
Paul Ryus, PE, Kittlelson & Associates, Inc.

Contributing Organizations

American Public Transportation Association
Institute of Transportation Engineers
Island Press
Summit Foundation
TransitCenter

Photo Credits

Adam Coppola Photography: 27 (Dexter Ave)

Tim Adams via Flickr: 95 (Toronto bus shelter)

Ben Baldwin: 25 (NW 23rdAve), 34 (SW Moody Ave), 47 (bus at stop), 104 (Bioswale), 132 (Asphalt)

Bill Bryant: 71 (N 45th St)

Bryce Giesler via Flickr: 99

Charlotte Area Transit System: 80 (Charlotte)

City of Cambridge: 95 (Cambridge bus shelter)

Dongho Chang: 102 (Seattle), 166 (Yesler St)

Chicago Department of Transportation: 69 (Washington St), 135 (Embedded color)

Payton Chung via Flickr: 80 (Sherbourne St), 167 (NW Lovejoy St)

CompleteStreets via Flickr: 115 (Santa Monica)

Caitlin Doolin: 95 (Baltimore BUS shelter)

Skye Duncan: 77 (Swanston St)

Bryce Geisler via Flickr: 87 (Houston Metro)

Green Lane Project: 189 (Halsted St)

Harbourfront Centre/Brian Medina: 35 (Queens Quay, bottom), 130 (Queens Quay)

Patricia Henschen via Flickr: 9 (16th St), 132 (Pavers)

Wikimedia Commons contributor House1090: 102 (sbX station)

Stephen Hui via Flickr: 106 (Vancouver)

Samuel Israel: 18 (Loop Link)

Corinne Kisner: 53 (Dearborn St), 155 (Dearborn St)

Roy Luck via Flickr: 137 (Bollards)

J. Daniel Malouff (Flickr user BeyondDC): 39 (Metroway), 47 (NW 11th Ave), 64 (NW 10th Ave), 65 (Mini-high platform), 85 (Metroway), 86 (Euclid Ave), 126 (Metroway), 132 (Concrete), 138 (Alexandria), 130 (Baltimore), 139 (Dynamic signage), 139 (Transit signal heads), 178 (Silver Spring)

Flickr user Merari: 137 (Low vertical elements)

Metro Transit: 33 (Washington Ave), 88

Stephen Miller via Streetsblog: 164 (86th Street)

Flickr user npgreenway: 187 (Portland)

New York City Department of Transportation: 37 (Webster Ave), 49 (Madison Ave), 53 (First Ave), 70 (34th St), 78 (New York), 80 (34th St), 97 (SBS shelter), 98 (Leaning rail), 99 (ticket machines), 101 (real-time information), 113 (125th St), 115 (First Ave), 134 (Red paint), 183 (SBS ticket machine)

Omnitrans: 31 (South E St)

Philadelphia Bike Coalition: 123 (Chestnut St)

Portland Bureau of Transportation: 67 (Portland), 75 (Moody St), 97 (Morrison St), 105

Carter Rubin: 33 (Main St)

San Francisco Municipal Transportation Agency Photo Library: 55 (Haight St), 59 (Mission St), 64 (Sidewalk/Curb Level), 65 (Level boarding), 74 (Duboce Ave), 82 (Market St), 92 (Folsom St), 95 (San Fransisco bus shelters, 2 photos), 113 (O'Farrell St), 119 (Church St), 121 (Sign in San Francisco), 131 (Market St), 134 (Red thermoplastic), 140 (Market St), 157 (Geary Blvd), 182 (Modern on-board PoP; Fare control officer), 188 (shelter), 190 (Market St), 191 (W Portal Ave)

Special thanks to Jeremy Menzies and the SFMTA Photo Library.

Photo Credits *(continued)*

Seattle Department of Transportation: ix (S Jackson St), 102 (Seattle), 117 (Parking sign; Streetcar image), 121 (Peak-only lane), 135 (Intermittent color), 135 (Brick & paver colors), 183 (Off-board RFID card reader)

Derek Severson via Flickr: 136 (roundabout)

Flickr user Sludgeulper: 137 (Plastic armadillos)

Flickr user SounderBruce: 43 (Second Ave), 95 (rapid service shelter on constrained sidewalk)

Christof Spieler: 4 (Powell St), 133 (SW Lincoln St), 169 (Peachtree St)

Natalie Stiffler: 12 (Santa Fe Depot), 105 (Boulder), 187 (Bike cage, 2 photos)

Salt Lake City Transportation Division: 104 (S Line)

Studio34 via Flickr: 21 (Baltimore Ave)

Studio 111: 51 (First St)

SvR Design: 45 (Bell St)

Natta Summerky, BlogTO: 35 (Queens Quay, top)

Wikimedia Commons contributor ŠJĐ : 102 (Kassel curb)

Craig Toocheck: 41 (K St), 82 (K St), 101 (Pushbutton)

Flickr user Teemu08: 133 (St Clarles Ave)

TriMet: 49 (SW 5th St), 88 (Marquette Ave), 89 (SW 5th Ave), 129 (Washington Ave)

Dan Tutt: page 55 (Eugene), 65 (Near-level boarding), 66 (Eugene), 102 (Eugene), 136 (Hard curbs)

Steve Vance via Flickr: 138 (Full-lane treatments), 172 (Concrete pillow)

City of Vancouver: 29 (Granville Mall)

Aaron Villere: 129 (University Blvd)

Oran Viriyincy via Flickr: 64 (Street Level), 95 (Seattle bus shelters, 2 photos), 97 (Seattle), 98 (Seattle), 100 (Los Angeles), 184 (Seattle), 186 (Orange line)

Flickr user vxla: 84 (New Orleans), 137 (rumble strips)

Dustin White: 158 (Third St)

Wikimedia Commons contributor xAtsukex: 51 (2nd St)

Kevin Zolkiewicz via Flickr: 23 (Roncesvalles Ave)

Island Press Board of Directors